In *Changing India* Robert W. Stern presents a comprehensive, provocative and highly readable introduction to contemporary India's modern history and social institutions. He takes his reader through India's family households and villages, its long-lived and little understood caste systems, venerable faiths and extraordinary ethnic diversity. He describes and analyzes India's modern agriculture and industrial economies and its evolving systems of classes. India's functioning as a democratic federal union of 850 million citizens, its electoral politics and parliamentary democracy are illuminated in Stern's discussion. He also traces the country's history as "the jewel in the crown" of British imperialism and contrasts its "third world" poverty and illiteracy with its technological sophistication and subcontinental predominance.

Changing India's central argument is that India's history and its institutions, both traditional and modern, are changing rapidly and profoundly. Yet these changes have been more adaptive to the remarkable continuity and vitality of India's underlying social systems than disruptive of them. This paradox may lie in the dominant pattern of change, which, Stern argues, is "bourgeois revolution": change resulting from the simultaneous development of capitalism and parliamentary democracy.

Changing India

Changing India

Bourgeois revolution on the subcontinent

ROBERT W. STERN

 CAMBRIDGE
UNIVERSITY PRESS

Published by the Press Syndicate of the University of Cambridge
The Pitt Building, Trumpington Street, Cambridge CB2 1RP
40 West 20th Street, New York, NY 10011-4211, USA
10 Stamford Road, Oakleigh, Victoria 3166, Australia

First published 1993

Printed in Great Britain at the University Press, Cambridge

A catalogue record for this book is available from the British Library

Library of Congress cataloguing in publication data
Stern, Robert W., 1933–
Changing India/Robert W. Stern.
   p.   cm.
Includes bibliographical references.
ISBN 0 521 42105 5. – ISBN 0 521 42106 3 (pbk.)
1. India–History–British occupation, 1765–1947. 2. India–
History–1947– 3. India–Social conditions. I. Title.
DS463.S73 1993
954.03′5–dc20   92–11675   CIP

ISBN 0 521 421055 hardback
ISBN 0 521 421063 paperback

To Andrea

"This whole book is but a draught – nay, but the draught of a
draught. Oh, Time, Strength, Cash and Patience!" (Herman
Melville, *Moby-Dick* [Harmondsworth: Penguin Books, 1972],
p. 241.)

Contents

Maps and tables

Maps

Tables

Acknowledgements

It was Andrea who first suggested that I write a book about India not for specialists but for adequately educated general readers; and appropriate to the occasion, as I wrote, she was the source of wifely consolation, good advice and acute criticism. *Changing India* is dedicated to her. Don Ferrell, Robin Jeffrey, Ravinder Kumar, Jim Masselos, Morris Morley and Leslie Stein have all been friends in need at various times and in different ways. Sue Folwell's editing skill and word-processing expertise turned my red-lined sheets of blue and white paper into a handsome manuscript. Macquarie University provided the usual bits and pieces of the wherewithal.

Glossary of Indian terms

ahimsa	Literally non-violence. A concept common to Hinduism, Buddhism and Jainism; and given modern currency by Mahatma Gandhi.
Akali Dal	Once the Sikh political party, now an agglomeration of factions which support either Sikh nation-provincialism or separatism, i.e., "Khalistan."
ashraf	Literally, nobility. Muslims of high social status. The north-Indian Muslim counterpart of the Hindu twice-born category. *Ashraf* membership is accorded to those Muslim quasi *jatis* whose claims to descent from the following are generally accepted: Sayyids (the Prophet's descendants), *Sheikhs* (Arabs), Mughals (Turkistan Turks), Pathans (Afghans) and, sometimes, Rajputs (Hindu warriors).
babu	Literally, father. A title attached, particularly, to a "white collar" bourgeois; may be used descriptively or disdainfully.
baniya	A businessperson, or a member of a *jati* whose traditional occupation is business; may be used descriptively or disdainfully.
bhadralok	Literally, gentlefolk; particularly, members of those Bengali *jatis* which cultivate the skills of literacy and numeracy and are inclined to educated employment.
bhakti	Hindu devotionalism; a medieval Hindu devotionalist movement.
Bharat	The official Indian name for India: appears on currency, stamps, etc. in *devanagari* script; may be used with nativist, folkish overtones.

Bharatiya Janata Party (BJP)	The major political party, these days, of *Hindutva*.
crore	Ten million. A *crorepati* is a millionaire.
dar al-Islam	A place ruled according to the sacred laws of Islam; or as second-best, ruled by Muslims who respect and partially abide by these laws.
deshi	Of the countryside, local, Indian provincial.
dharna	A traditional form of protest in which the aggrieved, through self-inflicted punishment, usually by fasting, gives witness to the rightness of his or her cause.
Dilli durbar	The regime in Delhi: of the Mughals, lately of the Nehru-Gandhis.
Dravida Munnetra Kazhagam (DMK) and All-India Anna – (AIADMK)	Parties of Tamil nation-provincialism, successors to the erstwhile Dravidian movement.
durbar	The regime in a former princely state, the court; also a public audience or reception.
filmi duniya	Literally, the film world; specifically, the Hindi film industry of Bombay, also called Bollywood.
Gorkhaland	A homeland-state which Nepali-speakers want carved from Darjeeling district of West Bengal and adjacent areas.
gotra	An exogamous division of a *jati*, a clan.
Hindutva	Literally, Hinduness; specifically, the urge to convert the Indian Union into a Hindu state, although what exactly this would mean is unclear.
jati	An endogamous social group of Hindus, a caste, whose referent ideology is the *varna dharma*. A quasi *jati* is a social group of non-Hindus with *jati*-like traits.
jajmani system	A traditional, heritable and ritualized relationship, now largely vestigial, of goods-for-services exchange and generalized superiority–subordination between a family of landed patrons (*jajmans*) and their client (*kamin*) families.
Jharkhand	A homeland-state which tribal people of the

	area want carved from contiguous parts of West Bengal and Bihar.
karkhana	A workshop, small factory.
Khilafat movement	Between 1919 and 1922, a popular, anti-British Muslim movement in support of the Ottoman *khalifah*, and to which Mahatma Gandhi attached Congress support.
mandir	Particularly, a Hindu temple.
mantra	A Hindu sacred formula, hymn, incantation; may be used disparagingly, i.e., an empty ritual.
masjid	Mosque.
mullah	A Muslim cleric-cum-legist.
nawab	In British India, the specific or generic title for a Muslim prince or princeling.
panchayat	A traditional council, of villagers or *jati* fellows, e.g. headed by a *sarpancha*.
panchayati raj	A statutory system of rural self-government and development instituted by Indian state governments in the late 1950s and afterwards.
pandit	A *brahman* title, e.g. Pandit Jawaharlal Nehru.
Punjabi Suba	Literally, a Punjabi language province. A euphemism for the homeland-state in northern Punjab, demanded by Sikhs and established – though incompletely – in 1966.
purdah	Literally, curtain; the seclusion of Hindu or Muslim women, either in their homes or in public by costumes of conventional modesty.
Quaid-i-Azam	Great leader, the title attached particularly to Mohammad Ali Jinnah.
raj	Regime; also kingdom, realm, rule, state, etc. *The* Raj refers to the former British government of India.
raja	Inflated to maharaja. In British India, specific or generic titles for, usually, Hindu princes, princelings or large warrior-landlords.
satyagraha	Literally, truth-insistence, Mahatma Gandhi's name for his *dharna*-based strategy of non-violent conflict and conflict resolution.
shari'ah	Islamic sacred law.
shastra	A work of Hindu injunctive scripture, i.e., sacred law.

Sikhism	A religion largely synthesized from *bhakti* and *sufism*, in Punjab from its founding by Guru Nanak in the sixteenth century. The Sikh faith is the *panth* (path) and the community is the *khalsa* – hence, "Khalistan."
sufism	The Islamic expression of devotionalism and mysticism.
swadeshi	Reference to goods made in India, particularly in cottage and handicraft industries. The term was popularized by nationalist movements, but is rarely used today.
swaraj	Literally, self-rule; popularized by Mahatma Gandhi and nationalist movements.
tamasha	Show, spectacle, entertainment; may be used disparagingly, i.e., a meaningless show.
Telegu Desam	A political party of Telegu nation-provincialism; founded by the Telegu movie star N. T. Rama Rao in the early 1980s.
twice-born	A reference to *jatis* of high social status, *jatis* which are generally accepted as belonging to the *brahman, kshatriya* or *vaishiya varnas.*
untouchables	*Jatis* and quasi *jatis* that are generally regarded as being so defilingly polluted or of such low social status as to put them beyond the pale of ordinary social intercourse. Referred to by British and Indian governments as "scheduled castes," by Mahatma Gandhi as "Harijans" (God's people), and, increasingly, by themselves as "dalit" (oppressed).
varna dharma	In Hinduism, a hierarchical order (*dharma*) of those categories (*varnas*) into which God divided humanity at the time He created it, viz. *brahman* (priest), *kshatriya* (warrior and ruler), *vaishiya* (producer of wealth), *shudra* (worker).

Introduction

Change, the societies of India and Indian society

Change and bourgeois revolution

This book is about contemporary Indian society and how it is changing. Of every seven people in the world now, one is an Indian. Contemporary Indian society is beneficiary and benefactor to one of the world's great and enduring civilizations. It permeates the entire Indian subcontinent; and of every five people in the world today, one lives there. At the subcontinent's political center, the Indian Union is one of the world's major powers.

Yet in the West even the barest knowledge of India is not usually considered to be part of an adequate general education. This book is addressed primarily to Western readers who have such an education and want to acquire some knowledge of Indian society. Readers who are knowledgeable may find some interest in my presentation and the argument that informs it.

I present Indian society as changing. Of course, it has always been changing: only the pace of change has varied from time to time, group to group and place to place on the subcontinent. I accept and apply to Indian society this insight of Hindu and Buddhist antiquity: change is the condition of every thing that lives. Change is the condition of social continuity. Change may be barely perceptible even to those who experience it directly or it may be, as it is in Indian today, self-evident, rapid and profound. There may be ideological or pragmatic reasons for denying that change has occurred or for exaggerating or disguising its occurrence. But there is always change.

It may, from a variety of causes, follow some dominant pattern. My argument is that nowadays the *dominant* pattern of change in India is what Barrington Moore, Jr. calls "bourgeois revolution." Moore defines his revolutions by the "broad institutional results to which they contribute."[1] Bourgeois revolution's essential institu-

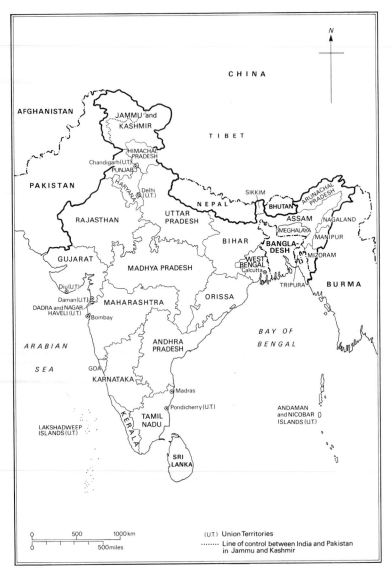

1. The Indian Union in 1993

tional contribution is to the development *together* (allowing for leads and lags) of capitalism and parliamentary democracy. In my meaning, this development is synonymous with bourgeois revolution. In India, it began and continues as a revolution from the top down; but increasingly as it proceeds, combining and incorporating elements in a society that long antedates it, it has become as well a revolution from the middle up.

In Moore's opinion, "much of the confusion and unwillingness to use larger categories," like bourgeois revolution, is because "those who provide the mass support for a revolution, those who lead it, and those who ultimately profit from it are very different sets of people."[2] There is little confusion but that in India bourgeois revolution's leaders, families who have profited by it or even experienced its changes, have come largely from the middle classes. In general terms, these classes are comprised chiefly of families whose incomes are derived from employment in the educated professions (including politics, many of whose practitioners these days were schooled at Hard Knocks), managerial and other higher salaried positions in modern industry and commerce and family farm-based commercial agriculture. While they have established their hegemony over most spheres of Indian public life, these classes are certainly not closed nor entirely self-perpetuating. Accompanying bourgeois revolution in India, and congruent with it, is substantial and accelerating embourgeoisement, i.e., the rush of new entrants into the ranks of the middle classes.

In the chapters of part I, my argument focuses on the basic institutions of rural India, on the four out of five Indian families which live in villages and country towns, and on how bourgeois revolution at their middle is contributing to changes in these institutions.

The chapters of part II contain some essays on the history, mostly from the urban top, of bourgeois revolution and change in India. In sum, its impetus came from British imperialism. It was domesticated, from the late nineteenth century, by the subcontinent's nationalist movements: most critically, the Indian National Congress's, led by Mahatma Gandhi. Since Indian independence in 1947, the governments of the Indian Union and its constituent states, most often formed by the Congress and Congress (I) parties, have been promoting and institutionalizing bourgeois revolution. Bourgeois revolution began to accelerate rapidly, to "take off" in the 1970s. The instigators of this history of change have come largely from urban elites, British and Indian; and the focus of part II is on them, though not exclusively, and on cities and urban institutions such as governments, parties and industrial enterprises. For whatever it lacks in what social scientists are wont to call "sophistication," the concept of bourgeois revolution makes up, for my purposes, in limited usefulness: manageability and malleability. I use the concept to serve the purpose of organizational economy, i.e., to organize into one small volume through its argument or arguments material that is virtually boundless. Arguments, it hardly needs to be said, are arguable. There are no definitive statements on the pages that follow. I use bourgeois revolution to serve the purpose of explanation. I do not imagine, however, that it explains everything. It is the *dominant* pattern of change in Indian society only in the sense that it describes the general direction of its political and economic development, and changes concomitant with it. There are crosscurrents and shores untouched by bourgeois revolution. It describes, but only in part, the recent revival of militant Hinduism, for example. Many changes in Hinduism, of greater concern to practising Hindus, it does not describe at all. It does not describe the proletarianization of modern Indian farm families, although their numbers may well exceed those of the families that have become *embourgeoisées*. The development in tandem, more or less, of capitalism and parliamentary democracy has not effected any fundamental structural change in Indian society. Indeed, a recurring theme throughout this study is of the compatibility, adaptability and, even, functionality of long-lived Indian social structures to bourgeois revolution.

Is it really a "revolution" at all, then? My best answer to this is twofold. First to concur with Moore that the "main problem, after all, is what happened and why, not the proper use of labels."[3] We are not unused to questionable labels in Indian studies. In chapter 2, one of our most useful concepts appears: "sanskritization." It is regarded as a questionable label, even by the distinguished anthropologist who devised it. Second, in chapters to follow, I hope this becomes clear. The development *together* in India of capitalism and parliamentary democracy has brought fundamental political changes and fundamental changes in their family economies to the rapidly growing middle classes. Their families now number in tens of millions and have become the directors and constituencies of political and economic change. Every revolution is partial, in its own way.

There is nothing inevitable about bourgeois revolution. Capitalism and parliamentary democracy, as Moore argues at great length, have not always developed together. They need not have in India. If, for example, the British had been more successful post-Mutiny in encouraging the collective participation in Indian politics of the landed aristocracy and it, in turn, had had the foresight to seek the alliance of the new classes of Indian industrialists, we might now have no Indian bourgeois revolution to argue about. From the perspective of 1992, it is also distinctly possible that what I have labelled bourgeois revolution may be only a passing phase in India's history. Certainly, bourgeois revolution has yet to profit (and, perhaps, even to affect critically) more than a minority of Indian families.

Although there is no agreed upon scholarly or official definition of what makes a family bourgeois in India, there is among informed observers of Indian society an apparent consensus that the bourgeoisie, the middle classes, constitute somewhere between 10 and 20 percent of the Indian population, somewhere between 85 and 170 million people. Indian economic statistics, which in this, as in most regards, can only be regarded as suggestive, indicate that the upper 20 percent of Indian households, rural and urban, control about 60 percent of India's agricultural land, earn about 50 percent of its income and consume about 50 percent of its goods. Given the prevalence within this privileged quintile of holdings in excess of legal land ceilings, "black money" and other under- and undeclared assets, its actual control of India's wealth is likely to be greater than the statistics suggest. To be sure, within this upper fifth of the Indian population, there is a wide range of economic difference from its lower to its upper edge, and the same income buys more or less of different things in different places. But so it is within middle classes, however designated, of other places. It is accurate enough and convenient to identify the Indian middle classes as the upper quintile of Indian households, minus their top 2 or 3 percent which belong to the wealthy (see table 1 for a similar, albeit more generous estimate).

That today's upper quintile of Indian households enjoys the economic advantages that were enjoyed by a considerably smaller percentage of Indian households in the past, i.e., that there has been embourgeoisement, is I think self-evident to most observers. For those who demand statistics, embourgeoisement can be fairly well inferred from the coincident increase over the past few decades

Table 1. *Household incomes in India 1989–90 (nos. and percentage are indicative only)*

Income group	Rupee income per annum	No. of people (Mn.)	Percentage of population
Low income	less than 12,500	420	59.0
Lower middle	12,500–25,000	192	27.0
Middle income	25,000–40,000	72	10.0
Upper middle	40,000–56,000	19	2.6
High income	more than 56,000	10	1.4

Source: Indian National Council of Applied Economic Research (based on average household of five persons). At current exchange rates US$1 = *c.* Rs. 26. But this is largely irrelevant to the domestic purchasing power of the rupee

of household savings – a statistically understated middle class phenomenon – and particularly middle class consumption: of electricity for domestic use, for example, which has more than trebled over the past twenty years. Or, production for middle class consumption: of motor cycles/scooters and domestic refrigerators, for example, which increased about ten-fold from 1970–71 to 1986–87.

While bourgeois revolution in India is likely to be a momentous event not only in its history but in the world's, it has as yet passed with little – though increasing – notice in the West. It has been partially obscured by the methodology and underlying ideology of post-World War II development economics, the rhetoric of Indian politics and economic planning, and our Western images of India.

Development economics tends to measure change in *per capita* terms. And in these terms, India's poverty is almost though not quite changeless. India provides the world with its largest national pool of poor people, and the amelioration of their poverty over the decades has been slight. But India's development is not taking place *per capita.* It is taking place in its upper quintile of households. The poor certainly outnumber the Indian middle classes, but the poor are not directors of change, nor the major participants in it, and certainly not its major beneficiaries. Neither are they likely to become so: not through proletarian revolution – whose occurrence becomes increasingly unlikely as bourgeois revolution proceeds – nor by "direct action" campaigns, e.g., general strikes, nor by capturing the instrumentalities of parliamentary democracy, nor by dragging bourgeois revolution to a halt with the inertia of their poverty.

The poor are certainly not passive. They are increasingly assertive, non-violently and violently. They affect the course of change and its pace, including the pace of embourgeoisement. They are the recipients of some varying and significant trickle-down effects of bourgeois revolution. But the engine of change is in the hands of the middle classes.

Measured in terms of the welfare of most Indians, bourgeois revolution is a stunning disappointment; although, perhaps, the predictable path of change, given the history of modern India and the structure of Indian society. In any event, things are as they are. I want to describe bourgeois revolution in India. I do not want to be mistaken for one of its apologists. I do not invite development economists to be its apologists. They would simply be of greater assistance in describing things as they are if, for example, they turned some of their efforts in refining "poverty lines" to the construction of embourgeoisement thresholds and trickle-down indicators.

In India's constitution, its eight successive five-year plans, hundreds of its party manifestoes, thousands of its laws and myriad speeches of its politicians there is a rhetorical commitment to a process of change whose chief beneficiaries are the poor. This reiteration of "socialism" or at least of some ideologically unspecific egalitarianism as the goal of Indian development is not entirely the meaningless hypocrisy and meaningful fakery of politicians and their minions. It serves, for example, to give governments a legitimate purpose and the governed of the nether quintiles legitimate demands. But it serves neither to describe the realities of change in Indian society nor the role of Indian governments in making them real. One economist has recently noted, for example, that in the mid-1980s the entire public expenditure on India's various poverty alleviation programs was roughly equal to that quintessential (but by no means, unique) government subvention to the rural middle classes: fertilizer subsidies.[4] Though never, of course, officially described as such, these poverty alleviation programs are only engineered (as opposed to "natural") trickle-down effects of bourgeois revolution.

India is in our Western image of it rather like a supermarket that specializes in exotica, that caters to our fantasies and our nightmares. We pick things off its shelves for our use, without knowing how they got there or where they came from. India supplied its poverty and superstitions to the vocations of Christian missionaries. It supplied its spiritual insights to the enlightenment of European scholars and litterateurs. Its "underdevelopment" supplied the United States for almost two decades with a cause in Asia worthy of its surplus wheat and university graduates. Its plans for development and their implementation have supplied Western economists of all persuasions with grist for their publishers' mills, consultancies and anecdotes. For the perplexed and disillusioned among us, India supplies the dispensations of its itinerant *swamis* and *guru*-entrepreneurs. Its horror stories of bride burnings and female infanticide and human sacrifices, apparently provide for readers of our afternoon tabloids some variation from more familiar horrors and some assurance that however bad things are in New York or Northern Ireland they are worse in Calcutta and Bihar.

We choose from the supermarket's wares things that are from time to time, on and off, here and there in vogue: food, fashions, Festivals of India. Stories about maharajas, British *Raj* romances and picture books about Rajasthan seem to enjoy an indefinite shelf life. Some years ago, a fairy tale biography on film revived our occasional interest in Mahatma Gandhi. But briefly. India's music, we may remember, inspired none less than Yehudi Menuhin and the Beatles, and its virtuosos electrified and bewildered audiences all over the West – for a while, a while ago. "It is the *sitar* here today," Ravi Shankar once mused in Sydney, "tomorrow it will be the *koto*."

And what of the day after tomorrow? Consider. The combined population of the twentieth century's two superpowers was never more than three-quarters of India's. As a consequence of governmental efforts that have succeeded in halving the general death rate and doubling the life expectancy of Indians at birth, India's population has more than doubled since it became an independent nation. To all but its Jeremiahs, this "population explosion" seems much less worrisome now than it did in the 1960s. India's population is larger than it has ever been. But it is also healthier and more literate. It continues to grow, but at a decelerating rate. If after it recovers from its current slump, the Indian economy resumes its late 1980's annual growth rate of about 5 percent, India's large population may well become in the next century one of its great political and economic assets.

India nowadays produces more than enough food to feed itself. During the two recent drought years of 1986 and 1987 – the latter, probably the worst in independent India's history – there was no famine; agricultural production declined by only about 10 percent and the economy in general, and particularly the industrial economy, continued to grow. In 1988, Indian foodgrain production was higher than it had ever been. There are still hungry people in India, far too many of them; but they are a shrinking proportion of the Indian population, and their plight is a consequence *not* of the unavailability of food but of its maldistribution: as poverty in the West is a product of maldistribution and not of scarcity.

Since 1947, foodgrain production in India has more than trebled. As has the production of rice. The production of wheat has increased more than eight-fold. These and other remarkable increases in virtually all food and other crops have been the result of government-led programs which have expanded the area of cultivation by more than one-third, consolidated the holdings of farmers in their villages, virtually eliminated non-cultivating landlords from the business of agriculture through land reform legislation, developed agricultural extension and research agencies, expanded credit and marketing facilities, established price and production incentives for farmers, introduced and encouraged the use of "green revolution" technology, facilitated a trebling of the area under irrigation and a hundred-fold increase in the consumption of chemical fertilizers. Except for its cotton, jute and tea, a rural slum of the British empire, India has become one of the world's four major producers of farm products and there is no foreseeable limits to its agricultural growth.

Agricultural development and political democracy have been the principal ingredients of bourgeois revolution in the Indian countryside. Its principal participants and beneficiaries are those households – the upper quintile – which operate four or more hectares, as proprietors or controllers. Most of them operate fewer than 8 hectares. In a generation they have ceased being "peasants," i.e., subject cultivators, and they have become capitalist farmers: legally secure in their tenure, acquisitive, enterprising, socially mobile, exploitive of their laborers, ambitious for their children, politically assertive and *the* force to be reckoned with in local and state politics. Proper bourgeois! But, for the most part, petit bourgeois: only relatively large small holders, rich only in comparison with the poor. The annual incomes of only the richest farm households would even approximate those of public works department superintendent engineers, for example, or specialist medical doctors employed by government.

Proper bourgeois! But not of closed bourgeoisies. Inheritance has taken its toll. Since 1970, the households which hold more than 4 hectares and the area operated by them have probably declined as percentages of the whole in favor of households with smaller holdings. The better-off of these constitute, roughly, the second quintile of farm households: "middle peasant" families which operate somewhere between 1.5 and 2 hectares each. The non-evidence of economies of scale in much of agricultural development in India, the increasing availability of developmental inputs and the crucial role of state governments in apportioning these inputs have set tens of millions of households in the second quintile on the route to embourgeoisement. A major political development in Indian politics since the 1970s has been the growth of "backward classes" and "farmers" movements. I shall have more to say about these below. By and large, they are caste-based or related movements of small holders with middle class aspirations: social respectability for their castes, "remunerative" farm prices for their families and education for their children.

In forty-five years of independence, the annual production of steel in India has increased more than ten-fold as has the production of commercial vehicles. The value of machine tools manufactured annually has increased from about a half-million US dollars to more than a quarter-billion US dollars. Installed capacity for the generation of electricity has increased from about 2,000 megawatts to more than 50,000 megawatts, and the generation of electricity has increased from about 5 billion kilowatt hours to over 200 billion kilowatt hours. Chemical fertilizer production has increased from less than 20,000 tonnes to over 7 million tonnes. There has been a four-fold increase in the length of India's road network and in the passenger- and freight-tonne kilometers travelled by its railways.

An electronics industry has sprung into being in independent India which produces a full range of computer hardware and software, modern communications equipment and consumer electrical goods, including about one million television sets each year. What was a virtually nonexistent motor cycle and scooter industry forty years ago, is now one of the world's largest: producing about a million vehicles each year. In general, industrial production in India has increased five-fold since independence. From the mid-1980s, until it was slowed by drought, and to 1991 when fiscal crisis and in its wake necessary economic restructuring brought it to a halt, however temporarily, India's annual industrial growth rate was more than 8 percent. India has become one of the fifteen or twenty major industrial countries in the world.

The "commanding heights" of the Indian economy are held by government-owned corporations: the railways and airlines, post and telecommunications, the major banks and life insurance companies, atomic energy, petroleum and munitions. For the rest, the economy is "mixed": government and private enterprise are both involved in the manufacture of steel, automobiles, heavy machinery and electrical equipment, the marketing of handicrafts and the management of hotel chains. Of the private corporations, the largest are family owned or managed conglomerates; and of these, the largest are of the families Tata and Birla. The paper value of their assets, considerably understated, are in excess of $US 5 billion each. The Tatas manufacture everything from soap to locomotives, the Birlas everything from the daily *Hindustan Times* to automobiles. Besides them there are scores of smaller big-business families, *crorepatis* (multi-millionaires).

In recent years, however, thousands of small-business families and entrepreneurs all over India have made small-scale manufacturing into the most dynamic sector of their country's economy. These industries of the urban petit and moyen bourgeoisie have increased their output more than five-fold since the middle 1970s, and now produce about one half of India's factory-made goods and one quarter of its exports.

In addition to small-business families, whose number has more than quadrupled over the past decade or so, two other groups have added their number to India's urban middle classes. First, university graduates whose numbers have increased more than ten-fold since 1947 and now provide India with one of the world's largest national pools of technically and scientifically trained personnel. In India, as elsewhere, universities have been a vehicle for embourgeoisement and for the addition of numbers and social variety to urban middle classes. Second, thousands of skilled and semi-skilled workers, particularly in Bombay, whose militant bread-and-butter trade unionism has produced pay packets large enough to nurture middle class aspirations.

Much of everything that is consumed in India is produced in India: food products, clothing and virtually all other household consumer goods, fertilizer and petroleum products, coal and steel, heavy electrical machinery and machine tools, locomotives and all other railway equipment, motor vehicles and ships. Since independence, India's industry has developed behind the political barriers of an "import-substitution" policy which, in effect, blocks foreign competition for domestic manufacturers and opens to them a vast and apparently insatiable market for almost anything that they can sell.

Import-substitution has come under increasing criticism in India for facilitating illegal and corrupt relationships between businessmen and bureaucrats, producing shoddy and expensive goods, under-utilizing India's vast potential workforce and thereby contributing to the maximization of unemployment at home and the minimization of India's competitive advantage of cheap labor in the manufacture of goods for sale abroad. Largely due to government prodding, Indian industry has been more and more seeking and finding foreign markets for its goods. In recent years, for example, engineering goods, and – largely from the small manufacturing sector – garments, leather goods and polished gemstones and jewelry have become some of India's major exports. An aim of India's economic restructuring in the 1990s is to increase its exports and export-led industrialization. Import-substitution, as a strategy of industrialization, has had its day. But it was certainly not without accomplishment. One of the goals of economic development in India was to provide it with the industrial self-sufficiency that characterizes a great power. And import-substitution did that.

Finally, with regard to Indian industry: although there are branches and subsidiaries of foreign multinational corporations in India and an increasing number of Indian corporations have licensing and other collaborative arrangements with foreign companies, India's industrial economy is overwhelmingly owned and operated by Indians.

Nor has Indian culture been colonized from abroad. It has, of course, borrowed from the European West over the past two centuries as it borrowed from the Muslim West in earlier centuries; but in almost all things, Indian culture is distinctively Indian. India's Christians and Muslims are no less Indian than its Hindus. Its great faiths are its own. So is its music: folk, popular and classical. In recent years, urban middle class families, and university students in particular, have provided growing audiences for Indian classical music and dance, and a growing custom for *deshi* (Indian provincial) chic in personal and home furnishings. Most of the books read by Indians are written by Indians and published in India. English is flourishing in India, but so are Indian languages. India is the largest film producing nation in the world. However slight the artistic merit and escapist the content of most Indian films – and like Hollywood's, a minority are of considerable artistic merit and not at all escapist – they provide the foundation for an extraordinarily powerful and pervasive popular culture that is distinctly Indian.

India can govern itself. The political center of Indian society has been occupied for the past forty-five years by the Indian Union. In form, it is a quasi-federal, democratic republic whose political authority is constitutionally apportioned between a central parliamentary government in Delhi and parliamentary governments in all twenty-five of the Union's constituent states and some of its territories (see table 3 for population distribution). Forty years ago, political democracy was an exotic transplant in India. Against all odds it has become successfully naturalized – less as an ideology, perhaps, than as a way of doing political business. In any case, and by any comparative measurement, parliamentary democracy in India is genuine, stable, and adapted to its social environment.

Unless disqualified for some particular reason, all adult Indian citizens are enfranchised to vote for the national parliament, their state legislative assembly and local or municipal council. The Indian electorate is the largest in the world. The proportion of it that usually votes is larger than it is in the United States and, I believe, no less well-informed or more gullible. It has four times in ten elections since 1952 for the national parliament and any number of times in elections for state legislative assembles turned governments out of power. And they have gone.

In India, as elsewhere, but perhaps more so in India, the interests of the middle classes are best served by political democracy. In India, as elsewhere, there have been lapses in its democracy. Ballot boxes have been stuffed and "lost," politicians' hirelings have "captured" polling booths, criminals have exerted political influence and become politicians, political workers have been beaten, politicians have been murdered, voters have been bribed and intimidated, campaign funds have been extorted and collected from the "black money" hoards of businessmen, politicians and bureaucrats.

Political irregularities have occurred not only in the hustings. There has been hardly a ministry in India, including the Union's, unsullied by scandal. Although their power, if they have it, is respected and feared, politicians, in general, enjoy no great reputation in India. On several occasions, including her infamous "emergency" of 1975 to 1977, Prime Minister Indira Gandhi used her constitutional powers in blatantly partisan and self-serving ways.

But again, by comparative standards, these lapses and irregularities, though condemnable, are no more than ordinary. What is extraordinary, by any standards, is that India has become one of the world's stable parliamentary democracies: that Indian politicians and bureaucrats have managed with more than workaday success to govern democratically and to more or less integrate into one quasi-federal union a population that is generally poor, illiterate, dispersed, parochial, anti-democratic in its cultural biases and larger and more socially diverse than the population of Europe.

Indian governments have been no less successful in suppressing domestic violence which threatens public order and their authority. Here too, of course, there have been lapses: police brutality, indiscipline and partiality; the insensitivity of politicians and bureaucrats to the demands of the poor and socially despised. But overall, there has been success. Though not without violence, to be sure, explosive tensions between castes and religious communities have usually been contained. In general, though not without violence, balances have been struck between the rights of Indian citizens to mount civil disobedience campaigns and the concerns of governments to dismount them. There have been a number of armed insurrections in independent India in districts of West Bengal and Andhra Pradesh, in Punjab, Assam and tribal areas of the northeast, in Kashmir. None have threatened the stability of the Indian Union. At no small cost in life and to human rights, all have been suppressed or contained. Some have been reconciled.

India can defend itself. It can make nuclear weapons and send them off by ballistic missiles of its own making. Its military services are well-armed, well-disciplined, well-trained, well-led and subordinate to their political masters. The Indian army is one of the world's largest and probably one of its best. Most of India's military ordnance is made in India, including (under license) Russian state-of-the-art aircraft. In recent years the Indian navy has been modernizing and expanding. It now has two aircraft carriers and a sizable air wing; a fleet of modern submarines, at least one of which is nuclear powered. Its military forces can not only defend India against any present or prospective threat, they can as well show the tricolor. India is clearly the great power not only in South Asia but on the Indian Ocean's littoral. That was the message of its political and military interventions in Sri Lanka from 1987 to 1989 and in the Maldives in 1988; and in 1989, of its partial economic blockade of Nepal.

Looking forward from the first decades of the nineteenth century, Tocqueville saw in the United States and Russia what we, looking forward to the twenty-first century might see in India and China:

There are at the present time two great nations in the world, which started from different points; [their courses are not the same] but seem to tend toward the same end . . . Both of them have grown up unnoticed; and while the attention of mankind was directed elsewhere, they have suddenly placed themselves in the front rank among the nations, and the world learned [of] their existence and their greatness at almost the same time.[5]

The societies of India and Indian society

When mankind's attention is directed to India, it will find a society that has, like Europe's, the diversities of a continent and the unities of a civilization. Moreover, these diversities and unities extend to the boundaries of the subcontinent which India shares with Pakistan, Bangladesh, Sri Lanka, Nepal and Bhutan. Within these boundaries, as within Europe's, political borders have changed over time and correspond only partially to ethnic boundaries and sometimes cut across them.

To take only the recent past: from Afghanistan, under Babur, the founder of his line, the Mughals began early in the sixteenth century to build their Indian empire from existing Hindu and Muslim principalities and their fragments. Before that empire began to disintegrate from the middle of the eighteenth century, Aurangzeb, the last of the Great Mughals, had extended his patrimony from Afghanistan to the Bay of Bengal, and from the Himalayas to the borders of what is now Tamil Nadu (see map 2). Then, from the fragments of the Mughal empire, the British began to build theirs. The British empire was partitioned into the republics of India and Pakistan in 1947. In 1970, after enduring more than two decades of exploitation, discrimination and repression in Pakistan, its eastern province rebelled and with the aid of Indian arms became Bangladesh. The republic of Sri Lanka, which until 1948 was the British colony of Ceylon and was not administered as part of their Indian empire, is certainly a political division of the subcontinent's society. India was ceded the French territory of Pondicherry in 1956; it seized the Portuguese territory of Goa in 1961; and it annexed its own protectorate, the Hindu kingdom of Sikkim, in 1975. The remaining Himalayan kingdoms are Indian protectorates: Bhutan less reluctantly than Nepal.

All the subcontinent's present international borders cut across ethnic boundaries. There is a Hindu majority and a Muslim minority of about 60 million Bengalis in India, most of them in the state of West Bengal. Across the border in Bangladesh there is a Muslim majority and a Hindu minority of about 100 million Bengalis. Until its recent discovery by cannabis and trekking enthusiasts, Nepal was best known to the West as the place from whence came those doughty mercenary soldiers, the Gurkhas. But over Nepal's eastern border, there are millions of Indian Nepali-speakers who have been demanding a state of ''Gorkhaland'' in the Indian Union.

Across the subcontinent, Punjabis, like Bengalis, were divided by the partition of the British Indian empire. There are about 21 million Punjabis in India, almost all Sikh and Hindu, mostly in the states of Punjab and Haryana. In the Punjab province of Pakistan, there are about 60 million Punjabis, almost all of them Muslims. Among Punjabis of all religions, in India and Pakistan, the dominant caste is Jat. Sind is in Pakistan, but there are about 2.5 million Sindhi-speakers in India. There are about 50 million Tamils in India, most of them in the state of Tamil Nadu on the subcontinent's southeastern tip. Less than 100 kilometers away, across the Palk Strait, in Sri Lanka there are another 3 million Tamils. In their rebellion against the Sinhalese majority-dominated government of Sri Lanka, its Tamils have been receiving moral and logistical support from Indian Tamils. In 1987, the Indian government became embroiled in two years of bloody ''peace keeping'' in north and northeastern Sri Lanka. Two thousand years ago, the Sinhalese were among the first people to receive the Buddha's message from India, and they are ethnically related to the people of the subcontinent's north.

Religion and things derived from religion spill across the subcontinent's political borders. Although less than 12 percent of India's total population, its Muslims number about 100 million. There are approximately as many Muslims in India as there are in either of the Muslim-majority states of Pakistan or Bangladesh. The largest geographical concentration of Muslims, more than one-third of their world population, is on the Indian subcontinent. And across its political borders, subcontinental Islam is as distinctively subcontinental, in its similarities and diversities, as is European Christianity distinctively European. Pakistan's Hindu population is minute, but

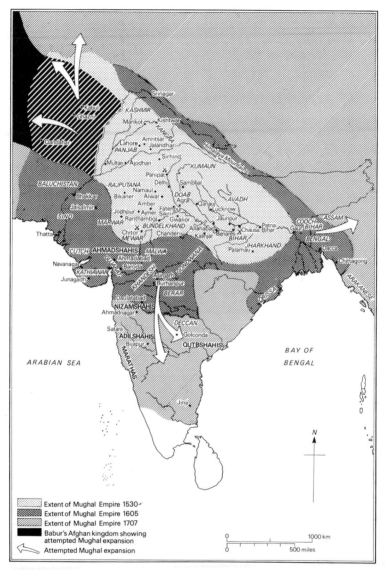

2. The Mughal empire, 1526 to 1707

Bangladesh has the second largest Hindu population in the world: about 13 million.

Political borders in South Asia even cut across the borders of "official languages." Bengali is the official language of West Bengal and Bangladesh. One of the earliest and most intense battles fought by the Bangladeshis, then East Pakistanis, against the government of Pakistan was to retain Bengali as their official language. Hindi is the official language of the Indian Union. Urdu is the official language of Pakistan. At the level of ordinary, day-to-day communications, Hindi and Urdu are basically the same language: except that they are written in different scripts and Urdu has a larger vocabulary of Persian and Arabic loan words and phrases. Because it is the language of Muslim high culture on the subcontinent, Urdu was chosen to be the official language of Pakistan. But Urdu is the mother tongue of fewer than one in ten Pakistanis, most of them migrants from India. The homeland of Urdu is around and about Delhi. There are more Urdu-speaking Hindus in India (although they would now identify their language as Hindi) than there are Urdu-speaking Muslims in Pakistan.

English is the distinctive and distinguishing language of the subcontinental haute bourgeoisie. It is their symbol. A mastery of written and spoken English is the *sine qua non* for entrance into the elite bureaucratic services, the officers' mess, the executive suite, the upper reaches of the professions, the circles of artists and intellectuals who are invited to international conferences, the editorial rooms of influential newspapers and journals, the professoriates of leading universities, the student bodies of "great public schools" and fashionable colleges, the company of the distinguished, the beau monde of the best people, the celebrations of the rich, the right clubs and so forth.

The use of English transcends the subcontinent's political borders, its official languages and its ethnic boundaries. When the prime ministers of India and Parkistan, Rajiv Gandhi and Benazir Bhutto met in 1988 to discuss the amelioration of relations between their countries, the language was English. Although they are only a tiny fraction of the subcontinent's population, English-language adepts are important because they are *the* elite. They are the directors of modernizing change. Their ostensible style is modern and they are the exemplars of modernity. In India, particularly, their society has become attainable to the upwardly mobile, the beneficiaries of bourgeois revolution. For better or worse, it is they who are leading India into the modern world and the modern world into India.

Table 2. *"Principal languages"* 1991 *(nos. and percentages are approximate: projections from 1981 census data)*

Language	Mn. persons speaking	Percentage of Indian pop.	MAJOR and secondary concentrations of speakers, by states and Union Territories (see Map. 1)
Assamese	12	1.4	ASSAM, Arunachal Pradesh[a]
Bengali	64	7.6	WEST BENGAL, Assam, Tripura
Gujarati[b]	41	4.9	GUJARAT, Daman and Diu
Hindi	326	38.6	BIHAR, HARYANA, HIMACHAL PRADESH, MADHYA PRADESH, RAJASTHAN, UTTAR PRADESH, Punjab, Delhi, Chandigarh
Kannada	33	3.9	KARNATAKA
Kashmiri	4	0.5	JAMMU & KASHMIR
Malayalam	32	3.8	KERALA, Lakshadweep
Marathi	61	7.2	MAHARASHTRA, Goa
Oriya	28	3.3	ORISSA
Punjabi	23	2.7	PUNJAB, Haryana, Chandigarh, Delhi
Sindhi	2	0.2	An expatriates' language in India. Sind is in Pakistan
Tamil	55	6.5	TAMILNADU, Pondicherry
Telegu	67	7.9	ANDHRA PRADESH
Urdu	44	5.2	HINDI-SPEAKING REGION, Andhra Pradesh

Notes: [a]States and territories in which other than – "principal languages" are prominent or predominant are: Arunachal Pradesh, Dadra & Nagar Haveli, Goa, Himachal Pradesh, Kashmir, Manipur, Meghalaya, Mizoram, Nagaland, Sikkim and Tripura. [b]Although Bombay is the capital of Maharashtra, the city's traditional language of business is Gujarati.

Within India itself, diversities abound: of ethnicity, religion and in regard to both the modes and means of production. Along with Sanskrit, which is of great cultural and sentimental significance, but spoken by hardly anyone, the Indian constitution lists fourteen "principal languages" (see table 2).

Of these, Hindi has the largest number of speakers, about 326 million; Sindhi has the smallest, about 2 million; the median, an average of Gujarati- and Malayalam-speakers, is about 36.5 million. Speakers of these "principal languages" are geographically concentrated, as they are in Europe. Other than Sindhi and Urdu, every "principal language" is the official language of one or more states of the Indian Union. In each of these "linguistic states," the majority of its population are reckoned to be speakers of its official-cum-"principal language."

Of India's ethnic diversity, however, its "principal languages" and "linguistic states" are only the surfaces. Language speaking in India, as elsewhere, is only a central trait in an ethnic complex of traits. Marathi-speakers, for example, belong to a society that is distinctly Marathi in its history, social structure, religious practices, literature and art, customs and manners, diet and dress. The ethnic distinctiveness of Marathis is no less than that of Swedes or Spaniards, for example, nor more than that of Telegus or Kannadigas.

Within any "linguistic state," the first language of most people is unlikely to be the "principal language" of that state, but rather one of hundreds of mother tongues which politicians and their linguists have grouped together to form "principal languages." Some mother tongues that have been grouped together are mutually intelligible and some are not. Some of them are themselves central traits in an ethnic complex, and some of these are more or less assimilable than others in the inclusive "principal language"-ethnic group. In every "linguistic state" there are minorities, sometimes troublesome or disaffected, whose mother tongues are included in other states' "principal languages" or in none.

Almost 100 million Indians belong to ethnic groups whose mother tongues are not included in any "principal language." Most of these people belong to tribal groups, of which there are hundreds in India. In the northeast, some tribal groups, most notably Nagas and Mizos, have fought protracted guerrilla wars against the government to prevent their ethnic identities and their interests from being submerged in an India of "principal languages." To keep the peace, the government has realigned state borders in the area with tribal boundaries. Here are the Indian Union's six "tribal states" – five with non-tribal minorities, and Tripura whose majority is non-tribal.

Other tribal groups and other-than "principal language"-speaking non-tribal groups are located throughout India. Of tribespeople in the millions, there are Santals in West Bengal and the Hindi region's

Bihar, Bhils in the Hindi region's Rajasthan, Gonds in Andhra Pradesh, where the "principal language" is Telegu. Konkani, which is not a "principal language," is the official language of Goa. The Gorkhas of Darjeeling district of West Bengal and Sikkim want Nepali to be constitutionally recognized as a "principal language."

Within virtually all non-tribal ethnic groups, smaller groups of Indians differentiate themselves from one another by caste. Ideologically, caste is an institution of Hinduism. But, in fact, there are castes and quasi castes among Muslims, Christians, Sikhs, Buddhists, Jains and Jews. Almost invariably, one becomes a caste member only by being born of parents, both of whom were born into that caste. Caste membership can be renounced or revoked, but one can never, or hardly ever, except through subterfuge, join or be joined into a caste other than that of his or her parents. Caste is the group into which one must marry to remain a member in good standing and to endow one's children with caste membership. Though less so now than in the past – it, too, changes – castes are differentiated as being of relatively high or low ritual-cum-social status, according to the traditional or prescribed occupations of their members, by sumptuary taboos and commensal restrictions.

Virtually all castes are areally centered and exclusive to the people of a larger ethnic division: Tamils have their castes, Bengalis theirs, and so forth. Castes are in Tonnies' famous term, *gemeinschaft*, "communities of fate": "us" as differentiated from "them." There are thousands of castes, and quasi castes, their fragments and aggregates in India. Second only to families, of which they are demonstrable or ideological extensions, castes provide the Indian countryside with its basic social organizations and political units.

Cutting across large ethnic and even caste differences in India, are diversities of religion. Sikhs belong to the same castes and often the same families as their Punjabi Hindu neighbors. Within the same non-Hindu tribal groups and certain of the same south-Indian castes, some segments are Christian and some are not. The most important lines of religious diversity, however, are between Hindus and Muslims. Muslims are everywhere in India. Forty percent of them live in the Hindi/Urdu-speaking north, where they are 11 percent; of the population. Other areas of Muslim concentration are: Jammu and Kashmir, which has a Muslim majority of about 65 percent; Kerala, West Bengal and Assam, where Muslim populations are between 20 and 25 percent. Everywhere in India, Muslims are part of their local society. They live in the same villages and towns as non-Muslims, they speak the same mother tongues and read in the same languages. Hindu castes and Muslim quasi castes, though generally separate from one another, are usually parts of the same local societies. Though less now than in the recent past, Hindus and Muslims of the same local societies sometimes professed more or less the same religious beliefs and performed some of the same or similar religious rituals.

Nonetheless, there is strife. And more than likely, there always has been, between Hindus and Muslims. Its monuments, from early times and still standing, and now a terrible political issue, are the mosques built by Muslim warriors on the ruins of Hindu temples they desecrated or destroyed. During the nineteenth century, the British imparted a political dimension to tensions between Hindu and Muslim middle classes. Muslim divines accelerated their efforts to purify their humble coreligionists' faith from the taints of Hinduism. Hindu revivalists fulminated against trespasses of Muslim conquerors and proselytizers on *Bharat Mata* (Mother India). While census takers and scholars began increasingly to appreciate the similarities between Indian Hindus and Muslims, they began increasingly to think of each other as different. From the middle of the 1920s, localized conflicts, "riots," between Hindu and Muslim communities became ordinary, recurring events on the Indian political scene. The partition of the subcontinent between India and Pakistan in 1947 was accompanied by a communal bloodbath in Punjab and Bengal. In independent India, communal riots are, again, ordinary and recurrent. Encouraged by increasingly militant, well-financed and ideologically oriented communal organizations, tensions between Hindus and Muslims have increased, particularly during the 1980s, and the incidence and destructiveness of communal riots have also increased.

India is as economically diverse as it is ethnically and religiously heterogeneous. It is like a vast museum of technology. Agricultural techniques vary from the slash-and-burn of some tribal people; to laborious subsistence cultivation by millions of "peasant" families; to "green revolution," capital-intensive, market-oriented farming by cultivating entrepreneurs. Through Rajasthan's towns, main streets spill over to their footpaths with carts, bicycles and rickshaws pushed and pulled and pedalled by men and boys; donkeys loaded with sacks of goods; vehicles drawn by horses and bullocks and camels; motor scooters, three-wheeled goods and passenger carriers; overaged and overloaded trucks and buses trailed by their stinking black exhaust; sleek new Japanese-model hatchbacks and light commercial vehicles.

Modern five-star hotels are built with the labor of women hod carriers who scale bamboo building frames with pots of bricks and mortar balanced on their heads. Modern technology is used to build modern engineering and electronic equipment. The small business sector includes *karkhanas* (workshops) that bang and clang with a family's labor on the ground floor of its living quarters and the trendy offices of computer software suppliers. Technological ages coexist in India today: and not only in how people make things and earn their livings, but consequently, in how they live their lives.

The lines that separate Indians into ethnic groups, castes and religious communities are hatched and cross-hatched with the lines of class. Among the 100 million or so Indians who live in cities with populations of over 100,000, and particularly among those in modern industrial and professional employment, class consciousness and conflict are facts of urban life, no less than they are in comparable cities elsewhere. In villages and small towns class consciousness is not so clearly articulated and class conflict tends to be absorbed or incorporated into patron–client relationships and factional and caste conflicts. But even here, in the countryside, wealth and power are intruding more heavily than they have in the past and even displacing the traditional caste criteria of social status.

How do the unities of civilization give coherence to a society so diverse as contemporary India's? What, in other words, makes an Indian society? It begs rather than answers the question, I know, to say its Indian-ness. But that is perhaps a way to begin. What constitutes Indian-ness? Certainly, it is no less a quality than European-ness, and like European-ness it is something like a complex of characteristics which those who share identify with themselves and each other, and by which they distinguish themselves from others and are distinguished by others.

I would include among these more or less shared characteristics, at least: myths and mythologies, memories of the past, the sense of a common fate – now and in the future; religious, philosophical and intellectual traditions, political ideologies and *modi operandi*, emotional and affective conventions, self-perceptions and notions about others and the world in general, prejudices and stereotypes, ideas about morality and propriety; affinities of social structure, language, physiognomy – actual and perceived; music, art and architecture; diet, dress and adornment. Indian-ness partakes of the sacred and the mundane; and arbitrarily, to be sure, and only for the sake of expository order, we might untangle, divide and consider these characteristics under these headings.

First, second and permeating almost all of the sacred, both giving life to the characteristics of Indian civilization and living in them, are Hinduism and Islam. Hinduism and Islam are not only different religions more or less separating their faithful but as well components in an Indian civilization more or less shared by Hindus and Muslims. Hinduism is first, both in its antiquity and its Indian-ness. A religious cosmography, Hinduism's concern is with the whole order of the universe and everything in it. Its location, however, is in India and among Indians. Eighty-five percent of India's population is Hindu. Ninety-five percent of the world's Hindu population lives in the subcontinent or is of Indian origin. All the world's major religions save Hinduism settled and resettled in places that already had long histories. The histories of Hinduism (or at least proto-Hinduism) and India began together and have remained, almost exclusively, together. Like other religions, Hinduism was the font of a great culture whose monuments decorate its world: in words and music, brick and mortar, metal, stone and paint. But, really, Hinduism lives in Hindus.

It lives in their daily lives all over India: in the families, castes and villages where most Hindus live. In no small measure, these are Hindu institutions. To be born into a Hindu family is to be born into a caste. To be born into a caste is to be born a Hindu, there is virtually no other way. To be born a Hindu is to have a place, according to one's caste, in Hindu society. Hindu society is for most Hindus their village. Its rules are for the most part Hindu rules. For example, proper relationships within a family between young and old, male and female, husbands and wives; legitimate marriages, births, adoptions, inheritances; appropriate behavior within a caste, among its members and between castes among their members; right deportment, occupation and exchanges of goods and services within a village – all are prescribed, thought to be prescribed, represented as being prescribed by Hinduism.

The great gods and goddesses of the Hindu pantheon are every-where in India. The rituals in their worship vary from place to place, they are known by various names and recognized in varying iconographies, they share their devotees' ardor with local gods and saints, they may be worshiped as idols or as emanations of the One that is the essence of All. But everywhere are Vishnu and Shiva,

Krishna and Rama, Parvati, Lakshmi and Ganesh. Their images are present and revered in homes and temples, shops and factories, government offices and schools, buses and rickshaws, bodily decorations and amulets, shrines by the wayside and in the middle of city streets. Their stories are celebrated in great festivals, commemorated by pilgrims, carved and painted, read, recited, acted, danced, sung and now, broadcast, screened, televised and videoed.

No less than great and folk culture, is popular culture in India infused with Hinduism. Though unhung in art galleries and museums, the most popular genre of painting in India today is graphic art: *par excellence*, the illustrations that decorate the tops of calendars. Mass-produced prints are available, with or without calendars, framed or unframed, in bazaars all over India. The illustrations are usually portraits and they usually portray Hindu gods and goddesses. They are in extensive use not merely as decorations but as icons. There is a group of sculptors in Jaipur city who have for generations carved marble idols for Hindu temples all over India. Nowadays, their models are calendar art portraits.

Calendar art merges and merges its Hinduism into the films: the visual art supreme of popular Indian culture. India's best known and most parodied films are the Hindi-language features of Bombay's *filmi duniya* (film world), but there are other film industries all over India that make movies in virtually all of its "principal languages" and have in the process contributed to their standardization. Together, India's film industries produce about one-quarter of the world's feature length films. Every day about 13 million Indians go to the movies.

There is a steady production of films whose themes are rather specifically *dharmik*, religious. One latter-day film of this genre and its video cassette reproductions have become icons in the worship of the goddess *Santoshi Ma*. She is a relatively new entrant into the India-wide Hindu pantheon. Her entrance has been via a Bombay feature of 1974, *Jai Santoshi Ma*, and the ubiquity of her calendar art portraits. For years, some while ago, in West Bengal, there was a noted resemblance between graphic art and amateur poster portrayals of the goddess Durga and a particularly popular Bengali film actress. In 1987, the Hindu faithful were presented with what has been the most widely attended recitation of the *Ramayana* in its two-millennia-old history: an epic television series of more than 100 episodes. It is typically *filmi*, the most popular series in Indian television history, a religous experience for many in its audience and now available on video cassettes. It was followed by a television event of equal magnitude: a serial presentation of the other major Hindu epic, *Mahabharata*.

Hinduism suffuses Indian politics and some of its most popular issues. To their operations as basic social units of Hindu societies, castes have readily added the function of representing their members' interests in the rough and tumble of Indian politics: as interest groups, vote banks, party blocs and even parties. Caste is an ordinary consideration in pre-selections of party candidates and post-election divisions of the spoils. Representatives of their castes contest for membership of virtually every institution that has access to public resources: state ministries, university councils, municipal corporations and village *panchayats*. Castes have become so integral a part of the Indian political scene that it is hard to picture it without them: these organizations of Hindu inegalitarianism that vitalize and are vitalized by Indian parliamentary democracy.

Hinduism has provoked some of the most contentious questions in Indian politics. Although Indian society is overwhelmingly Hindu, its government is constitutionally secular. To what extent should a secular Indian government try to support moral principles derived from the religion of most Indians, e.g., by banning the slaughter of cows? To what extent should it try to reform the social practices of Hindus which governments regard as harmful to Indian society, e.g., by prohibiting the giving and taking of dowries and the marriages of children? To what extent should it try to enforce its constitutional mandates to interfere in the socio-religious practices of the majority, e.g., by prohibiting the practice of untouchability? Really, secularism is a thin new crust beneath which Hinduism roils. *Hindutva* (literally, Hinduness) is certainly the most massive and turbulent force below the surface of Indian politics. Millions and millions of Hindus – young and old, left and right, rich and poor, high and low – would like their government to be not simply Indian but Hindu. They think of the national government, in particular, as secular in favor of the "minority communities" and excessively indulgent of them. The Sikhs have been objects of some current ire. But Muslims are the bane of "awakened" Hindus. Muslims are "them." In India, a pampered minority, of doubtful loyalty and with a past to answer for. In Pakistan and Bangladesh, at present and into the foreseeable future, menacing, subversion-abetting and dangerously volatile majorities.

But, the contributions over the centuries of Islam and Muslims to the society of India have been vastly greater than cohering an occasional "we" of Hindu revivalists. Indeed, second only to Hinduism, Islam is India's most powerful and pervasive "ism." And not only for Muslims. Over most of north India, Muslim *durbars* (princely courts) had come and gone over six centuries until the nineteenth. Things Islamic and Muslim and large populations of Muslims have been in north India for eight centuries. The social and religious practices of these Muslims have been profoundly, characteristically affected from their having grown over the centuries among converts from Hinduism and in a Hindu heartland. No less profound and characteristic have been the contributions to the Indian-ness of contemporary Hindu society from Islam: translated and transformed by Indian Muslim potentates and magnates, by Hinduized Muslim and Islamicized Hindu proselytizers and back-sliders. In art and architecture, language and music, dress and diet, customs and worship, high and popular culture in all its manifestations, the civilization of India is an amalgam of Hindu and Muslim contributions.

The amalgamators were, for the most part, men and women who were Hindu or Muslim devotionalists, *bhaktis* or *sufis*, or people who drew their inspiration from devotionalism. Of the latter, perhaps the most famous was the late-fifteenth-century poet, Kabir. He asks:

> O servant, where dost thou seek me?
> Lo! I am beside thee.
> I am neither in temple nor in mosque:
> I am neither in Kaaba nor in Kailash
>   [the abode of Lord Shiva]:
> Neither am I in rites and ceremonies,
>   nor in Yoga and renunciation.
> If thou art a true seeker, thou shalt at once see me:
>   thou shalt meet me in a moment of time.
> Kabir says, "O Sadhu, God is the breath of all breath."[6]

Bhakti, which had its beginnings in Tamilnadu as early as the seventh century, spread northward in the centuries that followed until it engulfed the subcontinent. Sufism came into India from the north. It shared with Hinduism a belief in God's immanence. Like Hindus, and particularly *bhaktis, sufis* expressed their devotion in music and dance. There were miracle-working *sufi* saints, like their Hindu counterparts. And to these were attached disciples (*murids*), like their Hindu counterparts (*shishayas*). Some of the *sufis* belonged

to religious orders, and some of these claimed and were acknowledged to be – albeit, not universally – orthodox in their Islam. But
there were orders outside the *shari'ah* (Islamic law). There were *sufis*
who belonged to no order: preachers of sermons, singers of songs,
God-intoxicated mystics who said they were neither Muslims nor
Hindus; visionaries, ecstatics, comforters, prophets, miracle-wor-
kers.

Not entirely but enough, *bhakti* and *sufism* melded into one
another, particularly in north India. Sikhism is an amalgamative
faith. But as such, it is only a reminder of the devotionalist ferment
that pervaded medieval India and produced a Muslim population,
now of about 300 million, from Pakistan across India and through
Bangladesh, that is distinctively Indian, and an Indian civilization
to which Islamic influences reach from village roots to high culture.
Even the recently accelerated attempts by both Hindu and Muslim
organizations to "purify" and separate their religious practices, one
faith's from the other's, have only been more or less. A few years
ago, I revisited at Fatehpur Sikri, outside of Agra, the tomb of the
sixteenth century *sufi* saint, Salim Chishti. One of Islam's busiest
holy places in India, his white marble mausoleum is best known as
a shrine to which wives go to implore the saint's intercession in
their prayers to become the mothers of sons. Among the supplicants
that day, there were at least as many Hindu as Muslim women, and
the suppliance and suppliant ritual certainly owe more to the *mandir*
(Hindu temple) than to the mosque.

In south India, in general, there are fewer Muslims and less of
Islam, but there too, they are part of the Indian fabric. Because
Arabs were in the spice trade from the eighth century and India's
Malabar Coast was one of its locations, Muslims are 20 percent of
Kerala's population. Andhra Pradesh, whose Muslim population is
about 8 percent, has its capital in Hyderabad: until 1947, the capital
of India's leading Muslim prince, the Nizam, its most famous
Muslim court and a major center of Muslim culture on the subcontinent. What is now the state of Karnataka with a Muslim population
of about 11 percent had been within the orbit of Muslim imperial
politics and religious proselytization from the early fourteenth
century, and during the eighteenth was ruled by a shortlived but
vigorous Muslim dynasty. Tamilnadu, virtually the only part of the
subcontinent that was beyond the furthest extent of even the Mughal
empire, has a Muslim population of about 5 percent.

No less than their coreligionists in the north, Muslims in south

India are integral parts of those local and regional societies that patch and blend into the fabric of Indian society. The creation of Pakistan ripped away only the edges. Often with tragic consequences, the Indian fabric has not been for Muslims everywhere and at all times protective and secure. Too often, it is rent with apparent suddenness some place or other by violent communal confrontations. Whatever the immediate outcome of any of these, their cumulative effect is to destroy Muslim confidence in the fabric. Yet they have no other. They are part of it, and it of them. Hinduism and Islam in India are analogous to Christianity in Europe in this sense: they are at once major sources of social conflict and cultural cohesion.

Indian-ness partakes of the mundane no less than of the sacred. Over the centuries, there have developed among Indians – as among Europeans, for example – ordinary continental similarities and familiarities. So for all their diversities, Indians are likely to recognize as Indian rather than something else the food that other Indians eat, how they look and act, their styles of life and ways of going about things, their histories and languages. In recent decades all of this has been made increasingly recognizable by rapidly expanding communications media and educational facilities.

Feature films shot on location all over India present to their audiences all over India unfamiliar people and landscapes, identify these as Indians and parts of India, and make them familiar according to the tried and true formulae of the Indian cinema. All India Radio's network has grown from six stations in 1947 to almost 100 now which reach almost 100 percent of the Indian population. Since 1959, India has built one of the largest television networks in the world. Over 20,000 periodicals circulate in India, of which about 1,600 are daily newspapers: published in English, every "principal language," and other Indian languages. The percentage of primary school age children who are enrolled in school has increased since Indian independence from less than half to almost all, the percentage of secondary school age children who are enrolled has increased from less than 10 to more than 40 percent. The language media in most mass communication and education are provincial, but most of the ostensible messages are Indian: in popular culture, current affairs, geography, history, the social sciences. The underlying message is: this is India and you are its citizens.

Parliamentary democracy and capitalist development have greatly enlarged the political and economic dimensions of Indian civilization. As bourgeois revolution proceeds, the Indian polity becomes more and more prominent as a cohering force in Indian society. Second only to religious celebrations, election campaigns and political demonstrations of one sort or another have come to provide India with its great public festivals. They are festivals in affirmation of Indian nationality, replete with their appropriate Indian luminaries, *mantras*, rituals, iconography, hagiography and demonology. These are well-known and immediately recognized – though taken with a grain of salt. Politics are an ordinary topic of conversation among ordinary Indians. Politicians and their *tamashas* (celebrations) may be held in general and increasing disrepute, but that politics translate into influence, wealth and power, loans and jobs, electricity, schools and metalled roads is widely appreciated. Widely appreciated, too, is that the prizes of politics go to those who can compete for them and that the competition takes place within the arenas of an Indian polity. To men and women who were, or whose parents were just a short time ago imperial or princely state subjects, citizenship in democratic India promises, at least, the rights and dignity of participants in the determination of their and their children's fate. To Indian bourgeois, in whose lifetime their country was scorned and ridiculed for its backwardness, the Indian Union promises citizenship in a great power.

Capitalist development has created an Indian market for goods and services. A perquisite of Indian citizenship is privileged access to these markets. And it is largely a privilege of the middle classes. The doctor from Tamilnadu who practices in Delhi. The manufacturer in Calcutta who sells his goods in Karnataka. The farmers in Punjab whose wheat is consumed all over India. In India's markets, the government is ubiquitous: a major regulator and participant. What can and cannot be made and sold, who can compete with whom, what can be imported and exported, what is the value of the rupee and how available is bank credit, how are security markets regulated, "black money" redeemed and laundered, the investments of NRIs (non-resident Indians) attracted to their homeland – to all these, and other questions relevant to middle class interests, the answers of the Government of India are likely to be important, if not decisive. In a word, the government has made Indian citizenship, at least for the middle classes, a crucial characteristic of their Indian-ness.

The changing countryside

My discussion in part I is of the basic social institutions of the Indian countryside, from the smallest to the most inclusive, and how they are all changing. Family household, family and village are the topics of chapter 1. Chapter 2 focuses on that unique Indian institution, caste. Class in its several manifestations, is the topic of chapter 3. In chapter 4, I discuss ethnic homelands-cum-states of the Indian Union. Religion, and particularly Hinduism, as it affects these institutions and is affected by them, is part of the discussion in most of these chapters.

Although the institutions of part I vary considerably in their structure from one Indian place to another, I have tried with whatever success to describe them generally for a non-specialist audience. Doubtlessly, my own experiences of India have given a north Indian bias to my descriptions. I describe the institutions in part I as changing and emphasize their participation in bourgeois revolution. In doing this, I have necessarily focussed my discussion, though not exclusively, on the rural middle classes.

sons partition the family's real and other property equally among themselves and establish their own, separate households. These give the appearance of being nuclear families when their children are young, but ideally they are joint families-in-becoming and will become so when sons marry and bring their wives home to live. As a customary general rule, only grandfather's sons or grandsons inherit any of the family's real property at his death. Although his widow may hold part of the family estate as a lifetime annuity. Her sons are bound in family duty to care for her and any other widows of the household and to assume responsibility for arranging their sisters' weddings and providing their dowries. If grandfather had had no sons or grandsons, the family's real property would have passed at his death to his brothers or more distant kinsmen in his father's line. Women's inheritances do not come primarily from their husbands' but from their fathers' families: when they marry and in the form of money, jewelry, clothing, household and other movable goods. Their dowries. In Hindi, dowry is called *stridan*: the gift to a woman.

Like all family ideals, this one affects reality more than it reflects it. In reality, the ideal joint family is in structure exceptional and real families do only imperfectly what they are meant to do ideally. Fortuitous circumstances and ordinary human imperfections account for some of the gap between the ideal and the real, but some of it – of particular concern here – is accountable to family adaptions to the exigencies and opportunities of life in contemporary India. In any case, however, the gap is not so wide as to separate the ideal from having its effects on the real. Far from it. For most Indians, family ties take clear precedence over all others, they bind closely and as a matter of course a more extended group than the nuclear family of parents and their unmarried children. Extended or extra-nuclear family organization is based almost invariably and exclusively – with some exceptions – on descent through the male line and male kinship. The exceptions are a few matrilineal groups of Hindus and Muslims in Kerala and among some tribal people.

Sometimes the gap between the ideal and the real is the apparent result of no more than family demography. There are families without sons, and sons without a father's family. There are families whose sons are unmarried children. Sometimes the gap is a matter of choice. There are fathers who choose not to have their sons live with them, and sons who choose not to live with their fathers. The ideal doesn't prevent such choices, although it might prompt and shape relevant explanations and rationalizations, inferences and gossip.

Where joint family households have been more or less established they may be more or less disestablished at any time before the patriarch's demise and with no anticipation of it. The proverbial saboteurs of the family's consanguinal jointness, the agents of subversive conjugality, are the household's daughters-in-law. They live within the interstices of the binding ties of blood, caught in them but apart from them. In the presence of the family's hierarchs, daughters-in-law are expected to show no particular concern for their children other than as children of the household, nor are they expected to show any signs of affection for their husbands or to court any. Joint family etiquette suits joint families. And privacy is hard to come by. The proper relationship of daughters-in-law to the patriarch is one of respectful distance. The proper relationship of daughters-in-law to the matriarch is one of obedience and deference to her status as their husbands' madonna. It is the duty of daughters-in-law to behave compatibly with their husbands' parents rather than their duty to behave compatibly with their sons' wives. If their brothers- and sisters-in-law are compatible, then well and good; if not, there are no sibling bonds to take the edge off even ordinary incompatibility. In a word, daughters-in-law are the most likely members of the family to be disaffected. Or to be blamed for the disaffection of their husbands.

The shoe may, of course, fit; or it may be purposely misfitted to disguise tenuous and attenuated ties among the household's men. Daughters-in-law live in the moral communities of their husbands' families and are expected to behave accordingly, but they are not really of them. The moral community's substance is the family's substance: the ties of blood among men. When these seem not to hold, a daughter-in-law's disaffection is a family affliction that merits sympathy and indicates a specific flaw rather than a general weakness. Scapegoats vary in kind but are universal in their use. Oblations to ideals! It will come as no revelation to observers of the Family of Man that fathers and sons and brothers are quite capable of mistrusting and despising one another without the connivance of their wives.

Disaffection can wreck a joint family household. Disaffection can also be one of any number of reasons for a household to vary from the joint family model. Convenience, preference and necessity are reasons. Household dynamics provide reasons, as do social and economic dynamics outside the family and beyond its control. The capacity of Indian families to contrive variations on and from the joint family model provides our first example of the Indian genius for preserving the valued substances of social institutions by allowing and even facilitating circumstantial changes in their form.

So, for whatever reasons, a husband and wife may live separately from his paternal household, with their children, under their own roof, taking food from their own hearth. But they may choose not to separate from his father's household the husband's portion of its holdings and they may continue to cultivate it as if they were unseparated members of his father's household. Or, they may choose to separate the husband's portion and cultivate it separately; but continue, for example, to accept his father's authority in making marriage arrangements for the couple's children and the husband's responsibility for contributing to his sisters' dowries. Or, they may not accept his father's authority or his responsibilities to his sisters, but for the sake of appearances, domestic peace, whatever, act as if they do.

In lieu of contributing his labor to the work of cultivation, the adult son of a farm family household may remit part of the income that he has earned from working in an urban occupation. Such remittances are common. For many farm families, they have become an important source of income. Usually, they secure for the remitter his coparcenary rights in the household's land holdings and otherwise his good standing as a family member. He may continue to live in his father's household and commute to work, depending upon its location and circumstances and his proclivities and those of his family. Or his wife and children may continue to live in his father's household and he may return to it regularly, irregularly, often, once in a while. Or his wife and children may live with him in an urban nucleated family: really a conjugal module more or less of his father's household. Or they may live with him in an apparently proper, sociologically standard urban nuclear family; although they may continue to be economically and, more than likely, otherwise tied to his father's household.

In contemporary India there has been an enormous growth in the number and variety of urban occupations and their accessibility to villagers. This is the consequence of any number of developments that we have yet to discuss: industrialization and urbanization, the development of transport facilities and services, the growth of education and the use of regional languages in occupations where

English was once the medium, and so forth. For village families, urban occupations are perhaps most notable as producers of remittance income. For poorer households, remittance income may mitigate underemployment. Often, in modest household enterprises, in land or otherwise, more people are doing the work that could be done as well or better by fewer people and, consequently, more people are being sustained by a family income that could better sustain fewer people. Sending sons off to work in town and harvesting their pay packets or postal money orders provide some relief. For better-off and well-to-do village households, income may be one among other substantial benefits they receive from sons who work in towns and cities across India and around the world – benefits of their participation in bourgeois revolution.

There is no evidence in the various studies of Indian village families to suggest that there are nowadays fewer households which approximate the joint family model than there have been in the past. The evidence also suggests that the greater a family's landholding or other wealth and the higher the local status of its caste – these often go together, of course – the more likely is its household to approximate the joint family model – minus remittance income earners. This is no different than one would expect. Where families are the basic social institutions, those that have a material interest in staying together and a stake in their respectability are more likely to stay together and behave respectably than families that have neither. They are also likely to vary their jointness in order to sponsor and collect the benefits from profitable and prestigious urban and modern careers for their sons.

More than one-fifth of India's medical students come from farm families.[1] A farm family that aspires to invest in a career in medicine, for example, for one of its sons, must be able to afford the considerable opportunity and out-of-pocket costs of his education through university. As a means of insuring its investment, among other things, the family may choose to arrange a suitable marriage for its doctor-to-be while he is still a dependent student, thereby precluding his own arrangement of an unsuitable marriage when he becomes an independent practitioner. Then, there will also be the costs to his family of maintaining his wife (off-set, to be sure, against her dowry) and, perhaps, children.

If the investment produces a successful urban medical practice, the household can look to it as a source of substantial remittance income. Some of this can be reinvested in land, in urban careers for other sons of the household and in substantial, good-husband-catching dowries for its daughters. Having a successful doctor in the family should also enable it to ask for substantial dowries and brides from well-to-do and well-connected families, otherwise facilitate its access to the well-to-do and well connected, provide a reliable hedge against life's contingencies and a cosy retirement for grandfather and grandmother.

However tied economically and otherwise to the village household of his father, our hypothetical doctor is almost certain to live apart from it. His lucrative medical practice will almost certainly be in a town or city, and he will live in a modern, urban, more-or-less nuclear family of his own. At least until his sons marry. Or until one or both of his aged parents come to live with him – another variation on the joint family model. Now, modern wives suit modern, urban, more or less nuclear families. Modern wives are educated women: women who can share their husbands' interests, be their companions, entertain their friends and colleagues, raise their children to succeed in the modern world, manage their households and cope with city life.

As India produces more and more modern men – it has, we know, become a supplier of doctors to the world's cities – the demand for modern Indian wives increases. To meet this demand and benefit from it, relatively well-to-do village families are doing what would have been unthinkable to them a generation ago: they are investing in university education for their daughters. Many of India's modern men are "new men," first-generation-up-from-the-village; and so increasingly are many of their modern wives. Some of these women will sooner or later do the work for which their education has prepared them: medicine (a good career for women in India), law, government service, university lecturing, business management, engineering and so forth. Whether or not an educated wife aspires to a working career, inflation and the increasing availability and attractiveness of modern consumer goods to modern families may simply be more than her bread-winning husband can handle on his own. It is fair to say, however, that village families send their daughters to university primarily to prepare them for careers as modern wives. For a village family that can hope to make an advantageous marriage for its daughter and sees the advantages of having a successful modern man for a son-in-law, its daughter's education is part of her family's negotiating package, along with her personal and familial attributes and her dowry.

In pages to follow, we will return often to a discussion of village families in the context of bourgeois revolution. A first, summary statement is perhaps appropriate here. Among the many other ways that better-off and well-to-do village families accelerate bourgeois revolution and reap its rewards are through their investment of family resources: first, to educate and accommodate the trained personnel that are necessary to that revolution; and second, to do this as a family enterprise, more-or-less assuring it thereby of some return on its investment.

To return to our hypothetical doctor's urban family: it may in time and depending upon circumstances become as completely nuclear, in reality if not in ideology, as its Western counterpart. Again, even in villages, nuclear families are common. In general, there is a sort of continuum in Indian village family organization. At one pole, there is the archetypical, model joint family: patriarchal, patrilineal and patrilocal. At the other pole, there is the model nuclear family of parents and dependent children. Between the poles and tending toward one of them are myriad variations, of which I have given only a few sketchy illustrations. These variations, however, *do not* ordinarily include organizational ties between a man and the families of his mother, wife or sisters. Within the joint family household and its extensions, however varied, organizational ties are lineal. And a man has no lineal ties to the families of his mother, wife or sisters.

Women are family members only individually and in their own right. Hindu women take their *gotra* (or clan) membership from their fathers, but it is no more than the inheritance of a prohibition against marrying a man of the same *gotra*. Otherwise these women are lineal members *de facto* of neither the families into which they were born or married. With the exception of that handful of matrilineal groups, extended family organization throughout India, within families of whatever caste or religion, accords only with the line of male descent.

It seems likely to me, that this remarkable consistency has contributed in no small measure to the equally remarkable preservation of the family as the basic social institution in Indian villages and in the society at large. Simply, the organizational unity of the family based on male descent, its integrity, is under no threat of being eroded by some competing organization, no spear-blunting invitation to enterprising sons-in-law and those who can't get on with their fathers, for example, to change their organizational

allegiances and interests. Where people's interests are in an organization their allegiances are likely to be there too. Again, the Indian
village household is an organization through which work is done
and its income is shared, property is passed on, marriages and
careers are arranged, children are reared, and life's contingencies
are provided for. And it is an organization of the spear *alone*.
On the distaff side there may be close *personal* ties, however. The
families of a man's mother, wife and sisters are, after all, kinsfolk.
To contain the ambitions of men of their lineages, Rajput princes
and noblemen, customarily sought alliances amongst their mothers'
and wives' male relatives. The affectionate relationship between a
brother and sister separated from him by marriage and his solicitude
for her children is proverbial in India. Proverbial enough to be
celebrated by a holiday in the Hindu calendar, *rakshabandan*, and to
invest the Hindi word for wife's brother – *sala* – with the additional
meaning of a term of abuse.

Depending upon their families and their families circumstances
and, of course, their own attributes wives may be regarded as
drudges in their in-laws' households or as important and powerful
members of them; daughters, as burdens or blessings; grandmothers,
as no more than their husbands' shadows or no less than their *maires
du palais*. Typically women of ordinary cultivating and artisan
families do not only the universal women's work of housekeeping
and childrearing, but contribute their toil to the household's work
of cultivation and artisanship. Well-born and well-to-do families
typically regard it as unseemly for their women to work in village
fields and lanes, or even to leave their courtyards more often than
they have to. Village families, Hindu as well as Muslim, give witness
to their respectability and affluence by more or less secluding their
women. Behind the household *purdah* (curtain) in village India are
kept those universal tokens of family honor and stability: women
who are supposed to be chaste, obedient and economically
dependent.

Purdah may be no less than an emotionally, intellectually and
physically harmful confinement. Or it may be no more than excusing
the family's women from tedious work outside their households.
Inside, women of middle-class village households are likely to be
busily engaged in a wide range of crucial family undertakings that
vary from the usual chores of homemaking and childrearing to those
managerial activities – like marriage arrangements – that enhance
a worthy family's worthiness and maintain its cohesion.

Ironically, the costs of family cohesion are borne disproportionately by its women. Indeed, unequal treatment of women, including their lineal exclusion, contributes to, if it does not sustain that cohesion. With some appreciation, no doubt, of this connection, but motivated by Gandhian and Western liberal solicitude for women's welfare, the government of India began in the 1950s to legislate in favor of greater equality between the sexes. Known generally as the Hindu Code, this legislation has been supplemented and complemented over the years by other laws, and together they form a comprehensive code of personal and family law for India's religious majority. Primarily, this code provides laws for marriage, separation and divorce, adoption of heirs and inheritance of family property.

In principle though not in practice, the Hindu Code and its extensions are radical reforms. They bring under the law matters, like inheritance in grandfather's household, which village families have customarily regulated themselves. Their regulations were generally based on time-honored caste usage and sanctioned, however knowledgeably, by Hindu injunctive scripture. When disputes arose, these were customarily adjudicated by such amorphous, *ad hoc* and extra-legal bodies as caste and village councils. Disputes over family matters were sometimes brought to British Indian courts. Here, too, judges handed down decisions based on their understanding of Hindu (or Muslim) injunctive scripture and relevant and applicable customs and usage. Nowadays, an Indian court would apply the appropriate provision of the Hindu Succession Act of 1956 and its amendments.

This and other acts of the Hindu Code and its extensions were meant not only to incorporate into one set of laws the myriad family customs of thousands of Hindu castes, but to reform them. With *shastric* (Hindu injunctive) sanction, customary usage regarding the inheritance of family property, for example, is much the same in most Hindu castes as it is in grandfather's: women have no right or only a limited right to inherit real property. According to the Hindu Succession Act and its amendments, however, grandfather's widow and daughters have inheritance rights to the household's real property that are equal to his sons. Other major legal reforms of customary Hindu family rules provide for civil marriage and divorce, a family's right to adopt girls, prohibitions on the giving and taking of dowries, a minimum marriage age for girls of eighteen and the right of a girl married during her minority to repudiate that marriage before attaining her majority.

These reforms are, by and large, only of the statute books. The Indian government and, even more, the governments of the Indian states are apparently unwilling or unable to enforce their legislation for the equal treatment of Hindu women within their families. For Muslim women there is not even a legislated code. Their family law is that of the *shari'ah*: the legal code of Islam. Under Islamic law, the women of a family have lesser rights, e.g., in the inheritance of property, than its men. Nowadays, still, in litigation over matters within a Muslim family, the courts of the Indian Union apply their understanding of the *shari'ah*. The government of India has the constitutional obligation to bring Hindus and Muslims under a "uniform civil code." Why after forty years there is still no such code; indeed, why in 1986, the government gave legislative sanction to the *shari'ah*'s rules on divorce *for Muslims* – these and related questions regarding Hindu–Muslim relations in contemporary India will be discussed in chapter 5.

There is concern within the growing women's movement in India that the benefits of development, through bourgeois revolution and otherwise, are going less to women than to men, and the costs of development are being borne more by women than by men.[2] Some of these costs have been overshadowed, at least to casual observation, by the prominence of a handful of *haute bourgeoises* in virtually all areas of modern Indian life. And particularly in politics: in positions of power. But with whatever irony, these few women are, I suspect, the beneficiaries of the general, gender-unrelated inegalitarianism of Indian society. Simply, Jack is *not* as good as his mistress in a hierarchical society, in a social order of castes. In this society, the exercise of power by "high" women over "low" men is commonplace: by high caste ladies-of-the-house over their families' sweepers and laundrymen, by matrons in transit over the "coolies" who carry their baggage, by women in white collar employment over office *peons* (menials).

Out of the shadow, too, the condition of Indian women in general has improved considerably in independent India. Women's life expectancy at birth, like men's, has increased by close to 100 percent – to about sixty years – in the last four decades. The female literacy rate has trebled to almost 50 percent. As percentages of their respective age groups, females enrolled in primary school have doubled and those enrolled in middle school through university have at least trebled. At every educational level, too, the number of females per 100 males has increased.

But. The condition of Indian women in general still compares unfavorably with the condition of Indian men in general. The female literacy rate is little more than half the male rate, and in the countryside less than 20 percent of girls and women are literate. In secondary schools and universities, there are about two males enrolled for every female. Outside of some areas of public sector employment, the proportion of women in the paid workforce has been declining over the years. This is the effect of a variety of causes. But among them, certainly, is the upward mobility of an increasing number of families, and their acceptance of the middle classes' usual preferences for women who are kept in housebound respectability and dependence on their men.

In their post-independence march to Hindu respectability and embourgeoisement, Hindu families by the tens of millions have ground to dust the Dowry Prohibition Act of 1961. The traditionally and generally accepted association of dowry marriages with high social status has not been effaced by Gandhian or liberal reformism. Almost certainly, there has been an increase of late in the practice of dowry marriages, largely through its adoption by upwardly mobile castes. Particularly among the middle classes, there has probably been an increase also in the monetary value of dowries; and the fiction that they are daughters' inheritances rather than the purchase price for sons-in-law becomes increasingly palpable. Indian women's groups have brought to light a number of hideous instances in which brides with discrepant dowries were brutalized and even murdered or driven to suicide by their married families. The extent of this horror is unknown, but like domestic violence elsewhere and in other forms, much of it may be hidden.

Hidden also, is the contribution of dowry marriages to the darkest secret of Indian family life: female infanticide. Known and ominous is an infant mortality rate for females that is, for India as a whole, about 10 percent higher than it is for males; and a continually declining proportion of females in the Indian population: per 1000 males, from 972 in 1901 to 929 in 1991.

It may be that bourgeois revolution in the Indian countryside has increased the value of sons as family resources and the cost of daughters as family liabilities. Nonetheless, it may also be that some of the trickle-down effects of bourgeois revolution are going to women. I can, perhaps, suggest this by comparing some relevant data from the states of Punjab and Bihar. It is a comparison that I will pursue in other contexts throughout this book, and, with a small diversion, I introduce it here.

Simply: of the major agricultural states in India, Bihar is the least well-developed and Punjab – the home, *par excellence* of both green and bourgeois revolutions – is the most well-developed. Bihar's per capita domestic product (at 1970–71 prices) is the lowest among these states: Rs.486, in 1985–86, up 21 percent from 1970–71. Punjab's domestic product is the highest: Rs.1621 in 1985–86, up 51 percent from 1970–71. (The per capita domestic product of India as a whole in 1985–86 was Rs.798, up 26 percent from 1971.)

What has this to do with bourgeois revolution's trickle-down effects to women? Here are some straws in the wind! In 1951, the number of females per 1,000 males in Bihar was one of the highest in India. But by 1991 it had steadily declined by 8 percent. (The decline in India as a whole over the four decades was 1.5 percent.) In 1951, the number of females per thousand males in Punjab was one of the lowest in India. By 1991, however, it had increased by 5 percent. In Bihar, the female literacy rate in 1991 was 23.10 percent, up 15 percent from 1971. In Punjab the female literacy rate in 1991 was 49.72 percent, up 24 percent from 1971. In 1985–86, the enrolment ratios of girls in Bihar was: 52.5 percent in primary school (ages 6–11) and 14.8 percent in middle school (ages 11–14). In Punjab, the comparable figures were: 94 percent in primary school and 53.1 percent in middle school. Finally, Punjab's per capita expenditure on health and family welfare in 1983–84 was more than two and a half times that of Bihar's.

The effects of this trickle-down are real and likely to be significant in time. That literate mothers are more likely than illiterate mothers to tend effectively to their children's health, for example, has been fairly well established. But trickle-down effects have neither eroded what Aldous Huxley called "the appalling dangers of family life" for Indian women nor the ties that bind Indian women, for better or worse, to their families: first natal, then married. Family ties have been varied by bourgeois revolution, even harnessed to it; but not slackened by it. In the Indian countryside, a family's successful participation in bourgeois revolution, as in everyday life, is facilitated by its cohesion and the support available to it, by virtue of its cohesion, from its caste or community.

Outside the countryside, the rich and powerful, too, are family people. Exemplary family men and women! They are important to villagers because they are rich and powerful, and because they have made it and provide social models for those who aspire to make it. Giant industrial conglomerates whose stocks are publicly traded on the Bombay exchange are managed in their every enterprise by generations of their founders' families. Business, whether of the *mandi* (local market) or of the Birla Brothers, is usually a family affair. In the ministry in virtually every Indian state, in the hierarchy in virtually every political party, politics too, is usually a family affair.

In the 1980s, the prime minister of India, a Hindu woman, and the chief minister of Jammu and Kashmir, Sheikh Abdullah, the legendary Lion of Kashmir, a Muslim, both modernists and secularists and political party chiefs, chose as their successors a politically inexperienced and apparently uninterested airline pilot and a medical doctor: their sons. In 1990, less than a year after it had come to power in one of India's most momentous elections, the second non-Congress government in the Union's history was badly shaken by the threatened resignation of its deputy prime minister, Devi Lal. At issue was the government's unwillingness to support the blatant rigging of a by-election by Devi Lal's eldest son in order to retain his father's bequest: the chief ministership of the state of Haryana. When he died in 1987 the charismatic, former movie star and chief minister of Tamilnadu, "MGR," left behind a party split into two factions: one led by his wife, the other by an old flame and protégée – a *filmi* variation on the theme! After Rajiv Gandhi's assassination in 1991 his lieutenants offered the leadership of the Congress (I) party to his widow: an offer that was generally regarded as appropriate however opportunistic, her family's legacy, after all, although Sonia Gandhi was not only inexperienced in politics but disinclined to public life.

Villages

The great and powerful, of course, have their protégés and minions. Ordinary villagers depend upon their families. Family ties are virtually the warp and woof of the Indian countryside's social fabric. The great majority of Indian families live in the countryside. Of every four Indians, three are villagers: about 600 million people. They live in 600,000 villages all over India. Another 25 million-or-so Indians live in towns with a population of less than 20,000. These are for the most part country towns: as much a part of the countryside, as integral to it as are their surrounding villages.

All along the 4000 kilometers of India's coastlines, there are villages of fisherfolk. Tribal villages dot the subcontinent, more heavily in some areas than in others. But all over India the great majority of villages are places of sedentary cultivation by families of small holders. They are ostensibly "peasant villages." Again, however, their middle classes, at least, are no longer peasants, i.e., they are no more or less the subjects of non-cultivating rulers than farm families in Iowa or Provence. Along with other village families that work and provide services for them, small-holding Indian village families are part of a wider civilized society: for example, as castefellows, coreligionists, language users; as producers and consumers of goods, services and revenues; and most recently, as citizens and voters.

Over most of India, villages are clusters of residences surrounded by fields that their resident families cultivate. Within the residential cluster, the village proper, in northern Indian an apparent warren of baked mud and brick buildings, neighborhoods are most frequently marked off by the lines of caste and religious community. A quarter, at some distance from other village neighborhoods is often marked off for families of untouchable castes. Interspersed within the neighborhoods there are more or less public facilities. These are, typically, places for worship, wells or reservoirs which are used to supply water for household use, small shops and, increasingly, a building or buildings which are used as primary school, medical dispensary, council chamber, accommodation for official visitors, and so forth.

Country towns are likely to have a large population of cultivating families who live and work in much the same way as do their village counterparts. Otherwise, country towns are the sites of a variety of facilities, run by local people and outsiders, which provide villagers with their closest substantial link to the wider Indian society. Places where they show movies are in country towns. Shops which sell goods made in factories all over India are there, as are merchants who buy villagers' produce for resale in distant markets. The police, offices of the civil bureaucracy, courts and lawyers, post and telegraph services, bus and train stations, branches of national and state banks and local *sarafs* (money lenders), highschools and hospitals, proper *pandits* (*brahman* priests) and *mullahs* (Muslim legists) are in country towns.

Apart from the transients brought by their work to country towns and migratory farm laborers, India's rural population is, in general, stationary. Families emigrate from villages to towns and cities; but not usually from towns and cities to villages, nor from one village to another. In northern India, marriages between children of the same village are usually taboo, so brides emigrate from their natal to their in-laws' villages. The men of a village are likely to have been born there, as were their fathers and grandfathers. Whether or not they are born in their husbands' villages, most Indian women are likely to spend most of their lives living in them and are less likely to venture from them from time to time than village men.

Autonomy and autarky are, of course, matters of more or less. Most Indian villages today are less to much-less autonomous and autarkic than they were in even the recent past, not to say in the golden ages of foreign and native romanticizers of Indian rusticity. Still, the ongoing, day-to-day and closest relationships of all sorts that most villagers are likely to have are within their villages, with people of their villages. Often these relationships have been inherited and will be passed on. They are relationships of generations.

The closest paternal kinsmen of a household's men are likely to live in their village: brothers, uncles, cousins, nephews. Castefellows within a village are often demonstrable kinsmen as well, although the kinship tie among some may be distant or attenuated. Although the geographical spread of castes is invariably wider than any one village, it is primarily within any one village that families and family members of the same caste relate to one another as castefellows. It is within their villages that people have daily experience of their caste and, indeed, the customs and usages that shape that experience may vary from village to village. It is primarily within any one village that families and family members of one caste or community relate to people of other castes and communities. The parameters of these relationships, their etiquette and taboos, and the hierarchical positions of some castes relative to others may well vary from village to village.

Political democracy, in particular, has extended the arena of intra- and inter-caste relationships to state boundaries; and while this extension has affected caste relationships within villages, the village centeredness of these relationships remain. So, for example, the castes that have benefited most from political democracy are "dominant castes." In general these are large, areally concentrated castes of relatively well-to-do, touchable Hindu farmers. Their considerable political power in the legislative assemblies of their states certainly affects their castefellows' relationships in their villages with one another and villagers of other castes. But the political bases of dominant castes' state-level political power are in their villages where their castefellows are well-to-do farmers and patrons of less well-to-do clients of other castes.

Relationships of production among villagers are still largely within their villages. In times past, all over India, these relationships were more or less regulated and given sacred sanction by what anthropologists call *jajmani* systems. These were systems of exchange within villages whereby landholding families received from families of occupational specialists and others, e.g., potters and laborers, certain specified services and remunerated these with certain specified quantities of grain or portions of land. On both sides of the exchange, *jajmani* relationships were heritable – in the male line, of course. These, too, were relationships of generations. I will return to a discussion of *jajmani* systems in chapter 3. Modernity in the forms, for example, of the increasing availability to villagers of cash, opportunities and compulsions to work outside their villages, factory-made goods, outside markets for their agricultural products, green revolutionary technology have partially dismantled *jajmani* systems now or wrecked them entirely in villages all over India.

Blending in with *jajmani* systems now or side by side with them or in their stead are purely secular relationships of superiority–subordination: between employers and employees, creditors and debtors, patrons and clients, masters and debt-bondsmen. What these have in common with *jajmani* relationships is this: they are centered in a village, most of their participants are likely to be villagers of the same village, the superior participants are likely to be landholders, and the more land they hold the more superior they are likely to be. The village centeredness of productive relationships may well have been increased by state-legislated land reform in the 1950s which virtually disestablished throughout India non-cultivating, absentee and urban landlords.

In the past, before Indian independence, the most regular involvement of baronial, princely and imperial regimes in the governance of the subcontinent's villages was to collect their taxes and, less dependably, keep the peace. Village government as such was usually supplied by *ad hoc* village councils: in northern India, *panchayats*. These councils and their *modi operandi* were either tenuously or not at all connected in any official or legal sense to the tax collectors' *raj. Panchayat* governance was largely a matter of arbitrating disputes among villagers whose lives were governed by their understanding of religious injunctive scripture and caste and communal conventions. If it seemed appropriate or prudent, village *panchayats* would arbitrate in consultation with elders of relevant families, castes or communities.

Panchayat government was of the village, by and for its well-to-do and well-born villagers. It functioned to maintain the order of things. It did this by holding to the ways things had always been and accommodating itself to the ways in which they were changing. The tax collectors' *raj* – its land tenure legislation, its law courts, its police and civil bureaucracies, its railways – changed things. But *panchas* – landed patrons and *panchayat* members – ruled.

They still do: in law, as members of state-legislated tiers of local self-government. These are often referred to as *statutory panchayats* to distinguish them from their conventional prototypes and counterparts, and the legal system of *panchayat* government is known as *panchayati raj*: literally, conciliar government. I shall have much more to say about this, too, in chapter 3. It is enough to say of *panchayati raj* here that, the intentions of its founders notwithstanding, the system has been less successful in filtering democratic development downward from state capitals than in percolating upwards to state capitals the village interests of well-to-do farm families. As *panchayati raj* has certainly maintained the political dominance of the middle classes in their villages, it has probably increased for them and villagers in their orbits the political importance of their villages.

Given the encapsulation of a family's life within its village, and therein its generational continuity and the memories of its generations, it is not surprising that people speak of their family's village as home. When they are away from home, villagers identify themselves and those whom they meet as belonging to their villages. Villages have histories and mythologies. They have reputations, general and specific to groups; and families partake of their villages' good or bad names. Generations, sometimes, after their families had come to the city and moved into the circles of the upwardly and outwardly mobile, Delhiwallas and Bombayites will tell you that their (paternal) families belonged to such-and-such villages. Villages have not only corporate identities, they are primordial locations.

Clearly villages are something other than societies in which families exchange goods and services and no more. But what other are they? Are they communities? If we keep to our definition of community as a group of people who think of themselves as "we" and act accordingly – often in juxtaposition or opposition to "them" – then villages are probably less communities than arenas in which communities meet. As families are the basic units of Indian society, so villages are its basic arenas.

In the Hindu ideal, the metaphor is otherwise: village arenas are really society's basic organisms, all maintained by the natural functioning of each of their parts in natural synergism with one another. Those who were born to treat with the gods, do so; those who were born to rule, rule; those who were born to produce wealth, produce it; and those who were born to toil, toil. The organisms they maintain are microcosms of the divine order of things.

In village reality, I have already intimated and will detail below, conflict and competition among groups are no less usual than cooperation. What is unusual in villages is villagers behaving as villagers rather than as members of their families, castes, religious communities and factions. In the rounds of their day-to-day lives, groups of villagers separate themselves from each other by what they eat and whom they eat it with, how they dress, where they live and obtain their domestic water supply, what work they do and won't do, whose patron or client they are, whom they defer to and who defers to them, what they worship, where and how. Even on village occasions, like weddings and *melas* (festivals), villagers are likely to participate as members of their group and in such ways as to demonstrate its separateness from other groups and, less now than in the past, its place in the village hierarchy. Government "community development" schemes failed to serve the poor in the 1950s and *panchayati raj* has served the middle classes from the 1960s, in some measure, because they were predicated on the incorrect assumption that villages are communities rather than arenas.

In these arenas, some of the oldest and most important communities are groups of families who identify themselves and are identified by others as belonging to different castes.

2

Caste: *varna* and *jati*,
Muslim quasi *jatis* and untouchability

What is caste? Of all Indian social institutions, caste is the most exotic to Westerners, the furthest removed from our experience. We may look through the forms of Indian family and village life to recognize the substance of Western lives. We may have no difficulty in recognizing from Western experiences the substance of patron–client and class relationships in Indian villages. But we have no castes. We speak of castes in Western armies and bureaucracies, in the societies of European cities, towns in the American south, in the Australian outback and the Republic of South Africa. But as a composite social form, caste in India is uniquely Indian. As a composition of parts, a tapestry – to choose a convenient metaphor – caste in India is unrecognizable to Westerners. Our discomfort with its strangeness tempts us either to disparage caste's uniqueness by fitting it to our experiences – of "social stratification" or, worse, "false consciousness," for example – or to devalue Western experiences because they seem irrelevant to an understanding of caste.

Negatively put, the central commitment of this chapter is to avoid these temptations. Caste is of the warp and woof of Indian civilization, and Indian civilization is of the warp and woof of caste. We avoid the temptation to social science hubris by understanding that the tapestry of caste is the work over millennia of a great civilization. By choosing not to understand in favor of fitting caste into some concept of Western sociology, we only denigrate our scholarship. Westerners may avoid the temptation to abandon as useless our own experiences by examining the tapestry's composition, by scrutinizing it for recognizable strands. Of these there are many: social hierarchy, ascription, race, ethnicity, status, class, power, snobbery, sumptuary regulations and taboos, ritual purity and pollution, notions of causality and contagion, things divinely ordained. By connecting our experiences to its parts, we may come to a recognition of the composite. Put positively, our commitment is to understand caste as something that is both peculiarly Indian and essentially human.

The first step to understanding is to make clear what we are trying to understand: simply, to name it properly. "Caste" won't do. We abandon it here. The term comes to us from the Portuguese, who were the first Europeans in modern times to colonize India and to become intimately involved with Indians in their colonies. But "caste" is a misnomer. In one word, cognate with "chaste," the Portuguese named a complex social system for what seemed to Europeans most exotic about it: the segregation of people into groups and their hierarchical arrangement on the apparent criterion of heritable, and unalterable religious purity. But religious purity is only one of caste's criteria and one of decreasing importance. More detrimental to our understanding, "caste" embodies a misconception. In one word, the Portuguese conflated two characteristics of any society that are best understood as distinct though related: referent social ideologies and the social groups that refer to them. Westerners, for example, distinguish between and relate Christianity and Christian denominations, Judaism and congregations of Jews, Marxism and communist parties. We are able to make (and refine) similar distinctions and relationships with regard to caste. Not with that European term, however, but with Indian terms. It seems sensible to prefer these to "caste."

In Sanskrit, the classical language of northern India and of Hinduism, the referent ideology is called *varna dharma*. According to it, mankind is divided into four categories, *varnas*, which are ranked according to their religious purity: there is an order, *dharma*, among them. The social groups that refer themselves to this ideology or are referred to it by their neighbors are numbered in thousands. They are localized in regions of the subcontinent where they comprise local society; and they are ranked, often indeterminately and contentiously, according to a variety of locally interpreted, determined and defined criteria. The generic names for these groups are different in the different regional languages of India and in their local dialects. But in the language of Indian studies they are usually called *jatis*: their name in Hindi pluralized in English. *Jati* membership is virtually universal among Hindu families. Among non-Hindu families, that 17 percent of India's population who profess Islam, Christianity, Sikhism, Buddhism, Jainism, Judaism, there are what might be called, for lack of a better word, quasi *jatis*. These are groups which follow some characteristically *jati*-like customs and usages, but do not, of course, sanction them with reference to Hindu sacred ideology.

Varna

Varna dharma is a religious ideology and ideal of Hinduism. Its essential claim to acceptance among Hindu believers is that it is ordained by God. It is sacred. Its historicity is uncertain and of no particular importance here. Scholars think, but are by no means sure, that *varna dharma* originated in the conquest and subjugation more than a millennium before Christ of the darker complected people of northern India by fairer complected Aryan invaders from central Asia. There are mythological descriptions of this in the earliest Sanskrit hymnals, and one meaning of *varna* – among others – is color. We have no idea whether *varna dharma* ever really existed as a hierarchy of social groups, based upon skin color or anything else. It doesn't now and even if it did sometime in the dim past, that would be quite irrelevant to its importance in India today. Unlike Christianity and Islam, Hinduism is disinclined to search the historical past for validation, and the validity of *varna dharma* is not as a memory of the past but as a living ideology.

Again, it lives in Hinduism. And that is worth emphasizing. Hinduism provides the vast majority of Indians with their social organization: their *jatis* and the *jati* systems in their villages. The ideological sanction for these is provided by *varna dharma*. Clearly we cannot understand *jati* without some understanding of *varna dharma*. But where, in an introductory essay, do we begin? Where do we end? The body of relevant literature – religious and scholarly, esoteric and contentious – is vast.

These are the questions and the obstacles that confront anyone who aspires to a terminable examination of doctrine in any religion. A preacher's style of doing the job is to choose a text, elaborate on it but not wander far from it. It is a style that aspires less to profundity and the exhaustive and definitive discussion of theologians than to making a point with economy, clarity and intelligibility to laymen. Without a preacher's purpose, it is a style appropriate to our discussion of *varna dharma*.

Our first text is a frequently quoted creation myth of Hinduism. It appears in the *Rig Veda*, the oldest of the Sanskrit hymnals and one traditionally revered by Hindus as the revealed and recorded word of God. According to this myth, the world and the *varna dharma* were created in the same primeval sacrifice. The Cosmic Spirit, called Purusha, whom we may think of in this context as the One, offered himself to the gods as an oblation, and:

When they divided [him], in how many different portions did they arrange him? What became of his mouth, what of his two arms? What were his two thighs and his two feet called?

His mouth became the *brahman*; his two arms were made into the *rajana* [i.e. *kshatriya*]; his two thighs, the *vaishiya*; from his two feet the *shudra* was born.[1]

Not all, certainly, but many of the parameters of any religion are set out in its creation myth. "As it was in the beginning, is now and ever shall be..." In the beginning, God tells His human creatures, or at least suggests to them subject to subsequent elaboration: I am who I am; you are who I made you; and this is the deal, the relationship between us. We know from the first chapters of Genesis, for example, that God of the Abrahamic religions – Judaism, Christianity and Islam – is omnipotent and transcendent, and that the progeny of His creature Adam are imperfect, free to make their own decisions and responsible for them, redeemable through God's mercy, and in His judgment essentially equal.

In much the same way, Hinduism's conception of mankind and its relationship to God is suggested in the story of Purusha's sacrifice. Purusha is the one source of mankind's ancestry, but mankind's ancestors are not one but four. Their progeny are the *varnas* whose ordained functions are unequally important to the maintenance of the organic whole: the cosmos created from Purusha. The *brahman* (priest) through the organ of speech, invocation, prayer and instruction maintains the divinely ordained order of things in which Purusha is immanent. The arms of the *kshatriya* (warrior-ruler) enforce among human creatures their acceptance of the divine order of things, including the *varna dharma*. The *vaishiya* generates the wealth which priests and rulers must have to perform their ordained functions. The *shudra* serves the whole by providing his toil in the service of the other, superior *varnas*.

These superior *varnas*, in subsequent elaborations of the *varna dharma* ideal, came to be known as "twice-born." *Brahmans*, *kshatriyas* and *vaishiyas* were thus grouped into another sacred category that increased the hierarchical distance between them collectively and non-twice-born *shudras*. The *shudra* category was in turn subjected to ideological bifurcation. There were those *shudras* who toiled at respectable, i.e., clean, occupations and lived clean lives. But there was a lower stratum of *shudras* whose toil, though necessary to the maintenance of social order, was so unclean, as were their living habits, to put them beyond the pale of ordinary social intercourse. They and their progeny were *panchama*, a fifth category of people who were *achhut*: untouchable.

What is self-evident is that in the ideology of *varna dharma* all men are created unequal; that they are endowed by their Creator with unequal capacities in order to perform functions of unequal importance to Him. Their positions in His hierarchy accord with their functions. Their functions and their positions are not only divinely ordained, however, but having been ordained by nature's God, God of the cosmic organism, they are also natural. The organism as a whole functions best when its parts perform those specialized functions that nature has equipped them to perform. The mouth can form the sacred, world-sustaining syllables, the arms cannot; the arms can wield the sword in defense of the *varna dharma*, the mouth cannot. Some functions are vital to the maintenance of the organism, and some are not. The parts specialized by nature to maintain the cosmic organism are the *varnas*.

This anatomical metaphor for the naturalness of inequality and hierarchy is succeeded in Hindu literature, and certainly in popular Hinduism, by a zoological metaphor. Its medium is the beast fable. You cannot train a tiger to nibble grass. You cannot train a goat to hunt. Capabilities and potentialities are in nature not in nurture. To act on the contrary belief is to invite disappointment, or embarrassment, or disaster. Like other animals or species of animals, men have their breeds and, of course, these have different and unequally important capabilities and potentialities. The generation of wealth is a more important social function than the performance of societies' menial tasks. *Vaishiyas* are the best generators of wealth because they are naturally acquisitive. *Shudras* are the best servants because they are naturally servile. In the Hindu ideal, the *varna dharma*, Man, as Louis Dumont argues, is properly *homo hierarchicus*.[2]

Inextricably connected to *varna dharma* and serving to reinforce it are two other Hindu ideals. These are the ideologies of *dharma* and of purity/pollution. Our use again of the word *dharma* is noteworthy. In *varna dharma, dharma* applies to society and its best meaning is "order." In the ideology of *dharma, dharma* applies to individuals and its best meaning is "duty." The two meanings are crucially related. When a society is properly ordered, people do their duty. When people do their duty, society is properly ordered.

Social order lies in *varna dharma*. But wherein does individual duty lie? That question takes us to the core beliefs of Hinduism, and back again to *varna dharma* as one of them. An appropriate place to begin the answer is in the law of *karma*. It is an "inexorable" law, according to Mahatma Gandhi, "impossible of evasion." "Whatever man sows, that shall he reap."[3] God does not determine our fate. Our gift from Him is the capacity to determine our own fate: to make choices, to sow as we will. The reaping takes place after we have experienced the incident of death and in the incident of subsequent birth or in a final release from these incidents. Depending upon how we sow in this lifetime we will reap in the next. The *brahman* who has sown badly will be reborn as less than a *brahman*. The *shudra* who has sown well will be reborn as more than a *shudra*. Whoever has sown perfectly will not be reborn, will attain *moksha*: liberation from the cycle of re-birth and re-death, oneness with God.

Wherein are the instructions for proper sowing? In the rule of *dharma*. Our text here is *The Bhagavad Gita*. Originally in Sanskrit, it is an epic poem of Hindu faith. Mahatma Gandhi cherished it, and it is doubtlessly one of the best known works of religious literature in India and in the world.

The *Gita*'s scene is a battlefield. The battle is about to begin. The opposing armies are in position. They are armies of opposing kinsmen. One of their chiefs, Arjuna, grieves. Whichever army wins, many brave warriors of both will be slaughtered, and it will be a slaughter of kinsmen by kinsmen. Whichever army wins, there will be mourning women, orphaned children and social dislocation, *adharma*. Arjuna confides his grief to his charioteer. His charioteer is Lord Krishna, God incarnate.

God comforts Arjuna, but instructs him, in effect, to get on with it, to prepare himself to fight the battle. That is his duty. Arjuna is a *kshatriya* and his *dharma* is to fight. The divine and even the social consequences of Arjuna's doing what he must do, fight, are neither within his capacity to determine nor to judge. The man who is concerned with consequences, attached in some way to the results of what he does is necessarily inhibited in the performance of his duty. The man who best serves God, society and himself performs his *dharma* and is detached from its consequences. Our duty is set out in nature: by sex, age and – notably, as in Arjuna's case – by *varna*. The general rule is:

Better is one's own *dharma* though imperfect, than the *dharma* of another well performed.[4]

The rule of *dharma* supports the *varna dharma* ideal largely by prescribing for the *varnas* proper and rewarding behavior. By contrast, the rules of purity/pollution support the *varna dharma* ideal largely by proscribing to the *varnas* improper and penalizing behavior. The sum of the rules is this: avoid pollution.

A concern with religious purity or cleanliness is not, of course, peculiar to Hindus. Leviticus (and its exegeses), for example, provide Jews with an elaborate set of dietary and sexual rules for doing that which is clean and not doing that which is unclean in the eyes of God. Although Hindu rules of purity/pollution are in substance of this religious genre, their systematic elaboration is in form so strikingly similar to our modern conceptions of health/sickness as to invite their use as an analogy.

Purity/pollution is *like* health/sickness; as applied not to the substantial body, however, but to its insubstantial essence: soul, for lack of a better word. Some people are relatively pure, others are relatively polluted. In Hindu ideology, an individual's state of purity/pollution is understood not as some metaphor but as an actual state of being; much as we regard an individual's health as an actual state of being. The ordinary and individual purity of people, like their ordinary and individual health, is from time to time adversely affected by circumstances. Women during their menstrual periods and families in mourning, for example, are in extraordinary states of pollution that pass in time and in response to the appropriate purificatory treatments. Much as flus and headcolds pass.

But there are also ordinary states of purity/pollution that are congenital and untreatable. These attach to people not as individuals, but as members of different species. The species are the *varnas*. The higher God has placed a *varna* in the *varna dharma*, the purer has He made that *varna*'s members. That purity is an attribute of high sacred status, and a requisite for the proper performance of the duties prescribed by that status. The *brahman*, who is highest and whose prescribed functions require the greatest purity is the most pure and least polluted. The *shudra* (particularly the untouchable *shudra*), who is the lowest and whose functions require the least purity, is the least pure and most polluted.

An individual cannot enjoy a purity greater than that ordained for members of his *varna*. But he can suffer a greater pollution. And that would necessarily and adversely affect not only his chances as an individual, in his lifetime and the next, but his abilities to perform his prescribed and organism-sustaining duties. The ways to keep from greater pollution are in the performance of one's own *dharma* and in the avoidance of pollution's contagion. Pollution, like some sickness, is understood to be contagious. It is primarily the conception of pollution as contagious that provides the reinforcing connections between the ideologies of purity/pollution and *varna dharma*.

The most widely recognized carriers of pollution's contagion are prepared food and water. There are Hindu dietary rules, rules about what to eat and drink, which in form similar to Leviticus', proscribe some food and drink as polluting. In Hinduism it is considered sinful to kill cows, and the consumption of beef is universally proscribed. A diet that is vegetarian and teetotal is generally considered to be less polluting for *brahmans* and *vaishiyas* than a diet that contains flesh and alcohol. Flesh and alcohol, on the other hand, are an appropriate diet for *kshatriyas*. Nature prescribes different diets for different breeds of men. In substance, the dietary rules of Jews distinguish them from gentiles, the dietary rules of Hindus distinguish the *varnas* from one another.

There are also Hindu commensal rules, rules about whom to eat and drink with and from whom to accept food and water. These are, in effect, rules for the maintenance of purity and the quarantine of pollution. In sum, relative levels of purity/pollution are maintained and pollution is quarantined when *varna* members dine and drink only with one another, take prepared food and water only from a member of their *varna* or a purer one, and give prepared food and water only to a member of their *varna* or one that is less pure. Pollution is not contagious among those who are equally polluted, nor can the contagion be spread from those who are less polluted to those who are more polluted. Here is the nexus between the ideologies of purity/pollution and *varna dharma*: rules about eating and drinking affirm the separateness of the *varnas* and the hierarchy among them.

Jati

Some of the most obvious differences between *varna dharma* ideology and *jati* societies we have already noted in passing. There are four *varnas,* but thousands of *jatis. Jatis* don't function as synergic parts of one organic whole, one great society. Rather they work in opposition to one another no less than together as parts of separate and overlapping little societies, i.e., villages, or slightly bigger than little societies. The ideologies are Hindu, but *jatis* are Indian. Groups convert from Hinduism, change their faith; but in the ideology of *varna dharma* they cannot change their breed. In fact, they can and do. But only to become in time another breed. The best translation of *jati* is breed.

The divisions of *varna* go to the borders of Hinduism. *Jatis* are rarely found beyond the borders of ethnic regions and often do not extend to these. Until fairly recently, *jatis* which were large and widespread served to identify their members, but were not groups in which their members regularly interacted with one another. The regularly interactive groups within these *jatis* lived and still live in one village or cluster of villages. It is within these that *jati* members are related or personally known to one another, marriages arranged, *jati* rules of ritual purity pronounced and enforced by *ad hoc panchayats* of *jati* elders.

In this century, and particularly since India's independence, face-to-face interactions within small groups of *jati*-fellows have been supplemented by *jati*-wide activity. The loci of these activities are usually in state politics. Associations of *jati*-fellows have become welfare societies and interest groups; they have established colonies in bureaucracies, blocs in political parties and *panchayati raj* institutions, and factions within ministries. Association leaders are *jati*-fellows with the requisite skills and state-wide prestige rather than the requisite age, genealogy and local reputation. *Jati* associations are based on shared identity and interests among *jati*-fellows rather than personal identification, and their concerns are more with irrigation and electrification than ritual purity.

Nowadays state legislative assemblies sometimes resemble *panchayats*-of-the-whole in which every *jati* in the state is represented, albeit unequally. Best represented, almost invariably, and most powerful though often in factions are the large *jatis* whose leading members are well-to-do farmers. The coming to political prominence in the states of these dominant *jatis* and, more recently, the challenges to their prominence from other *jatis* amalgamated as "other backward classes" are post-independence phenomena, crucial events in bourgeois revolution and matters to be discussed in subsequent chapters. In the *varna dharma* ideal, *varnas* are separated from one another and hierarchically arranged. In the *jati* reality, *jatis* are separated from one another and hierarchically arranged, but neither are done with the ideal's consistency or determinacy. *Jatis* keep separate from one another primarily through the arrangements by *jati* families of their children's marriages. *Jati*-sanctioned marriages are between brides and grooms of that *jati* only, and *jati*-legitimate children are born of such unions only. A *jati* is an endogamous group, whatever else it may be.

It is a commensal group – one whose members dine only with one another and on food prepared only by one another – much less categorically. The ideology of purity/pollution is particularly Hindu. Part of the quasi-ness of Muslim and other non-Hindu *jatis* is their non-acceptance or non-ideological acceptance of commensal taboos. Among Hindu *jatis* the ideology of purity/pollution is accepted almost universally. Indeed, it provides (or provided) not only a widely accepted theoretical justification for the separation and ranking of *jatis*, but actual guidelines for villagers' daily behavior in their little societies: with whom should men share their water pipes and thereby recognize as equals, who should women allow in their kitchens, to whom should villagers permit access to their wells. But nowadays, villagers live not only in their little societies but in the Indian world outside their villages, and their villages, too, are parts of the world outside.

Some scholars argue, it might be noted in passing, that *jati* endogamy is merely an historical or logical corollary of *jati* commensality. In a word, a man is in greater danger of becoming polluted from eating impure food or drinking impure water than from having sexual contact with a woman whose *jati* is less pure than his own. Food prepared by a wife of the same *jati* as her husband and shared by her children is pure, almost by definition. Sexual contact outside of marriage between men and women of different *jatis* is generally considered to be improper. But it is nonetheless commonplace and often winked at, particularly when the contact is between a man who is relatively powerful and of a higher *jati* and a woman who is relatively powerless – frequently, the man's servant or dependant – and of lower *jati*. This sort of exploitive sexual relationship does not, of course, imply an invitation to dine or the acceptance of such an invitation. *Godan or The Gift of a Cow*, is an epic novel of Indian village life written in 1936 by the foremost Indian novelist of his times, Premchand. In it, the mother of an untouchable girl chides her *brahman* lover:

You think you are very pious. You'll sleep with [my daughter] but you won't touch food cooked by her.[5]

Corollary or not, *jati* rules of endogamy have become virtually absolute within all – and particularly – Hindu *jatis*. *Jati* rules of commensality, on the other hand, have become increasingly situational. Simply, there are more and more situations in which more and more villagers, particularly men and their grown children, find it difficult or inconvenient or unpleasurable to abide by their *jatis'* commensal rules. More and more, as I have noted, villagers travel. At a tea stall near a railway station or a bus terminal, in a market town hotel or on an Indian Airlines flight, how can one know the *jati* of those who prepare and serve the food? And even if one did know, how can one not eat or resist the temptation to eat or refuse the invitations of companions to eat with them; or why, away from the eyes and tongues of the village, should one? For the millions of village men who remit income to their families and live without them in the city, who prepares the meals and in what company are they eaten? For the millions of young villagers who attend colleges and universities away from home and live in hostels and digs, who prepares the meals and in what company are they eaten?

Hindus have adjusted their commensal rules to the compulsions and temptations of the world outside their little societies in much the same way that many practising Jews have adjusted their dietary rules to their lives in diaspora: rules are observed at home, but observed less well or not at all away from home. If the logic of the rules is to be internally consistent, then, of course, both compromises are at least irrational. Food that is prepared by someone who is polluted is polluting wherever it is eaten. Meat from an unclean animal is unclean wherever it is eaten. But if the logic of the rules is to facilitate the survival of the group, then both compromises are not only rational but functional.

Within the little societies that are the customary habitats of *jatis*, where circumstances are more or less controllable by them, the observance of commensal rules by *jatis* contributes to maintaining their separate identities, their members' sense of being secure among their own kind, and probably some order within their villages. Beyond village borders, *jatis* cannot control the observance of their commensal taboos. Rather than discredit their authority by exercising it futilely, they forgive non-observance and profit from the non-observant. The dining habits of villagers who work in the city may be suspect, but their remittances are welcome and contribute not only to their families' wealth but to their *jatis'* prestige.

There is some evidence, I have it from Rajasthan and West Bengal[6], that even within villages, customary commensal taboos are giving way, at least in part. Members of touchable Hindu *jatis* are apparently loath as ever to take food or water from members of untouchable *jatis*. But among touchable villagers, twice-born and not, there seems to be in their villages' public places, at least, more eating, drinking and smoking together across *jati* lines. It may be that villagers' non-observance of commensal taboos in town and *en route* is weaning them away from observance inside their villages. The new political *modus operandi* of democracy is taking on some ideological overtones that may be shading however lightly the landscape of purity/pollution. High *jati* politicians who would win the votes of their lowest *jati* constituents must woo them over tea. Untouchable *jati* ministers, and there are many of them, expect invitations to dine from twice-born favor seekers.

It may be that as village hierarchies become increasingly secular and less sacred, a change that I will discuss in the next chapter, *jatis'* observances of sacred commensal taboos becomes increasingly less functional to the maintenance of those hierarchies and therefore increasingly irrelevant to villagers. Much of the fabled conservatism of Indian villagers is, I believe, the usual preference for the tried and true of those who believe that they must cleave to it in order to hold on to what they have and even to survive. Such preferences are not irrational. Nor is abandoning them when what *was* tried and true no longer *is*.

In the *varna dharma* ideal groups are separated from one another by the inherent capacities of their members: capacities which manifest themselves in the hereditary occupations of their groups. *Jatis*, in general, have and are usually known by their hereditary occupations: priest, warrior, merchant, farmer, mason, smith, potter, carpenter, tanner, sweeper and so forth. Nowadays, however, many and in some cases most *jati* members, do not follow their hereditary occupations or follow them only in part. The inherent capacities on which these occupations are theoretically based continue as ever to be differentiated in terms of purity/pollution; but with some exceptions, people are not expected or compelled to do what they were born to do. So, for example: two families which have for generations cultivated land of approximately the same value may belong, one to a *brahman jati* and the other to a potter *jati*. No one regards this as anything but ordinary. However, the cultivating family whose inherited occupation is temple priest may regard itself and be regarded by its neighbors as belonging to a higher and purer *jati* than the cultivating family whose inherited occupation is potter.

Although farming and trading are the hereditary occupations of some *jatis*, villagers, in general, regard these as occupations open to members of any *jati*. Some villagers, from choice or necessity, combine their hereditary occupation with other work. A well-to-do farmer will also lend money. An impoverished tanner will also work as an agricultural laborer. Villagers reserve, more or less and in one way or another, some hereditary occupations for members of the appropriate *jati*. Usually, but not always, the job of temple priest is reserved for *brahmans*. The job of making clay pots is reserved for the members of *jatis* whose hereditary occupation is potting, if they are still following that occupation and can meet villagers' demands for clay pots. The jobs of hauling dead animals away and disposing of their carcasses is reserved for members of *jatis* whose hereditary occupation is leather working. And they may be coerced to do these jobs by villagers who regard such work as necessary but too polluting to be done by anyone other than untouchables.

Apart from these occupations of the countryside which villagers regard as the hereditary occupations of particular *jatis*, there is in India today a full range of occupations that no one regards as the hereditary occupations of any *jati*. These are the occupations of towns and cities, of modernity: rickshaw pulling, bus and truck driving, railway and airline employment, working in factories and offices, civil and military service, shopkeeping and manufacturing, acting or dancing in the movies or on television, business administration, advertising, teaching, marriage counselling, medicine, law, and on and on.

There is usually some connection between a person's hereditary *jati* occupation and his modern job, and it is often something like this. To some degree, the hereditary *jati* occupation of a person's family affects, for better or worse, its and his chances in village society. In general terms, applicable not only to Indian villagers, people with higher status and more valued skills enjoy greater potential access to wealth than do people with lower status and less valued skills. Conversely, people with more wealth enjoy greater potential access to high status and valued skills than do people with less wealth. The status, skills and wealth enjoyed by a village family affect its capacity to prepare its children for modern jobs. But, in all this there is also a disconnection. The valuations of purity/pollution that are attached to hereditary *jati* occupations are not attached generally to modern occupations.

For example, because for generations some of the men in a *brahman* family had been trained as temple priests, literacy is one of the family's skills and intellectual training one of its experiences and a contributor to its status. Because it is a *brahman* family of temple priests, it has also for generations enjoyed the income from a landholding which had been donated to support their temple. The sum of all this for our purposes, is that the family is well situated to choose and pay for a medical career for one of its sons. Another hypothetical doctor! That doctors may be in regular contact with death and human excreta takes nothing away from this doctor's *brahman*hood nor the very high status of medicine as a modern occupation. In the doctor's village, *jatis* whose hereditary occupations, practiced or not, involve regular contact with death or human excreta – like leather workers and sweepers – are untouchable.

Much the same observation that we made earlier about the non-application by *jatis* of their commensal rules to eating and drinking away from home can be made about the non-application of their usual assessments of purity/pollution to modern occupations: they are compromises which at some ideological cost benefit those who compromise and their *jatis*. The costs are minimized and the benefits optimized because the compromises are not general. They are reasonably specific to those situations and spheres of activity in which *jatis* exercise no control or in which their attempts to exercise control would likely be unsuccessful, unprofitable and undermining of their authority.

Like the *varna dharma*'s ideal of *varna* separation, its principles of hierarchy are applied by *jatis* to their little societies and on the bases of criteria that are, at least notionally, sacred. But again, applications in practice vary from principles. Some of the variations have already been suggested in our observations about practical applications of the principle of separation. At the furthest extent of their existence, *jati* hierarchies are – like the *jatis* which comprise them – regional. Within regions there are variations, village by village. The places that *jatis* and *jati* families enjoy in their regional and village hierarchies are ultimately determined not by what they say or do, but by the ways in which they are regarded and treated by their estimable and influential neighbors. As it is with us, so it is with them.

Chitpavan *brahmans* of Maharashtra, Nambudri *brahmans* of Kerala, *Rajputs* of any of the major clans in Rajasthan: these are *jatis* which are so generally regarded as high and pure within their regions, that families belonging to these *jatis* are likely to be at the top of their village hierarchies. The Mahars of Maharashtra, the Chamars of the Hindi-speaking states, the Paraiyans of Tamilnadu: these are *jatis* that are so generally regarded as low and polluted within their regions, that families belonging to these *jatis* are likely to be at the bottom of their village hierarchies. Between high and low, however, in that middle hierarchical range occupied by many and often most *jatis* and their families, rank order is less than determinate and ranking criteria are other than sacred.

In different and sometimes even neighboring villages, the same cultivating or artisan *jati* is ranked differently. Sometimes these differences appear to be the consequences of sub-regional or village-to-village variations in the reputations of *jati* families for doing what is pure and avoiding what is polluting. But as often as not purity/pollution has little to do with it. Variations in a *jati*'s ranking seem to correlate most closely with variations in the value of the land owned by the *jati*'s families. A cultivating *jati* of middle rank whose families own more land in one village is likelier to be thought of as higher there than in another village in which its families own less land. Because of the extension of *jati* activities into local and state politics, there has probably been some standardizing in *jati* rankings, particularly with regard to large cultivating *jatis*. So, for example, ordinary cultivating families may now enjoy the reputation in their villages of belonging to a *jati* of consequence in the state government and, perhaps, of being connected in some way to one of its ministers.

There are always *jatis* which claim more exalted hierarchical positions than are accorded to them by their neighbors. These claims are sometimes manifested in a process which the anthropologist M. N. Srinivas calls "sanskritization."[7] Typically, the sanskritizing *jati* begins to refer to itself as having a more exalted place in the *varna dharma* than that accorded to it by its neighbors. They, more than likely, refer to the sanskritizing *jati* as a group of *shudras*, or imply such a reference in the regard and treatment that they accord to the *jati*. But they are mistaken, say *jati* leaders. The *jati* suffers *shudra* status because of some cruel twist of fate or the machination of some malign force in the immemorial past, or because of the enmity of its neighbors or their jealousy or their self-interested persistence in error. In God's truth, appropriately documented, the *jati* has always belonged to the *vaishiya* or *kshatriya* or *brahman varna*. Having made this claim, *jati* leaders then encourage *jati* families to model or remodel their behavior – dietary and commensal, familial and occupational, sartorial and so forth – on the behavior of another local *jati* which is generally regarded in the region or village as enjoying the twice-born status to which the claimant *jati* aspires.

And then in the sanskritizing model, there is usually a fight. Where status – whether of being a *kshatriya* or a member of the right club – is valued as a resource or as a means of access to resources, those who enjoy it and even those who don't are likely to guard it against the claims of arrivistes. These confront not only those who say "they are not as good as we are," but those who say "they are no better than we are." In Indian villages such confrontation takes the forms of social ostracism, economic boycott, harassing litigation, political vendettas and physical violence. In order to vindicate its claims – even partially, here and there but not everywhere, after many confrontations over many years – the upwardly mobile *jati* must be able to give as good as it gets. And that means it must have resources: situational, political, psychological, and particularly, economic. In sum: Although the sacred hierarchy of the *varna dharma* is the model for regional and village *jati* pecking orders, contested places in them are likely to be decided not by arguments about purity/pollution but in clashes of secular interests. At the same time, however, sanskritization more or less affirms the *varna dharma* model of *jati* hierarchies by processing in sacred form the substance of upwardly mobile *jatis'* secularly motivated and advanced ambitions.

Though strewn with obstacles, winding, full of pitfalls and traversable only by the most determined and resourceful travellers, the path of sanskritization, as Srinivas lays it out, goes up. Even, perhaps, to the *village* top. But not to the *India* top. That top is urban. From the village's social boundary, where sanskritization breaks off, the road to the India top is called by Srinivas "westernization." Its travellers are reasonably well-to-do urban families of unquestionably twice-born *jatis*, and the road leads to membership in the modern elite of India's great cities. The distinctions sought by sanskritizing and westernizing families are different and sometimes contrary. So, in the Srinivas model, for example, as the women of sanskritizing village families move into relative seclusion, the women of twice-born westernizing urban families move out into practising medicine, publishing magazines, managing boutiques. Families of the urban elite are not our concern here. As it applies to village families nowadays, Srinivas' model is too dichotomous and too equating of sanskritization with village upward mobility. Nowadays, as the matrons of sanskritizing village families move into relative seclusion, their daughters are being sent to universities to learn to be modern wives. More or less secluded in their villages, the wives of *panchayati raj* headmen act as hostesses when their husbands entertain important representatives of modern, urban India; e.g., university educated bureaucrats. Upwardly mobile village families are sanskritizing *and* westernizing: taking from both what serves them best.

Though customarily accorded no more than the sacred status of touchable peasants, many dominant *jatis* nowadays seem to feel no great compulsion to sanskritize, or to sanskritize any more than they need to in passing. They needn't fight their way to the village top. They are there. Not sanskritization, but parliamentary democracy and capitalist economic development were their vehicles. Distinctions of economic class among *jatis* which have always been a feature, however thinly veiled, of local hierarchies have become an outstanding characteristic and one that accords less well, more ambiguously than it has in the past with distinctions of sacred status. Outside of places like Tamil Nadu and Maharashtra where anti-brahmanism is an old and widespread sentiment, newly prominent cultivating *jatis* seem to find such social ambiguities well within their capacities to tolerate. They have not found it in their faith or in their interests to challenge directly the sacred *status quo* or even to spend much energy in jockeying for better positions in it. Except where it impinges on their pursuit of wealth and power. It is this pursuit and the demands of those who succeed in it for status in accordance with their wealth and power that makes the sacredness of *jati* hierarchies increasingly notional and the process of sanskritization increasingly irrelevant to social mobility. Next to the well-to-do *Jat* agricultural entrepreneur, son in a Canadian university and in-law in the Haryana ministry, who after all is his family's *pujari* (priest) but a *brahman* servant?

In addition to the particular relationships that we have already noted between the ideologies of *varna dharma*, *dharma* and purity/pollution, on the one hand, and the realities of *jati* societies, on the other, there are some general relationships of great importance that we ought to note. In a civilization in which religion is still *the* vital force, referent ideologies that are sacred give unimpeachable credentials to the social groups that refer to them. The *varma dharma* is sacred. *Jatis* and the local societies of *jatis* partake of its sacredness. To be sure, *jati* realities are imperfect copies in an imperfect world of that which is perfect, ordained by God. But no more so than are our multitude of different churches copies of The Church.

Imperfect copies though they are, *jati* societies refer not only to an ideal but to other imperfect copies. Particularly between north and south India, there are notable regional variations between *jati* societies. But certainly more striking than these are the similarities of the copies one to another in all the basic characteristics – and even variations from them – that we have attributed to *jati* societies. It is no less striking that these similarities are probably more than anything else the consequences from time immemorial of countless references and cross-references of separate *jati* societies to a common ideal. Until recently *jati* societies in different regions of India were barely aware of each other's existence, much less were they in direct contact with one another. Except to some limited extent at pilgrimage centers. Hinduism has never had a subcontinental church ruled from its center, nor has there ever been a subcontinental state which sustained the Hindu *dharma* from its center. What has been subcontinental are the sacred ideologies and their imperfect realities, and nothing has contributed to the cultural identity of India more than these.

Socially, India is an identity of particles. People belong to particular families, villages, *jatis*, ethnicities, communities; and, in general, it is as such that people think of themselves and behave, and are thought of by others and treated. The major particularizing institution is *jati*. It particularizes families, their places in their villages, Gujaratis and Tamils, Hindus and Muslims. Indian society is vast: but it does not, in the countryside, certainly, have masses. It is not a mass society. It may be that a society of particles is less amenable to mobilization for proletarian or ethnic revolution than to adaption, however coincidental, to the opportunities of parliamentary democracy and capitalism.

Nowadays in India, the relatively new secular ideologies of parliamentary democracy and capitalism and the social realities that refer to them – legislative assemblies and elections, factories and class conflict, for example – impinge increasingly on the lives of Indian villagers. But, as I have suggested, the new has not so much challenged the old as been accommodated by it. Not only has the accommodation been successful thus far, but there has evolved a system of accommodation – with regard to commensality and work, for example – whose capacities have no apparent limit. The little societies of Hinduism have centuries of experience in accommodating themselves to the new and secular, or non-Hindu: to Muslim and British rule. Too, it might well be that people who believe that *homo hierarchicus* is the essential and natural order of things are better able than others of us to sustain their faith while accommodating it to changes which alter inequalities but seem always to retain them.

I have said that *jatis* provide villages with their pecking orders, but they do much more than that. Over the centuries, they have performed the functions of sodalities and regimes. *Jatis* are demonstrable or conventional extensions of the family in a family-centered society. The family has been the bastion, and the *jati* its walls. Without relinquishing their usual defensive function, *jatis* nowadays have also moved to offensive positions, to assault on their members' behalves the citadels of the modern world. However driven by clan feuds, family vendettas and personal hatreds, a *jati* enjoys the status of that mystical bond of blood which is so difficult to deny to those who claim it, and even to our dismay and discomfort identifies those of our own. In Rajasthan, another name for *jati* is *khun*, blood.

Until Indian independence, virtually all activities within villages, of hearths to fields, were regulated by *jati* families and the *panchayats* of *jatis* and dominant *jatis*. The tax collector's *raj* intruded into village life, and sometimes crucially, e.g., in matters of land revenue; but was usually no more than tangential to it. Captains of empire were intelligent enough to leave well enough alone. *Panchayats* and *sarpanchas* were intelligent enough to want to be left alone. Nowadays, of course, they have adjusted themselves to intrusive national and state governments. The adjustments have been variable. They have taken irrigation loans and primary schools with enthusiasm, land reform and family planning measures more selectively; they have compromised with the laws that bar untouchability and ignored those that ban dowries. And more and more they have intruded on, colonized in their own interests, the tax collector's *raj*.

The domestication of parliamentary democracy in India since the 1950s has largely displaced from state legislative assemblies reformers who represented modern and Western values. Their places have been taken by representatives of villagers and *jatis* and their values. Politics is not a new game to *jatis;* only there are new rules today, and new arenas. Of their success in playing the game, their survival over the centuries and their demonstrated capacity to adapt to changing circumstances are the evidence. In general their *modus operandi* has been neither to force change nor to oppose it beyond reason and self-interest but rather to accommodate it, situate it, profit from it or make the best of it, endure.

Muslim quasi *jatis*

We know that as Christianity developed in Europe it was profoundly influenced at its high cultural level by the Greco-Roman civilization that preceded it and at its popular level by the folkways of the pagan villagers and townsmen who became Christians. It should not surprise us that Islam as it developed on the subcontinent was similarly influenced by Hinduism and Hindus and that their influence was profound. Indeed, probably more profound than the influence of pre-Christian Europe and Europeans on Christianity. After all, Islam did not develop on the subcontinent as successor to a moribund Hinduism, but as another faith in a vibrant and forever changing civilization of Hindus.

Islam on the subcontinent is the faith of Muslims who are in their overwhelming majority the progeny of converted Hindus. Their conversion was effected largely by a variety of regular and irregular *sufis* or influenced by *sufism.* At its most orthodox, *sufism* has important theological and ritual similarities to Hinduism. At its most heterodox, *sufism* was virtually indistinguishable from the Hindu devotionalist (*bhakti*) movements of medieval India. Typically, Hindu converts came to Islam not as individuals but in groups: in *jati* or *jati* subgroups, usually of middling to lowest Hindu rank. Like Hindu *jatis*, these groups of Muslim converts have over the ages fragmented or fused with other groups to become new groups. But groups they remain, hundreds of them, in an Indian society tessellated into groups. In social terms, at least, there is no Muslim community in India. Only Muslim communities.

For the most part, these Muslim communities live among Hindu communities. Both live in the same villages. In these, Muslims are likely to have their own social structure, but as well to occupy places in village social hierarchies and to participate as families in relationships of production with other village families. In the twentieth century, still, there were Muslim communities which were virtually indistinguishable from their Hindu neighbors even in their professions of faith and religious rituals. M. Mujeeb in his celebrated *Indian Muslims* gives a number of examples of such communities. Here is one example, recorded in 1911, from Purnia district in what is now Bihar.

> In every village could be found a . . . shrine dedicated to the worship of the [Hindu] goddess Kali, and attached to almost every Muslim house was a little shrine called . . . God's House, where prayers were offered in which the names of both Allah and Kali were used. A part of the Muslim marriage ceremony was performed at the shrine of the [Hindu] goddess Bagvati. Goats, fowls, pigeons and the first fruit of trees and crops were offered [by Muslims] to purely Hindu deities, in particular the village godling . . . The most popular deity, among both Hindus and Muslims, was [the Hindu] Devati Maharaj, with his door keeper, Hadi.[8]

The conversion of Hindu *jatis* and *jati* subgroups to Islam was rarely epiphanous or otherwise immediate. But usually through a long slow process, two steps forward and one step back, of acculturation from Hinduism: of "Islamicization," a process of generations that for many Muslim communities is still ongoing. For some, particularly poor and newly converted communities, the process may seesaw and zigzag inconclusively; or even, over time, from neglect or under the influence of Hindu revivalism, reverse itself. For some the process may end in literate, well-articulated Islamic heterodoxy; as it did for the Khojas of Gujarat who believe that the Prophet's son-in-law, Ali, was the tenth incarnation of the Lord Vishnu, and the Ahmadiyyas of Punjab who revere Allah's revelation to a prophet successive to the Holy Qur'an and the Seal of the Prophets. Some have and others will doubtlessly become communities of more or less orthodox Sunni or Shia Muslims. For none is "Islamization" likely to efface the Indian-ness that they share with their Hindu countrymen.

I have called these Muslim communities quasi *jatis*. Called by their members *quam* (ethnic group), *beradari* (brotherhood) *jati, zat* (alternative to *jati*) and so forth, these Muslim quasi *jatis* exhibit to some degree some *jati*-like traits. Such traits among Muslim quasi *jatis* enjoy the sanction of custom and usage; but not, as they do among Hindus, the sanction of religion. To the contrary, Islam shares with the other Abrahamic religions a belief in the essential equality of male believers, if not of all Adam's progeny.

As it is with Hindu *jatis*, the trait most invariably exhibited by Muslim quasi *jatis* is endogamy. Marriages sanctioned by the quasi *jati* are between brides and grooms of the quasi *jati*. Exceptions to this rule, as among Hindus, are almost invariably hypergamous marriages, i.e., between grooms whose quasi *jatis* are of higher social status than their brides'. Muslim quasi *jatis*, though less so among the elevated, are socially attached to traditional occupations as are Hindu *jatis*. As among Hindus, actual and traditional quasi *jati* occupations may differ, and both are likely to affect the community's social ranking. Muslim quasi *jatis* generally rank each other as do Hindu *jatis*, and with much the same indeterminacy and lack of consensus. Social relationships of any intimacy are more likely to take place within ranks than between them; but, of course, among Muslim quasi *jatis* there are no prohibitions supported by injunctive scripture against interdining.

It may be, as some argue, that Indian Muslim social structure has been influenced, and not only in its ideology, by the concern of Arab Muslims with purity of descent: their legacy from the pre-Islamic Middle East. In which case, that concern meshes neatly with Hindu concern for ritual purity which is, of course, maintained over time by purity of descent, i.e., descent from *jati*-endogamous marriages. In any case, the social structure of Muslim Indians resembles much more the social structure of their Hindu neighbors than that of Muslim Arabs. Except that, undetermined and unfixed by anything sacred, the positions of quasi *jatis* in their Muslim local societies are probably more susceptible to change through the influence of money, power and pluck than are the positions of Hindu *jatis* in their societies.

A widespread, particularly in northern India, though by no means universal, means used by quasi *jatis* to bring about such positional changes is, in effect, a Muslim variant of sanskritization. It is sometimes called "ashrafization." In Indian Muslim social ideology, the *ashraf* are the functional equivalents of the twice-born in the ideology of *varna dharma*. Defined as pure by descent, the *ashraf* constitute the Muslim category of, literally, "nobility." Its subcategories, hierarchically arranged are: *Sayyids*, descendants of the Prophet, from the line of his daughter and son-in-law, Ali; *Sheikhs*, descendants of the Prophet's tribe or tribes associated with him; *Mughals*, scions of warriors from Turkestan who gave the world Tamerlane and India its greatest Muslim dynasty; and *Pathans*, the dominant tribesmen–warriors of Afghanistan. It is an illuminating insight into Indian Muslims' self-perceptions of their origins and subsequent careers, I think, that they should conceive of their nobility as entirely foreign. The one Indian exception to this rule tends to prove it. *"Rajputs"* are sometimes accepted as a fifth *ashraf* category. The Bhutto family of Pakistan, for example, claim Rajput genealogy. Muslims who call themselves *Rajputs* are claiming Hindu ancestry of pure warrior stock, from a twice-born *jati* renowned for its purity of descent.

Like *varna dharma*, then, the classification of *ashraf* is best thought of as a referent ideology. It is not a group and its subgroups of people, but rather a social category and its subcategories to which groups of people, Muslim quasi *jatis*, may refer themselves and others. Quasi *jatis* that aspire to *ashraf* status "discover" that they have a *Sheikh* (or some other *ashraf*) ancestor, document and publicize their discovery, call themselves *Sheikhs*, model their social behavior after that of some quasi *jati* of unquestionable *Sheikh* status, try to arrange marriages with them or failing that with some other quasi *jati* of less unquestionable *Sheikh* status, and so forth.

Imtiaz Ali regards ashrafization as the "structural implication" for and among Muslim quasi *jatis* of their tendency toward Islamization.[9] To what extent it is an increasing or decreasing implication of Islamization, I do not know. Certainly, the rush to middle-class respectability and its material benefits that nowadays characterizes aspiring Hindu *jatis*, characterizes aspiring Muslim quasi *jatis* as well. And more and more, in the countryside, among Muslims no less than Hindus, models of respectability and its symbol are taken from the Westernized *ashraf* and twice-born of modern urban India as well as from ancient faith.

Untouchability

I have already alluded to untouchability but said little about it directly. It is the condition of more than 120 million Indians. Their *jatis*, ubiquitous throughout India, number in the hundreds and in all their characteristics are like other *jatis*. Except that members of untouchable *jatis* are regarded by their touchable neighbors as carriers of pollution so dreadful as to necessitate extraordinary quarantine.

In theory, untouchables are the sources of dreadful pollution either because their *jatis* customarily have had particularly unclean living habits, e.g., eating carrion, or particularly unclean occupations, i.e., those which involve regular physical contact with death or human excreta. *Jatis* whose customary occupations are attending to funeral grounds and tanning are usually regarded as untouchable, for example, as are *jatis* of sweepers and launderers. These *jatis* may, in fact, no longer practice their unclean habits or occupations. Nowadays, untouchables are usually agricultural laborers who hold little or no land and work for village landholders. But that is theoretically irrelevant to their status as untouchables. That such habits and occupations were customarily theirs indicates that they are naturally unclean.

Extraordinary measures are necessary to quarantine the contagion of untouchables: more than the usual restrictions on interdining and food handling among touchable *jatis*. Typically, untouchable *jatis* are kept residentially segregated in their villages and forbidden ordinary access to village temples, the homes of touchable villagers and the wells and tanks that are the sources of their domestic water supply. The poorest of the village poor are usually untouchables. They live in squalor and misery. Touchable villagers keep them in their lowly place by holding them in debt bondage or otherwise paying them as little as possible for their labor, sexually exploiting untouchable women, discouraging the education of their children, routinely subjecting untouchables to verbal and physical abuse, and demanding that they acknowledge their lowliness in the ways in which they refer to themselves and defer to their betters. For touchable, and particularly landholding, villagers, untouchables provide the economic services of an exploitable labor pool, and the social and psychological services of *untermenschen*: people to be better than, to look down on, despise, humiliate, ridicule, reduce to servility and grovelling.

For the Indian government, however, untouchability is a national disgrace. Its constitutional and legal commitment is to rid India of it. That is not only the approved and intended direction of change, but the actual direction. Though the pace is slow. I want to discuss untouchability in terms of getting rid of it. To clarify the discussion we can distinguish sacred ways of getting rid of it and mundane ways; and, of course the ways often cross.

Ironically, the same Hinduism which apparently sanctions untouchability, also promises untouchables relief from it. Simply, the sweeper who accepts his *dharma* as a sweeper in this life, will be reborn into the next as a sweeper's better. We can only guess at the extent to which this promise has been a source of consolation and hope to untouchables over the ages. And a device for keeping them in their places. Not all have been happy to stay in their places, however. We know that much. There are untouchable *jatis* that have sanskritized their way into touchable Hindu status, although rarely. In general, untouchable *jatis* lack the resources, psychological as well as economic and political, to sustain a sanskritizing campaign; and their attempts to do so are often met with particularly bitter resistance from touchable Hindus.

But Hinduism does not provide the only sacred way for untouchables to get rid of their untouchability. It is generally agreed, that of those *jatis* which have over the centuries converted to Christianity and Islam, a substantial, if not a major proportion were untouchable. I assume that one motive at least of many of the converting *jatis* was the desire to rid themselves of their untouchability or of its consequences, e.g., hunger. To what extent the tens of millions of descendants of these converts are materially better off for their having become Christians and Muslims, is, again, something about which we can only guess. They are, in general, two of the poorest religious groups in India; and to boot, there are *jatis* of untouchable Christians and Muslims – so regarded by their coreligionists, as well as by their Hindu neighbors. Still, it is probably true that upward mobility from a Hindu untouchable base is less likely to have occurred and to occur through sanskritization rather than through conversion first, and then social climbing up through Christian ranks or by ashrafization. Doubtlessly, there are perfectly respectable Muslim quasi *jatis* whose ancestors were Hindu untouchables.

From the founding of the Arya Samaj in 1875 to the recent establishment of the Vishva Hindu Parishad (world Hindu association) as an umbrella organization for Hindu revivalist groups, these groups have been keenly aware of Christianity's and Islam's attraction to untouchables. Hindu revivalist associations, in general, now argue that untouchability is an excrescence on Hinduism rather than something sanctioned by it, sponsor programs for untouchable welfare, and make some efforts at reconverting untouchable Christian and Muslim *jatis* back to Hinduism.

Two major crossings of the sacred and mundane ways to get untouchability out of India were marked in the decades before its independence by Mahatma Gandhi and Bhimrao Ramji Ambedkar. Gandhi described himself as a *varnasramadharma* Hindu: one who believes in the major tenets of the faith. Untouchability was, to him, a corruption of the faith. He was a passionate preacher and active campaigner against the "sin" of untouchability. He worked and lived among untouchables, whom he called "Harijans," God's people; and in his various *ashrams* (headquarters-cum-model communities) there was no untouchability. He forbade the practice of untouchability to Congressmen. But his way of getting rid of untouchability was much the same as that of the twice-born Hindu reformers who preceded him. It was the way of reconciliation within Hinduism. Untouchables were encouraged to give up, insofar as possible, doing those things, e.g., carrion eating and whisky drinking, that supposedly offended touchables; and touchables were encouraged to revalue the work done by Harijans and accept them as ordinary members of the Hindu fold. In effect, untouchability would be got rid of by dissolving it into Hinduism, undoing the ancient bifurcation of the *shudra varna*.

Gandhi, of course, was not only a *mahatma* (a Hindu saint; literally, great soul) but also the Indian National Congress's supremo, and there were good political reasons – which he would not distinguish from good religious reasons – for keeping within the Hindu fold almost one-fifth of its members, safe from British divide-and-rule tactics to entice them out. Safe for the Congress.

But not safe *from* the Congress, Ambedkar argued, as the powerless wards of a nationalist movement whose reins were held by twice-born and dominant Hindu *jatis*. The oppressors! Not safe for lack of the opportunity to develop outside of touchable Hindu domination, as had the Muslims with British patronage, into a separate and powerful constituency in Indian politics. Ambedkar was an untouchable: from the very large Mahar *jati* of Maharashtra. He was one of the remarkable men of his age: an economist trained at Columbia University and the London School of Economics, a leading barrister, distinguished academic lawyer and chief draftsman of the Indian constitution. As both an intellectual and an activist, he was the outstanding untouchable leader of the twentieth century. He wanted the untouchables out of Hinduism and out of Congress. Only outside could they be powerful, and only if they were powerful would their Hindu oppressors heed them.

In the years of discussion before the landmark India Act of 1935 was passed by the British parliament, Ambedkar lobbied the British government to establish for untouchables the same sort of separate political identity that they had established for Muslims earlier in the century. When in 1932, the British agreed to Ambedkar's demand, Gandhi went on a "fast unto death" until either the agreement or the demand was withdrawn. Ambedkar unhappily withdrew the demand in favor of a compromise with Gandhi. This "Poona Pact" between them more or less indicated the mundane way for ridding independent India of untouchability. Untouchable *jatis* were to be regarded as an integral part of Hindu and Indian society. But in order to realize that integration, they would be made the beneficiaries of compensatory and protective discrimination.

Before we investigate that way, however, a final paragraph about Ambedkar and the sacred way. Although he believed in and actively promoted the political mobilization of untouchables – to fight their own battles, to be self-reliant and independent of the unreliable solicitude and benevolence of touchable Hindus – Ambedkar understood that people lacking in self-esteem are unlikely to mobilize themselves successfully for political action. In order to hold untouchables in thrall, Hinduism had imposed a *dharma* on them which forbade self-esteem, and they could gain it only by choosing not to be Hindus any longer. After scant success as an organizer and leader of untouchable political action, Ambedkar in the last years of his life led a mass conversion of untouchables to Buddhism. There are now about 5 million Buddhists in India. But they are almost all Mahars. It has become a major faith of Ambedkar's *jati*-fellows, but not of untouchable rebellion against Hinduism. Except that the Mahars have also produced the Dalit (oppressed) Panthers: a group committed to "direct action." Still, whatever the Mahars may have gained in self-esteem from their conversion and whatever they may gain in future from their Buddhist self-esteem and *dalit* assertiveness, nowadays in their villages their social positions and material conditions are those of untouchables.

In independent India, the mundane ways for ridding India of untouchability are more or less government sponsored or autonomously political and they are basically four:

First, through the law. The Indian constitution expressly abolishes untouchability. It prohibits any government agency or private establishment from discriminating or acting in any way *against* any Indian citizen on the grounds that he or she is an untouchable; and the constitution and its pursuant laws make any such discrimination or action a criminal offense.

Second, through compensatory and protective discrimination. The Indian government pioneered in this area, now widely known among English-speakers by its American euphemism, "affirmative action." Although untouchability is officially no longer existent in

India, the government maintains a schedule, i.e., register, of *jatis* all over India which were customarily and are now illegally considered untouchable by their neighbors. Hence, "scheduled castes": an Indian euphemism inherited from the British. Scheduled caste representation in the Union parliament and state legislative assemblies is guaranteed. This is done by reserving for untouchable candidates *alone* the right to contest about 15 percent of parliamentary and legislative assembly constituencies. All adult residents of these constituencies are enfranchised, but the candidates – of all parties and none – must be untouchables. *Panchayati raj* institutions are usually obliged to co-opt scheduled caste members if none are elected.

Places in educational institutions, including universities, are reserved for untouchables, in proportion to their numbers; and relaxed terms of admission and scholarship schemes are available to them. Places in all grades of employment, from executive to menial class, in Union and state public services and in all government-owned corporations are reserved for untouchables. To facilitate their employment, particularly in the higher grades, ordinarily applicable qualifications – age limits, educational requirements, experience and so forth – are relaxed for untouchable applicants. Tribal people, i.e., "scheduled tribes," are also the beneficiaries of Indian government-sponsored programs of compensatory and protective discrimination (see table 3 for scheduled castes and tribes distribution).

Third, through poverty alleviation measures. In recent years the Indian government has instituted a number of programs for providing direct relief to that 51 percent of India's population which in 1979–80 was living below the officially defined poverty line. A disproportionate number of India's poor are untouchables, about 20 percent, and there is greater poverty among untouchables than among touchables.[10] The poverty of untouchables is one of the major obstacles to ridding India of untouchability. Scheduled castes, then, (and scheduled tribes) are particular targets for poverty alleviation programs and these are of particular concern to untouchable *jatis*. The largest of these programs is the Integrated Rural Development (IRDP) Program under which poor families are supplied with income-generating assets, e.g. goats; and to maintain them, access to credit and other facilities. Under other programs there are schemes for technical training, guaranteed employment and the provision of basic village amenities.

Fourth, through untouchable political action. This is not so

Table 3. *Population 1991 and percentages of scheduled castes (untouchables) and scheduled tribes and their distribution (see map 1)*

	Pop.	Scheduled castes	Scheduled tribes
		(approximate %)	
India	843,930,861	15.3	7.5
States			
Andhra Pradesh	66,304,854	14.9	5.9
Arunachal Pradesh	858,392	0.5	69.9
Assam	22,294,562	6.2	11.0
Bihar	86,338,853	14.5	8.3
Goa[a]	1,168,622	2.1	0.9
Gujarat	41,174,060	7.2	14.2
Haryana	16.317,715	19.1	none[b]
Himachal Pradesh	5,111,079	24.6	4.6
Jammu and Kashmir	7,718,700	8.3	none
Karnataka	44,817,398	15.1	4.9
Kerala	29,011,237	10.0	1.0
Madhya Pradesh	66,135,862	14.1	23.0
Maharashtra	78,706,719	7.1	9.2
Manipur	1,826,714	1.2	27.3
Meghalaya	1,760,626	0.4	80.1
Mizoram	686,217	0.0	93.7
Nagaland	1,215,573	none	84.0
Orissa	31,512,070	14.7	22.4
Punjab	20,190,795	26.9	none
Rajasthan	43,880,640	17.0	12.2
Sikkim	403,612	5.7	23.1
Tamilnadu	55,638,318	18.3	1.1
Tripura	2,744,827	15.1	28.4
Uttar Pradesh	138,760,417	21.2	0.2
West Bengal	67,982,734	22.0	5.6
Union Territories			
Andaman and Nicobar Islands	277,989	none	11.7
Chandigarh	640,725	14.0	none
Dadra and Nagar Haveli	138,542	2.0	78.6
Daman and Diu[a]	101,439	2.1	0.9
Delhi	9,370,475	18.0	none
Lakshadweep	51,681	none	92.5
Pondicherry	789,416	15.9	none

Notes: [a]Percentage of undivided Goa, Daman and Diu. [b]"None" means none scheduled by the Government of India.

much government sponsored as are the preceding ways, but rather government tolerated and facilitated by parliamentary democracy. Like political action among touchables in the Indian countryside, political action among untouchables is usually organized *de facto* in *jati* and *jati* subgroup units. And like touchable political action, it takes many forms. *Jati* associations mobilize *jati*-fellows for political action and act as interest groups in state politics. There are *Harijan* blocs in state branches of the Congress (I) and in provincial parties. From time to time, most recently in Uttar Pradesh, a political party of untouchables appears. Or an untouchable direct action group, like the Dalit Panthers of Maharashtra. Government-funded non-government organizations (NGOs) have promoted non-violent political activity among untouchable *jatis* all over India. Government, chronically in Bihar, has used paramilitary police to suppress violent political protest among untouchables, whether organized in fact or in politicians' fantasy by revolutionary communist groups.

To what extent has India rid itself of untouchability? To some extent and in ways that are consistent with the general pattern of bourgeois revolution. No more than for the general population has change for untouchables been from the bottom up. At the bottom, according to Indian government calculations, the percentage of Indians below the "poverty line" has declined to somewhat more than half of what it was in 1977–78. The incidence of poverty among untouchables has decreased accordingly but not much more than accordingly. The contribution of the various poverty alleviation programs to this decrease cannot be more than marginal. It is common knowledge that a substantial proportion of the funds allocated to the various poverty alleviation programs have been misdirected and misspent. Between 1980 and 1985, according to government evaluation reports, IRDP funds reached about 5 percent of untouchable families who were living below the poverty line, and of these less than 20 percent benefited substantially. More important apparently than the engineered trickle-down effects of poverty alleviation programs are the natural trickle-down effects of prosperity. More than two-thirds of Bihar's untouchables live in poverty, less than one-third of Punjab's do.

Untouchability is still widely practiced in the Indian countryside, the constitution and the laws notwithstanding. But reports of vi⸺ and other outrages on untouchable men, women ar⸺ touchable villagers and stories of *jati* warfare betwe⸺ and touchable villagers are more likely to come from u⸺

states in which untouchables are particularly poor and degraded: Bihar in particular. They are less likely to come from developed states in which untouchables are relatively well-off and relatively well-able to defend themselves. The better-off they are and the better-off their states, the better positioned are untouchables to better their conditions in their villages and in the world beyond through their access to discriminatory reservations.

Given the dominance of landholding farmers in virtually all states, any substantial redistribution of land to the landless, untouchables and others, is likely to remain the unfulfilled goal of an earlier generation of Indian rural reformers. But, of course, the better-off untouchables are, the more able they are to buy or rent land. In places where green revolution technology is well-established, even small holdings can be profitable. The wages of agricultural laborers "increase in real terms wherever growth and the diversification of the local economy are sufficiently strong."[11] So too, the opportunities increase for untouchables to avail their families of medical care and to educate their children.

Education is the untouchable's key to the opportunities of employment provided for them by compensatory discrimination. Uneducated, their chances, alternative to agricultural labor, are those of urban drudgery and servility or, worse, virtual helotry in stone quarries and brick kilns. Nowadays, where advanced education is requisite for untouchables to hold positions reserved for them, in the higher grades of public service and government-owned corporation employment, untouchables are underrepresented because of their lack of education. But this will certainly change as more and more untouchables attain advanced education, in part because of reserved places for them in universities and colleges. Including members of parliament and state legislative assemblies, there are already tens of thousands of untouchables who have made it, though rarely to the top, through reservations. Doubtlessly, their numbers will increase. But to date and in the foreseeable future, this has done and will do more to create an untouchable bourgeoisie rather than to raise the general socio-economic level of scheduled castes.

Of course, it need not end there. Untouchable bourgeois have used their organizational skills, their income, power, influence, prestige, connections and so forth to prime social lift pumps for their *jati*-fellows. By their example, they contribute presumably to untouchable self-esteem and discredit the belief that untouchables are naturally inferior. But in the operation of lifting tens of millions of impoverished and degraded untouchables by tens of thousands of middle-class untouchables, progress is bound to be slow. Its direction, toward amelioration of the conditions of untouchables, if not the abolition of untouchability, is clear. Untouchable political action, violent and non-violent, pushes in the same direction: not toward proletarian revolution, certainly, but toward embourgeoisement and bourgeoise reconciliation.

3

Class: primordial group representation, stimuli-response, patron–client relationships

In the last chapter I indicated that the notionally sacred systems of Indian villages – ideologically sanctioned by *varna dharma* and mediated by *jatis* – have, in fact, substantial and growing secular components. These are, primarily, of wealth, power and influence. They are likely to be enjoyed by village households to the extent that they control the productive assets of their villages. In most villages the primary productive asset is land. To the extent of their holdings, then, households which control land are likely to enjoy wealth, power and influence. These are also likely to be enjoyed by households to the extent that they control capital: money, for example, which can be loaned, bullocks or tractors for hire, access to state or cooperative society development funds or urban remittance income earning employment. Some, though not all village households that control capital also control land.

Then, of course, there is the "other half" – more or less. To the extent that their households lack control of both land and capital they are likely to be poor, of course, powerless, without influence and readily exploitable by households which control land and capital. Between a village household that holds 10 hectares, for example, and one that is landless there exists in its implications as stark a contrast between rich and poor as we are likely to meet in London or Manhattan.

Can we discuss class relationships among villagers? Certainly. They exist, and in my experience and from reports of scholars and journalists, it seems clear that villagers nowadays are acutely conscious of class differences, among themselves and between them and non-villagers. Our discussion, however, encounters a major obstacle and one that it must negotiate. It is this. While villagers doubtlessly have their class relationships, these are mediated largely by affiliations that are derived neither from the class positions nor the class consciousness of their members.

It seems to me that there are two principal ways in which other-than-class-based affiliations larger and more inclusive than families mediate class relationships in the Indian countryside. First, they are mediated by *jatis*, quasi *jatis* and other primordial groups such as tribes or religious communities; and/or they are mediated by associations of these groups. Second, class relationships are mediated by the same or different responses or anticipated responses from different classes to class-related stimuli. In addition, patron–client-cum-factional affiliations mediate class relationships. But this mediation is essentially class-based, however rationalized.

A general assumption in my discussion is that the states of the Indian Union are the largest and most inclusive arenas in which there are rural class relationships. Within these, of course, there are smaller arenas. The definition of class most comfortable to my discussion is one of Max Weber's.[1] A class is a group of people whose "typical chance for a supply of goods, external life conditions and personal life experiences" is determined by their similar capacities "to dispose of goods or skills for the sake of income in a given economic order." In other words, and in Indian rural terms, a class is a collection of households which are similarly situated economically. Which share a "market situation." Class groups may or may not be communities or societies. Their members may or may not be conscious of belonging to a class.

Primordial groups as mediators of class relationships

There is perhaps an implication here that *jati* relationships as such and relationships of class are somehow distinct, although both may be mediated by *jatis*. Indeed, it may be useful in some of our discussion to treat them as distinct *for purposes of analysis*. To relate sanskritization and Islamization, for example, to the role of economic change in facilitating social mobility. Our distinction is akin to the physiologist's treatment of circulatory and respiratory systems as analytically distinct. Of course, in neither social nor physiological reality do such distinctions exist. Villagers experience their social systems holistically; as our bodies experience the respiration of air and the circulation of blood. In real relationships among villagers, those of *jati* and class are *not* a duality. They patch in here and there, usually overlapping, in the variegated, variegating fabric of village social life. The pathwork includes, for example, and now more than ever, well-to-do families of quite ordinary *jati* and well-born families of quite ordinary income. This, to villagers, is not anomalous but commonplace. To us it is the first clue to an understanding of the role of *jatis* and communal groups in the representation of their members' class interests. For well-to-do villagers and poor ones, well-born villagers and ones who are lowly born, *jati* and class are not distinct but composite parts of their identities. As our status groups and classes are composite parts of ours.

Jatis and communal groups are the primary organizations of the composite. To be sure, *jatis* are neither derived from the class consciousness of their member families nor is the consciousness of class the primary bond among these families. Apart from some untouchable *jatis* in which poverty is general, *jatis* and quasi *jatis* generally include families of different classes and exclude families of the same class. Still, however imperfect the fit, near enough has been good enough for *jatis* and communal groups to establish for themselves in democratic and developing India a relatively new, secular and modern *raison d'être*. They have become interest groups, representing their members' political and economic concerns.

The representation has taken place in a variety of ways. There are *jati* associations: more-or-less modernly organized societies with elected office bearers, dues-paying memberships, accounts, by-laws, and so forth which function to cater for their *jati*-fellows' interests. There are some well-established *jati* associations, like the Service Society of the Nair *jati* and the Sri Narayana Dharma Paripalana Yogam of the Ezhrava *jati*, both in Kerala and both founded in the early twentieth century. These are formidable interest groups in state politics and provide their members with a wide range of educational, job and welfare services in addition to political influence. Democratic politics and their intimate connection to economic development has prompted the formation, fragmentation and reformation of associations of *jatis, jati* segments and *jati* alliances all over India.

A relatively new form of association in India, now enjoying an exponential growth, is the NGO, non-governmental organization. NGOs are of varying effectiveness, credibility and freedom from political party control. Many receive government funding and funds from philanthropists and philanthropic organizations in India and abroad. Almost all are the products of middle-class activists who have organized local and specific groups of poor people in an effort to ameliorate their living and working conditions by measures of self-help, including industrial action and political activity. The groups are usually specified by their organizers in terms of what their members do: agricultural labor, work in cottage industries, brick kilns and sweatshops in the "unorganized sector" of manufacturing industries. The members of these organizations, however, usually specify themselves in terms of what they are: their *jatis*, communal groups and tribes. And these primordial affiliations underpin the class organization of their members.

There are *jati* and quasi *jati* blocs in virtually every state political party organization, legislative assembly and government ministry. Inter-*jati* conflict is a major component of state politics. Another is intra-*jati* conflict: between *jati* factions led by competing *jati* politicians. *Jati* politics of both sorts may (and may not) be related to sacred ends, e.g., sanskritized status, but the means are secular and in the clash of secular interests. Moreover, while *jatis* and other primordial groups retain their interests in Hindu or other social respectability, they increasingly define respectability and mark the routes to it in class terms. Who takes water from whom becomes less and less important, and who has how many irrigated hectares becomes more and more important.

In the struggle for hectares, primordial groups, by themselves or in alliance, have established or captured political parties at the state level. The Akali Dal is a party of, by and for Sikhs – unabashedly so. Its concerns, however, are not only with defending the *panth* (faith) against absorption into Hinduism, but with securing irrigation waters for Sikh farmers and places in the Indian army for their sons. Nowadays, in the bloody turmoil of Sikh politics, the Dal has become an agglomeration of factions that vie with each other and with factions of armed militants to be the most uncompromising defender of the *khalsa* (Sikh community) and its secular interests.

Since 1967, Tamil Nadu has been ruled by parties, the Dravida Munnetra Kazhagam (DMK) and the All-India Anna Dravida Munnetra Kazhagam (AIADMK), both of which developed from factions of an anti-*brahman* coalition of non-*brahman jatis*. Originally, this Dravidian movement was not only a reaction against the sacred status of *brahmans* but against their dominance in Tamil Nadu as landholders and in public administration and the professions.

In the late 1970s, the Gujarat branch of the Congress (I) came to be dominated by a backward classes coalition of aspiring *jatis* and quasi *jatis*. These are a number of touchable Hindu *jatis* which call themselves, collectively, *kshatriyas*, plus untouchable Hindu *jatis*, tribal groups and Muslim quasi *jatis*. This improbable alliance of Hindus and Muslims, touchables and untouchables, "peasants" and tribals has challenged the economic and political power in Gujarat of twice-born and dominant Hindu *jatis*. Specifically, what the backward-classes-dominated Congress (I) state government did in the 1980s was to extend to its touchable Hindu and Muslim constituences the compensatory reservations in state government employment enjoyed by untouchables and tribal people, but constitutionally allowable as well to members of "other backward classes," and practiced, most notably, in Tamil Nadu in favor of non-*brahmans*. The reaction from the middle classes of twice-born and dominant Gujarati *jatis*, particularly students, was violent: as it would be in various parts of India when in 1990 the National Front government in New Delhi decided to reserve positions in central government employment for other backward classes' applicants.

For decades, Naga and Mizo tribesmen of the northeast fought guerrilla wars against paramilitary forces of the Indian government. Now they have states of their own in the Indian Union, Nagaland and Mizoram, and their own political parties. Naga and Mizo leaders, as insurgents and now politicians, have wanted to protect not only the tribal identities of their groups but also their economic interests against the incursions of non-tribal farmers, moneylenders, timber contractors, and so forth.

In central Bihar's villages there has been for some time now a state of simmering class-cum-*jati* warfare that periodically comes to the boil in bloody violence. The warfare is three-sided. We can identify the sides in class terms as: large land holders, small farmers and landless laborers. But they are organized for battle in *jati* lines. Touchable landholders and farmers have their *jati senas* (literally, armies); and untouchable *jatis*, as such, have been trained and organized for combat by revolutionary communist cadres.

It is enough, I think, to recall and restate some of our earlier discussion about *jatis* to understand why they (and communal groups) have become primary mediators of their members' class relationships in the Indian countryside. In sum, *jatis* are communities. They embody consciousness, in depth and breadth, to a degree that is unattained and probably unattainable by class-conscious associations in industrial societies. *Jatis* enjoy the sanctions of religion, custom and usage, longevity and reliability. In a society in which family ties are particularly salient, all the legitimate members of people's families, however distant, are their *jati*-fellows and their *jatis* are demonstrable and ideological extensions of their families. Intimate social relationships are sanctioned by *jatis* and only among *jati*-fellows. Occupational specialization, insofar as it exists, is *jati* occupational specialization. All this, and more, that creates and maintains *jatis* as communities, as self-conscious groups, groups "for themselves" to use Marx's phrase, inhibit the creation of interor intra-*jati* associations based on class. In other words, *jatis* tend to monopolize their members' group life. And even traditionally this includes its economic – class as well as occupational – aspects. Frequently and in effect, sanskritization and ashrafization, for example, are ways by which *jatis* demand sacred status consistent with their class position.

The modern mediation of class relationships by *jatis* tends: first, to over-represent the interests of dominant *jatis*; and second, to overrepresent the interests of well-to-do households in virtually all *jatis*. Dominant *jatis* combine the virtues that characterize powerful interest groups in most parliamentary democratic systems: they are large, generally well-to-do, respectable, self-confident, attractive as allies, well-connected politically and spokesmen for their own interests. In the prevalent relationships of patronage–clienthood in Indian villages, about which I shall have more to say later in this chapter, dominant *jati* households are usually patrons, and this enhances their other interest group virtues. Clients, for example, are amenable to their patrons' voting instructions. At the bottom of village hierarchies, by contrast, untouchable *jatis* combine the disabilities of the powerless: poverty, disrespectability, low self-esteem, illiteracy and lack of education, sickness, a lowliness which serves the economic and status interests of their neighbors, dependence on others. In addition, they are often clients, and this is a disincentive and an obstacle to their organized representation of their interests.

The mediation of their class relationships by dominant and twiceborn *jatis* tend to favor the interests of their most powerful and prosperous members. They tend to be the mediators: village patrons, local- and state-level politicians. But, even the reservations demanded by spokesmen for backward classes' *jatis* are likely to be of greatest benefit to their most advanced households; in much the same way as the benefits of compensatory discrimination have been distributed among untouchables and tribals – and probably to the same effect of embourgeoisement. Of course, *jati* politicians who ignore the interests of their poor and less-well-off relations share the same perils as any politicians who disregard the concerns of large sections of their constituencies. Households are bound to their *jatis*, to be sure, and poor households as much, if not more than rich ones. But there are few *jatis* or other primordial groups of any size or consequence whose political manifestations are not factionalized, and few of their factions operate without dissent and opposition to their leadership. *Jatis* expect their politicians to deliver the goods. Still for reasons that will become clear, I hope, by the end of this chapter, the mediation of class relationships by *jatis* tends not only to over-represent but to aggregate higher-class interests in the countryside. Conversely, such mediation tends not only to under-represent but to disaggregate lower-class interests.

Class interests as mediated by stimuli responses

My observations in this section are meant to be another way of looking at what I have already written about classes in the Indian countryside: not an alternative way, but rather a complementary and supplementary way. I propose to do this looking in two stages: I want, initially, to construct a rough and ready class taxonomy comfortable to my definition of class and applicable to an hypothetical Indian village. Then, I want to explain how these classes – without consciousness, neither communities nor societies, entirely the constructs of analysis – are nonetheless capable of acting like classes.

At the base of my taxonomy is the table to which I have already referred. It is presented by Pranab Bardhan as a "crude approximation," and as such I accept it and reproduce it in slightly modified and abbreviated form as table 4.[2] It will do. Incidentally, this portrayal of the distribution of agricultural wealth, i.e., area operated, in the Indian countryside bears a striking resemblance to "crude approximations" of the distribution of wealth in bourgeois industrialized societies. A recent survey in Australia, for example reports that: "the wealthiest 20 per cent of individuals owns about 70 per cent of the nation's private wealth . . . The bottom 50 per cent of Australians owns less than 8 percent of the nation's wealth."[3]

From Bardhan's table, I build my model class structure, firstly by reducing his categories to three, more or less as follows: his "very large" and the upper range of his "large" into my "upper"; the lower range of his "large," his "medium" and the upper range of

Table 4. *Distribution of farm families in India in 1975 by farm household land size categories*

Farm household land size categories	Range of holdings in hectares (1 ha = 2.47 acres)	Percentage of rural agricultural population	Percentage of rural agricultural area operated
very large	8.10 or above	7.9	40
large	4.05–8.09	10.7	20.4
medium	2.02–4.04	16.3	19.8
small	1.01–2.01	18.5	12.4
marginal	0.51–1.00	15.7	4.0
sub-marginal	0.01–0.50	18.6	3.0
landless	0	12.3	0

his "small" into my "middle"; the lower range of his "small," his "marginal," "sub-marginal" and "landless" into my "lower." Secondly, I refine my categories by adding to the incomes of land-holding households their incomes derived from sources other than their holdings, and adding to the incomes of landless households their incomes derived from sources other than the sale of their labor. Village households derive income from urban remittances and investments, from interest on loans extended to other village households, from rents and other payments collected from lands they hold but do not operate, from goods and services supplied by landholding household members to fellow villagers, from goods sold to fellow villagers by members of households of landless laborers, and so forth. Finally, if there are in my hypothetical village any households which are entirely non-farming, i.e., derive no income from landholding or agricultural labor, I place them into one of my three categories according to their income. My product is something like the following simple taxonomy:

> upper village households
> middle village households
> lower village households

Analysts of actual rather than hypothetical class relationships among rural families might want to use fewer or more, different or more widely based categories. That would depend on who they were looking at and what they were looking for. It is worth reiterating, however, that their categories, like mine, would be the constructs of analysts. They are not the constructs of village households. We categorize in order to better understand villagers' social realities. But our categories are not their social realities. Our categories are the product of our consciousness and not theirs. We cannot, of course, expect conscious action from classes that are not based on their members' consciousness.

We do expect our classes to have different "market situations," and in an actual research project, we would test that expectation and categorize or recategorize accordingly. In my hypothetical village, I expect these "market situations" to be roughly as follows, starting from the middle.

Middle village households are generally secure in their sources of income: in their tenure, if they are landholding. Because of ordinary, foreseeable misfortune – a bad season or two – a middle village family is likely to be pressed but not ruined. A middle village household will hire in and hire out labor, let in and let out land, but primarily by operating the household's holdings (and/or other enterprises) with family labor it is usually able to produce a better-than-subsistence income. "Better-than subsistence" is at least in part socially defined and would vary from locality to locality and group to group, but I would generally include in its definition for example, savings: to hedge indebtedness, cover contingencies like the death of a bullock or the payment of a dowry and, perhaps, provide for an investment in a water pump or a son's higher education. Middle village households are at least potentially vulnerable to social, economic and political assertiveness from below and power from above.

Above, upper village households hold enough land and/or capital to make their livelihoods not merely secure but profitable. They are, more or less, the countryside's upper quintile; although by Western standards, only the most prosperous upper village households are rich. Landholding upper village households are the regular and usual employers of villagers who sell their labor. As well, these households may also be suppliers of capital to other villagers: as moneylenders, for example. And as such they pose a threat to the tenurial security of small-holding households. It is the upper households of the village who are likeliest to derive substantial income, influence and prestige from the urban employment of their sons and other relatives and profits from investments in such extra-village enterprises as sugar mills and transport companies.

Increasing embourgeoisement of upper village households' life-styles, in and of themselves and in relation to the market situation of the households, further differentiates these households from those of their neighbors. Upper village households own tractors and television sets. The roles of their men in cultivation are likely to be those of entrepreneur and manager. Some of these households' men have prestigious and well-paying urban careers. Upper village households aspire to both traditional and modern respectability. They take and give large dowries; and send their sons and, increasingly, daughters to university. In their villages, the wives of upper households observe the *purdah* of respectable matrons, and become increasingly familiar with the modern world in order to perform their traditional roles as household managers. Patron households are likely to be upper village households; and nowadays, their webs of patronage and clienthood are likely to extend beyond their village walls. I will discuss patron–client relationships in the next section of this chapter.

Finally, with regard to upper village households, I have not provided a category separate from theirs for "landlord households." The great estates of non-cultivating landlord households – of either rentier or aristocratic varieties – were, in general, broken up by state government land reforms in the 1950s; and in the 1990s, there are no differences in the market situations of landlord and upper village households and decreasing differences in their lifestyles and even their *amour propre*.

Lower village households are insecure in their livelihoods. If they own any land, it is not enough to sustain them. As a group they are effectively landless. If they own any capital, e.g., goats, it is not enough to sustain them. All or most of the livelihoods of lower village households are earned by selling the labor of their men, women and children. From their labors, they earn a subsistence or less-than-subsistence income. They are readily exploitable in their villages by upper and middle village households. Often lower village households survive only in clientage, which at its worst is debt bondage.

Now, if these classes are the products of our categorization rather than their consciousness and we cannot, therefore, expect conscious action from them; what sort of class action can we expect? For the answer that I propose, I am indebted, again, to a suggestion by Max Weber.[4] We can expect of households which are similarly situated in economic terms similar responses to the same economic or economically related stimuli. So, for example, to the stimulus of some state government's hypothetical decision to enforce that usual provision of land reform legislation that sets minimum wages for agricultural labor, we can expect similar responses from households that I have classed together and different responses from each class: opposition from the upper, ambiguity from the middle and support from the lower.

As I indicated earlier, these responses are likely to be mediated by *jatis, jati* factions and other primordial groups and their factions. They are also mediated through the expectations of state politicians. Indeed, we can only hypothesize about class reactions to any state government's decision to enforce the payment of minimum agricultural wages, because state politicians have been almost unanimous in the expectation that any such decision would be an act of political suicide. The same expectation has inhibited state politicians from enforcing other provisions of land reform legislation which disserve the interests of landholding households, e.g., ceilings on their landholdings, tenurial security for subtenants, maximum shares for sharecroppers, special protection for small holdings of untouchable and tribal households. In response to the same expectation, state governments do not tax agricultural incomes – although agricultural production accounts for about 30 percent of India's gross domestic product.

The political predominance, across India, from villages to state legislative assemblies, of landholding interests over the interests of the effectively landless, i.e., my lower village households, the salience of land in Indian villages as the marker between "haves" and "have-nots," and, perhaps, some misapplication of Marxian class analysis have inclined both scholars and journalists – often unconsciously and implicitly – to assume a two-class division in the Indian countryside. There is the upper and the lower, the top and the bottom, those who own land and employ labor, and those who are effectively landless and are employed by the landed. There is, to be sure, an ambiguous middle *something* of small holders, our middle village households, but insofar as they are effectively landed, so the assumption has it, their households constitute the top's bottom.

However correct that may have been in the past, a manifestation of rural embourgeoisement in recent years has been the assertion of their own particular interests by middle village households. That assertion, as usual, is mediated in combination by primordial groups and through stimulus-response. Whatever its socio-economic profile, the backward classes' coalition of *jatis* that now dominates the Congress (I) in Gujarat, for example, has its political center, its dominant force, in its class of middle village households. The stimulus to which the coalition responded was a political vacuum: the mass desertion of the Gujarati Congress (I) in 1977 by its usual twice-born and dominant *jati* supporters. Their political center is in the class of upper village households. Relatively advanced in their climb to wealth and status, twice-born and dominant *jati* families and their children are bitterly and violently opposed to the central demand of the backward classes' coalition, for access to that vehicle *par excellence* of government-sponsored embourgeoisement: reserved places in universities for their children. Again, such reservations would most likely benefit the better-off-households of backward class *jatis*.

In the 1980s, "farmers' movements" appeared in various parts of India. Of these, the largest and apparently most cohesive and best organized are the Shetkari Sanghatana (farmers' union) of Maharashtra and the Bharatiya Kisan (Indian farmers') Union of western Uttar Pradesh. Both bring out farmers in the tens and even hundreds of thousands to participate in their rallies and agitational campaigns. Both are mixed-*jati* and mixed-class movements. In terms of "effectively landed" as opposed to "effectively landless," both represent the interests of landholding households.

The movements are manifestations of the political power of land-holding farmers in their states. They are self-defensive responses to what landholding households see as official, and particularly Union government, bias in favor of urban industrial interests as opposed to those of the countryside. The movements want government support for higher farm prices. They complain about farmers' "negative terms of trade" for manufactured goods. There is also in their movements recognizable responses of the "folk" to "the city" and all the hateful and fearful things it represents in changing times: politicians with foreign wives, capitalists with accounts in foreign banks, men without caste, women without shame, the denigration of tradition and alienating modernity.

Emergent from the farmers' movements, however, is a class division being made by middle village households, on which the movements depend for their mass support, and upper village households. Note, for example, what were reported in late 1987 to be the basic demands of the Shetkari Sanghatana's supremo, Sharad

Joshi. First, ostensibly because of drought conditions, a government declaration freeing farmers from indebtedness to public and cooperative sector creditors; from which freedom "only loans taken to buy trucks, tractors and drip irrigation equipment will be exempted." Second, "a reassertion of the demand for more remunerative prices for agricultural produce." Third, "higher minimum wages for farm laborers . . . , roughly doubling the minimum wage to Rs.25 a day."[5]

The first and third demands are, at least in part, contrary to the interests of upper village households: they are the principal purchasers of trucks, tractors and so forth and the major employers of farm laborers. Middle village households employ farm labor less, and are themselves suppliers of farm labor. Lower village households, particularly of farm laborers, which must often purchase substantial portions of their food supply, would find the second demand contrary to their interests. Except that the contrariness would be mitigated if their wages were doubled, largely at the expense of upper village households. All three demands, in a word, are most favorable to the interests of middle village households.

The decision in 1990 of the National Front's prime minister, Vishwanath Pratap Singh to reserve places in central government employment for applicants from *jatis* which are classified as belonging to "other backward classes"; the bitterness and violence that his decision occasioned among twice-born and dominant *jatis*; his loss of office through the desertion from his parliamentary majority of the party of Hindu "awakening," the Bharatiya Janata Party (BJP), in part because it feared that the reservation issue would pare its Hindu vote; Singh's strenuous efforts to keep alive the issue (and his political career) by campaigning on it for the 1991 parliamentary elections; and in spite of the National Front's relatively poor performance in those elections, growing awareness in the victorious Congress (I) of backward classes as political forces to be reckoned with – all this has put the strivings of middle village households and their *jatis* on the agenda of India's *national* politics, and is likely to keep it there.

Patron–client-cum-factional affiliations as mediators of class relationships

In the Indian countryside, I suggested earlier, the interests of the upper, generally landed, classes tend to be over-represented and aggregated and the interests of the lower, effectively landless, classes tend to be under-represented and disaggregated. Here is the place to pursue that suggestion. And once again, we begin with the exposition of an ideal.

In the Hindi-derived vocabulary of Indian studies, the ideal is called the *jajmani* system. We have already referred to it. Like the joint family ideal, it is best thought of these days as affecting rather than reflecting reality. A village's *jajmani* system was meant to function as its sacred economic order, much as its *jati* hierarchy was meant to function as its sacred social order. They were interrelated parts of the same *dharma*.

At the center of a village's *jajmani* system were its households of *jajmans* or patrons. They were usually the village's largest landholders. Although their *jatis* were likely to be relevant to their positions as landholders, they were *jajmans* not because of their *jatis* but because of their holdings. Supplying them with various goods and services were households of *kamins* or clients. Ideally, the goods and services they supplied were according to the *kamin* households' traditional, customary, divinely ordained *jati* occupations. So, a household of potter *jati* provided its *jajman* household with a fixed supply of baked clay pots. The *jajman–kamin* relationship was properly heritable, familial, ritualized and performed within the context of a reciprocal, albeit asymmetric, relationship: a relationship of general social superiority to general social inferiority between the landholding and the potter households. A patron–client relationship.

In the *jajmani* ideal, the potter's ancestors would have supplied pots to his *jajman*'s ancestors, and the *jajman*'s descendants would receive their pots from the potter's descendants. The potter made the pots, but as part of a household enterprise; and the *jajmani* relationship was between the potter's household and the *jajman*'s household. Members of the two households acknowledged and demonstrated in their social and ritual interactions their relationship of reciprocity between unequals: in modes of address, patterns of precedence and deference, exchanges of symbolic gifts, participation in each others' ceremonies, and so forth.

In times of need, potter clients were expected to appeal to their *jajman* households for help: a loan, an introduction, the exercise of some influence. Landholding *jajmans* were expected to call on their potter *kamins* for extra-occupational services: as witnesses in a court case, partisans in a dispute over land, messengers. For their services as potters and otherwise, the *kamin* household had a recognized right to a fixed quantity of the produce from its *jajman* household's fields. Because the patron–client relationship between a particular *jajman* household and particular *kamin* family household of potters was regarded as an integral part of the village's social order, it was a matter of concern to a group wider than the two households: at least, to their *jatis* and their village *panchas* (elders, members of its *panchayat*).

Ideally, this same patron–client, *jajman–kamin* relationship pertained between landholding households and sweeper households, at the bottom of the village hierarchy, and *brahman* households, at the top. Both sweepers and priests were patronized to perform their *jati* occupations, to do what they were born to do. As it had been with their ancestors so it was with them and would be with their descendants. Members of the sweeper household were treated with the appropriate etiquette of contempt, and they were poorly remunerated – usually in kind – for their demeaning (however necessary) services. The *brahman* household was not, certainly in a social sense *kamin*: a lesser. It might well have been of a higher *jati* than that of its *jajman* household. It was treated with the appropriate etiquette of respect – even of deference, however ceremonious. For their priestly services, *brahmans* were well remunerated: sometimes with their *jajmans'* most significant gift, a grant of land, an oblation (*maf*) from his holdings.

Thus *jajman* households separately and their heads together as members of the village's customary *panchayat* enjoyed a surrogate *kshatriya*-hood. Their little, village *rajs* worked, ideally, as organic wholes. Their separate parts performed the functions that they were meant to perform and were valued according to their sacred worth. Whoever sat on the Delhi or Simla *gaddi* (throne) or held the *durbar* (regime) in the princely states, the economic and political as well as the social centers of most villagers' lives were in their villages.

Village reality doubtlessly approximated the *jajmani* ideal more closely in the past than it does now. By now *jajmani* systems have been effaced by virtually all of modernity's encroachments on village life and intrusions into it: increasing availability to villagers and their use of cash, factory-made goods (like aluminum pots and plastic buckets), urban occupations and remittances from them, specialist services of all sorts. The effacement has not so much destroyed *jajmani* systems as gradually converted them into secular patron–client relationships.

Things change, but remain the same. As it was in *jajmani* systems, landholding households are still at the center of village patron–client relationships. These are still relationships of property, and even more so than before: between households that hold land and those that don't. Nowadays, clients may take at least some of their pay in cash, they are likely to be employed as farm laborers rather than in their traditional *jati* occupations – which many of them no longer follow anyway. Clients may or may not have any inter-generational ties to their patrons' households. They are likely to be their patrons' clients on his terms rather than on any *jajmani*-like terms of patron-weighted reciprocity. Their clientage is unlikely to be thought of as serving any sacred purpose and therefore worthy of any protection other than the sweet will of their patrons.

But clients still need or want patrons. Clientage is the refuge of lower village households, and it can become their prison. Clients need patrons as sources of relatively secure employment in what is usually a buyer's market for agricultural labor. They need or want patrons to help them deal with the often unfamiliar and unfriendly world outside their villages: the world of politicians, bureaucrats and police. Because they have little or no land or capital to serve as collateral, clients need patrons for unsecured loans. Their labor is their collateral, and debt bondage is the most extreme form of clientage. There are millions of Indian village households which live in debt bondage. Patrons may need clients as assured sources of labor during peak periods in the agricultural cycle. They may want clients because it is a good and pleasing thing to be a patron, to have others beholden to you, touching your feet, fearful of your wrath, dependent on your whims. Patrons also need clients to fight their factional battles. Patron–client relationships are the bases of factions.

Village factions are contentious affiliations led by patron house-holds in pursuance of their interests. Their client households are their followers in factional strife: because it is beneficial for them to follow or costly for them to do otherwise. Contentious patron households might be of *jati*-fellows, even of relatives – families of estranged brothers, for example – or they might be of different *jatis*. Where they are of different *jatis*, factional and *jati* conflict may be patched in together. Some client households may be of their patron's *jati*, and some not. Some may even belong to the *jati* of their patron's factional opponent. It doesn't matter. If there are no other options, the prudent client is true to his salt. Factional contests may be fought in deadly earnest and, *jajmani* ideals notwithstanding, they are commonplace in Indian villages. They are pursued through defamation, harassment, litigation, boycott and violence. Conventional wisdom, or at least the convention of alliterating wisdom, has it that the usual causes of factional strife in the Indian countryside are: *zamin* (land), *zevar* (movable wealth; literally jewelry) and *zanan* (women).

Since Indian independence, conflicts between village factions have been incorporated increasingly into the inter- and intra-party conflicts of democratic politics in Indian states. They were first incorporated into those politics whose centers are state legislative assemblies. From the early 1960s, they have been incorporated into the politics of *panchayati raj*. I referred to *panchayati raj* in chapter 1. But it is necessary to describe it in some more detail here; before discussing its effects, in particular, and parliamentary democracy's, in general, on the nexus between village factionalism and the representation of class interests.

From its beginnings in an official report in 1957,[6] the intended result of *panchayati raj*, literally, conciliar government, was to quicken the Indian government's largely unsuccessful, village-based ''community development'' program. *Panchayati raj* was meant to stimulate development by devolving some political authority for it on to a new system of local self-government in the countryside, encouraging and funding its developmental efforts and co-ordinating them with the efforts of bureaucrats and state politicians. *Panchayati raj* was to provide India's villages with local government that was statutory rather than conventional, democratic rather than oligarchical and oriented to change rather than to keeping the *status quo*. Although details and names vary from state to state, the general scheme of *panchayati raj* is as follows:

By universal adult suffrage, villages in a small cluster of villages elect a village *panchayat*. From the *panchayat* level upward, *panchayati raj* councils are often obliged to coopt women members and members from untouchable *jatis* or tribes if none are elected. In some states, village *panchayats* elect their *sarpanchas* (presidents). In other states, they are elected separately by popular vote. Statutory village *panchayats*, in general, have not been particularly effective. Their *sarpanchas* however, have been: for better or worse. The *sarpanchas* of all village *panchayats* within a development bloc meet together with bloc development officers as a *panchayat samiti* (committee). In most states, *panchayat samitis* are the institution in *panchayati raj* structures with most immediate effect on rural development. From its elected members, *panchayat samitis* elect their own presidents. The presidents of all *panchayat samitis* in a district meet with district development officers as a *zila parishad* (district council), which chooses its president from its elected members.

Given the prevalence of patron–client relationships in the Indian countryside, it will come as no surprise that the *sarpanchas*, who virtually monopolize *panchayati raj* systems at all their effective levels, are overwhelmingly members of upper-village-cum-patron households: often their youngish, better-educated sons rather than their rustic patriarchs. The factional leader who is or has at his hearth a statutory *sarpancha*, nowadays, enjoys a considerable advantage over his rival patron households. His clients constitute his vote bank. And particularly through his *panchayat samiti* membership, he uses his access to development funds and political influence to maintain and enlarge his clientele, enrich his household and fight his factional battles. One effect of *panchayati raj* has been to give village factions access to public funds: to fight over them and with them.

Other effects of *panchayati raj* have been to enlarge the arenas in which village factions contend and to make political influence more readily available to them. The members of *panchayat samitis*, for example, are almost invariably divided into factions which battle over the spoils of development for themselves and their constituents. The president of a *panchayat samiti* and his chief rival, the candidates of opposing factions, are patrons of patrons, in effect: with client-patrons and their clients extending over perhaps 150 villages. Their political influence is considerable, as are its pay-offs to them. Ministers, civil administrators and police officers do not underrate their capacities either to be helpful or to do mischief.

The following description from Haryana of the election for president of a *panchayat samiti* gives us some insight into the institution:

The rival groups which cut across party lines, caste identities and religious affiliations are based on personal networks or coalitions of factions formed after hard bargaining. [These groups] try to gain the majority by . . . appeals to parochial sentiments and primordial loyalties, official pressure, threats of reprisal, promises of patronage, bargaining for offices, kidnapping and physical violence.[7]

Finally, *panchayati raj* has become a major contributor to the over-representation and aggregation of landed interests in India's states, particularly of their upper village households. Concomitantly, it has contributed to the under-representation and disaggregation of the interests of lower village households. However bitter and deadly the contests between rival factions on *panchayat samitis* and *zila parishads*, they are contests among members of the same landed classes, and they proceed from the aggregation of those classes' interests. It is not their question, for example, whether or not there should be some subsidy or another to landed farmers, but what the subsidy should be and to whom it should go.

Lower village households have no *panchayati raj* institutions in which their interests are represented and aggregated. Rather, *panchayati raj* helps to maintain their clientage. Without it, their patrons would be neither *sarpanchas* nor *zila parishad* members, so some pay-offs of *panchayati raj* are trickled down to maintain the clientage of lower rural households. They are poor people, and something is better than nothing. But the cost of that something is the disaggregation of their interests, even as these might be represented by their *jatis*. Hands pressed together, the landless laborer goes for a loan or a political favor to his patron and not to his equally impoverished and powerless *jati*-fellows.

In every parliamentary democracy, the interests of the well-to-do tend to be better represented than the interests of the poor. In Indian state politics, this tendency is exaggerated because of the pervasiveness in villages of patron–client relationships between the well-to-do and the poor. *Panchayati raj* has institutionalized this exaggeration. That was not, of course, the intention of its founders. Nor must it always be so. More and more, men from backward-class *jatis* and middle village households are contesting and winning elections for positions of *sarpancha* and even of *panchayat samiti* and *zila parishad* presidents. The prospect is not of *panchayati raj* becoming an institution of the poor, but rather of its enlargement as an arena open to the not-quite-so-well-to-do: families with middle-class aspirations.

4

Homelands, "linguistic" and tribal states: nation provinces and bourgeois revolution

For families and villagers, *jatis*, classes and factions, their most inclusive arenas, in general, are those regions that we refer to variously as their homelands, linguistic or tribal states and nation-provinces. The references vary according to context and over time. So, *jatis* have homelands. It is within these that they mount sanskritizing campaigns, for example. Social customs vary from homeland to homeland. Homelands are ethnic regions. Ultimately, they are subjectively defined and their boundaries are indeterminate. Some groups of people think of Karnataka as their homeland. In that part of south India, the homelands of other people are different parts of Karnataka, outside of Karnataka, or even the area through which the Indian government has drawn the border between the states of Karnataka and Maharashtra.

States are political regions. The Indian government has formed homelands or parts thereof into quasi-federal states of the Union. State borders drawn ostensibly on linguistic or tribal lines endow homelands with borders that are politically determinate and economically significant. These borders are necessarily and sometimes purposely drawn with more or less arbitrariness. They contain within them residents who more or less or not at all think of themselves and are thought of by others as folk of their officially defined homeland-states. Homeland-states settle provincial political authority on elected representatives of their folk. Under the Indian constitution, the states have the primary authority to legislate in areas closest to the folk's interests: for example, the rural economy, urban development and education. The state is, concomitantly, a political arena in which sections of the folk – *jatis*, for instance – contend for the benefits of legislation: power and wealth.

A symbiotic relationship, familiar to Europeans from their own history, begins to grow between ethnicity and political power. The folk sustain and develop the political unit, the political unit sustains and defines the folk. In India, at some point in this process, if it is successful, the ethnic homeland-cum-quasi federal state of the Indian Union becomes, conceptually, a "nation-province." I regret the neology. But I cannot find a concept in use that adequately conveys my meaning. I mean something analogous to the Western nation-state (a neology of *c.* 1918 and in general use only post-World War II): a similar, stable relationship of mutual benefit between ethnicity and political power. Except that in India the related power is provincial rather than sovereign. India is becoming a multi-nation state of nation-provinces, or so it seems.

In turn, these nation-provinces have become incubators of bourgeois revolution in the Indian countryside. To see this, however, to fit it into the picture that we began in previous chapters to paint upward from little societies at the bottom of our canvas, we must now – to pursue the metaphor – complete by painting downward from the top. In previous chapters our picture has been of ordinary people doing ordinary things, albeit under changing circumstances: ordinary people responding to changing circumstances. Here, our picture, working its way downward, is of great events and political decisions which changed circumstances for ordinary people.

From homelands to linguistic or tribal states

The British made positive use of India's ethnic diversity to shape their ideology of empire. Relatedly, they either ignored or made negative use of India's ethnic diversity to draw their provincial borders.

Like Europe, India was a geographic term. That, in general, was the prevailing British view. The subcontinent was a vast mélange of people who spoke different languages, had different customs, belonged to different races, were members of different castes and tribes, enjoyed different levels of civilization and worshiped different gods. There was no Indian nation. Indian nationalism was a chimera; worse, it was a self-serving fantasy of the subcontinent's microscopic minority of English-educated "babus" (in Anglo-Indian English, a contemptuous reference: to "*mere* clerks"). From time to time, in its pre-British past, large parts of India had been brought together in the imperium of some dynasty of despots. When imperial despotism lost its effect, the subcontinent fragmented into petty despotisms: its usual condition. The old races of Asia were incapable, perhaps, of putting and keeping in place a political system more sophisticated than personal or, at best, dynastic autocracy. Only British administration, European genius for administration, had built and sustained in India an empire – not a nation, certainly – that was systematically and legally governed.

So, whate'er the British best administered was best for India; and, ostensibly and ideologically, if not in fact, it was according to this criterion that the captains of empire determined India's provincial borders. The ethnicity of those who lived within these borders was not in general, an official consideration of the tax-collector's *Raj*. Consider only those ethnic homelands now defined according to the Indian Union's list of "principal languages." So, for example, the British province of Madras contained Tamil regions and some Malayalam and Telegu regions. Others were in the princely states of the Malabar coast and Hyderabad. Bombay province contained some Kannada, Marathi and Gujarati areas. Others were in the princely state of Mysore, the British Central Provinces and scores of petty principalities in what is now Gujarat. Only the provincial borders of the United Provinces within the Hindi/Urdu region and Bengal followed language lines.

Bengal had not always been thus. Prior to 1905, Bengal province had been a vast sprawling area which included the Hindi region of what is now Bihar and the Oriya region, Orissa. Then, for what he said were administrative reasons, that remarkable person, Curzon, the viceroy, bifurcated the province by drawing a line through its Bengali region. Thereby he divided Bengalis between two provinces, east and west; a Muslim majority in one and a Hindu majority in the other. This first partition of Bengal, undone seven years later, provided the Indian nationalist movement with its first *cause célèbre* – and its foreshadowing of Indian nationalism's entanglement in Hindu and Muslim communalism. It also gave a clear indication of the possibilities of bringing nascent Indian nationalism and India's ancient and diverse ethnicities into a mutually supportive opposition to British imperialism. Even earlier, at the turn of the century, the nationalist firebrand, Bal Gangadhar Tilak, set out to popularize Indian nationalism in his native Maharashtra, the Marathi region, through the idiom of local Hindu worship and mythology.

But it was Mahatma Gandhi who, systematically and for all of India, wedded its ethnic diversities to Indian nationalism. In 1920, at its meeting in the central Indian city of Nagpur, the Indian National Congress confirmed Mahatma Gandhi as its supremo. He presented it with a new constitution which, among other things, delineated the Congress's provincial units *not* on the imperial map of India but on an overlay which divided the map into more or less unilingual "linguistic provinces."

Under Gandhi's leadership, the Congress was embarking on a mass non-violent non-cooperation movement whose stated goal was nothing less than to compel the British to grant *swaraj* (self-government) to India. Dividing Congress into "linguistic provinces" was part of turning Indian nationalism into a mass movement. Gandhiji's trusted lieutenants, Congress stalwarts, committed nationalists, would become the leaders of Pradesh (provincial) Congress Committees in the "linguistic provinces" to which they belonged, in which they had their *jati* and communal ties, of which they were eminent bourgeois who had made good on the stage of nationalist policies, whose languages they spoke, literally and figuratively. They were the Congress's officer cadre, and their "linguistic provinces" were to become nationalism's recruiting grounds. The media of recruitment were provincial, but only to better convey messages that were at least meant to be national: Indian.

I have kept "linguistic provinces" captive in quotation marks to suggest that it is a euphemism for ethnic provinces. Again, in India, someone's mother tongue is only an important trait in a complex of traits that identify him or her as a Gujarati or Tamil or Bengali or whatever. To be sure, Gandhi organized Indian nationalism from ethnic clusters; but to say as much would have conceded too much to British – and Indian Muslim – ideologues who denied that there was an Indian nationality. After all, is it not a contradiction in terms to argue that diverse ethnic groups can share a common nationality? In ordinary usage, "nationality" was widely meant as a synonym for what we mean by "ethnicity." Indian nationalist ideology avoided the question by readily conceding that Indians speak many different languages. But it insisted that India was their nation. India was a multi-lingual nation. What kept it from becoming a nation-state was not its *linguistic* diversity but British imperialism and its policy of divide and rule.

Gandhi's reconstitution of his nationalist movement into "linguistic provinces" became a Congress commitment to reorganize the actual provinces of India on "linguistic" lines once *swaraj* was attained. This commitment was reiterated any number of times over the years in various Congress documents, and as late as 1946 in its manifesto for the last Indian election held under British auspices.

The British were certainly going. *Swaraj*, which the Congress had since defined as "complete independence," was certainly coming. And then the subcontinent exploded. A communal firestorm raged throughout northern India. Hindus and, in Punjab, Sikhs murdered, maimed, brutalized and pillaged Muslims: men, women and children in the hundreds of thousands. Muslims visited the same horrors on Hindus and Sikhs. From what were to become West and East Pakistan millions of Sikhs and Hindus fled in terror into India. From what were to become the Indian states of Punjab and West Bengal millions of Muslims fled in terror into Pakistan. Indian and Pakistani troops, only yesterday soldiers of the same British Indian army, fought each other in Kashmir in 1948.

Swaraj came to India in tragedy and violence. Their underlying message, so read by Jawaharlal Nehru and his colleagues, was that the forces, however irrational, that held Indians to their thousands of diverse ethnicities were greater than the sentiments that held them to India. If unchecked, these sentiments were likely to blow away India's nascent nationalism and sunder its Union. The fear was this: that the establishment of East and West Pakistan would be the first moves in the subcontinent's balkanization. They had to be the last. The leaders of the new Indian Union were determined to make sure of that. The Dravidian movement in Madras was still secessionist and its goal was nothing less than detaching from the Union all of south India and making it into an independent state of "Dravidinadu" (land of the Dravidians). Tribal groups in the northeast were also secessionist.

Congress's commitment of thirty years to organize independent India into "linguistic" provinces or states was summarily abrogated by its leaders. Certainly, they had always known that Tamils were not simply several million Indians who spoke Tamil, nor Bengalis several million who spoke Bengali. After 1947, they were confronted by what they knew, by the ethnic reality that underlay the ideology of "linguistic provinces." They appointed the appropriate investigative and advisory bodies, at the highest levels of government and ruling party. "Nationalism and subnationalism are two emotional experiences which grow at the expense of each other," warned the government commission headed by Judge S. K. Dar. The Congress committee – two of whose three members were the Union's duumvirs, Nehru and Sardar Vallabhbhai Patel – demanded "the stern discouragement of communalism, provincialism and all other separatist and disruptive tendencies." Both commission and committee, of course, recommended against the formation of "linguistic states," at least until a more "opportune time."[1]

For many Indians, however, in the late 1940s and 1950s, the opportune time was then. The Union government had not merely broken its party's long-standing promise, but in so doing it had taken the wrong side on a genuinely popular issue. It had taken a step that seemed to confound the ambitions and expectations of the Congress faithful: ambitions and expectations that had had three decades to incubate. In the wake of widespread violence and the threat of more to come the opportune time to carve an Andhra Pradesh (state) from the Telegu homeland in Madras province and the former principality of Hyderabad was hastened to 1953.

In South India, two years later, former British provinces and princely states were merged and the lot carved up into four "linguistic states". Along with Andhra Pradesh, they are Karnataka (formerly Mysore), Kerala and Tamil Nadu (formerly Madras). Bombay state was not realigned for some more years because of the question of how that might affect Bombay city. Of that great port and industrial metropolis, Maharashtra is the hinterland and most of the city's ordinary citizens are Maharashtrian. But its capitalists are Gujaratis, Parsis and Marwaris (originally from Rajasthan). There is also a large south Indian population in Bombay.

Would the city continue to serve India as its business capital and entrepôt on the Arabian Sea if it were made the capital of a Maharashtra state? Probably so. It is the goose that lays the golden egg, and Maharashtrian politicians had no plans to kill it, however much they wanted a state of their own and railed against Gujarati "colonialism." Would Congress continue to be the ruling party in western India if Bombay were not made the capital of a Maharashtra state? Probably not. Popular sentiment was overwhelming in favor of a Marathi language state, opposition parties were united in its support, Maharashtrian Congressmen were worried and wavering and even in Gujarat there was a movement for a Gujarati language state. Benefits weighted the balance. In 1960, Bombay was bifurcated into a Gujarati language Gujarat and a Marathi language Maharashtra.

Before Nehru died in 1964, his government had acceded to all major, widely supported demands for "linguistic states" save one; and India had become for the most part a union of homeland-states. The exception was the Sikhs' demand for *Punjabi Suba* – Punjabi language state – to be carved from the northern half of the state of

Punjab, as it was then. India's first prime minister correctly understood that Sikh politicians were using the "linguistic state" euphemism to disguise a trait of ethnicity which Indians of Nehru's secular persuasion think is particularly corrosive of Indian nationality: religious communalism. Pakistan was a product of Muslim communalism. *Punjabi Suba* was the demand of Sikh communalists for a state in which the *khalsa* (the Sikh community) would rule. Nehru wouldn't hear of it.

But by 1966, the Sikhs had demonstrated their loyalty to India in its wars with Pakistan and China, and the Congress Party was facing a difficult election. Nehru's daughter gave way. Punjab was divided: a new, Sikh-majority Punjab in the north, a Hindu-majority Haryana in the south. However, the new Punjab was still in Congress ideology *Punjabi Suba*: another "linguistic state." 'No,' ideologically unequivocal but practically ambiguous and portentous, was the official answer to the question of whether "religious community" was an attribute of ethnicity on the basis of which a legitimate demand could be made for a homeland-state in the Indian Union.

One of the striking, in retrospect, perhaps the most striking, characteristics of the process by which most of the Indian Union was divided into "linguistic states" was that it took place almost entirely within the Congress Party. To be sure, demands for "linguistic states" were almost always accompanied by threats of opposition unity and serious violence in which lives were lost and property destroyed. But these in themselves did not create a single "linguistic state." Rather they served as gauges by which Congress hierarchs could measure the seriousness of such demands; and if they were sufficiently serious, the lines on which they had to negotiate a settlement *among themselves.*

The demand for a "linguistic state" was read as particularly serious if it threatened Congress hegemony in the region. While demands for "linguistic states" have been invariably troublesome, they have not all been serious. Those that have not threatened Congress's hegemony have not been serious, and they have been ignored or suppressed. Congress hegemony was regarded by Nehru and his colleagues, I think correctly, as essential to the survival of the Indian Union in its first decades. The men who negotiated the division of India into "linguistic states" were leading provincial politicians and Pradesh Congress Committee hierarchs. But they were also oligarchs of the *national* Congress Party and Indian nationalists of unimpeachable credentials. It was an oligarchy on Nehru's sufferance; and he suffered it not gladly, but wisely.

In the last years of Nehru's life, "tribe" was added by the ruling Congress Party to "language" as a trait which sanctioned the demands of relevant ethnic groups for homeland-states. The guerrilla war against the Indian government fought by Naga tribesmen, who enjoyed Burmese sanctuary and Chinese arms, was more or less terminated by the establishment in 1963 of Nagaland as a state of the Indian Union. In India's national ideology, in its constitution and under its laws, there is expressed a special solicitude for those 60 million Indian citizens who belong to more than 400 "scheduled tribes." They are acknowledged to be the victims not only of British imperialism, but of the venality of their fellow Indians: sedentary cultivators, money lenders, timber merchants and contractors, corrupt forestry officials and so forth. In no small part through armed insurgencies in a strategically sensitive and militarily vulnerable corner of the Union, tribal groups of the northeast have encouraged the Government of India to express its solicitude by turning "tribal areas" into homeland-states for tribal people. In the 1970s and 1980s, all on India's northeastern borders, the "tribal states" of Arunachal Pradesh, Manipur, Meghalaya, Mizoram and Tripura were created. The total population of these tribal states, including Nagaland, is small: fewer than 8 million people, only about half of whom are tribals.

Nation-provinces

When does a homeland-state, of either the "linguistic" or "tribal" variety, become a nation-province? Unlike nation-state which is a political-cum-legal designation, nation-province is a political designation *only*. It has no legal meaning; and, thus, our question is similar to queries about when to designate a polity as feudal or democratic, or socialist or fascist. We have few precise and consentaneous answers. Mostly, we have indications. India's political history over the past four decades provides a set of crucial indications relevant to our question. It is the gradual distintegration in the Indian states of the "one-party dominance" of Congress and Congress (I) and the development of provincial parties.

Briefly, postponing a fuller discussion until chapter 6, in the first two decades of India's independence, during which time there were three general elections, the Congress Party ruled: not only as the Union government but, with one brief interval in Kerala, as governments in all states. There was no shortage of opposition parties and independent opposition candidates, and elections were free and fair by ordinary democratic standards. But the Congress Party always won enough seats – usually with less than a majority of votes – to form ministries in parliament and state legislative assemblies. This one-party dominance was India's major variation on the democratic theme.

Then in the 1967 general elections, two things of relevance to our discussion here occurred. First, in several states, the Congress Party was voted out of power and non-Congress ministries were formed. Second, for the first time since she had been made prime minister by her party, Indira Gandhi led Congress to election victory. It was anything but a great victory, but it was enough. Congress became, in fact and then in name, Congress (I): (I) for Indira.

The most significant and long-lasting of the non-Congress ministries that were formed in 1967 was of the Dravida Munnetra Kazhagam (DMK) in what it renamed Tamil Nadu. It used to be Madras. The DMK was then the most recent manifestation as a political party of the long-lived Dravidian movement. Its first modern appearance was as the Justice Party, organized in the years between the world wars: a period of great political activity all over India. The *weltanschauung* of the Dravidian movement was that Dravidians, the folk of south India, were systematically expropriated and enslaved by *brahmans* and their ideology of brahmanical superiority, which they – originally migrants from north India – derived from the Sanskrit texts of north-Indian Hindu injunctive scripture. The Dravidian movement was anti-*brahman*; anti-Sanskrit, the language of brahmanism; and anti-north India, the homeland of *brahmans* and brahmanism. For the first decade or so of Indian independence, the Dravidian movement was secessionist. Then, having renounced secessionism, it became the most vociferous and active opponent of any attempts by the government of Jawaharlal Nehru – a north-Indian *brahman* – and his successors to enforce the constitutional provision that made Hindi – a north-Indian language derived from Sanskrit – the official language of the Indian Union.

After 1967, there was a schism in the DMK and it was succeeded in government by the breakaway All-India Anna Dravida Munnetra Kazhagam (AIADMK), which claimed to be the True Church of the Dravidian movement. For a decade until he died in 1987, the AIADMK chief minister of Tamil Nadu – indeed, his party's one of one – was Maruthur Gopala Ramachandran: "MGR" to his fans, the all-time superstar of the Tamil silver screen. After his death, the AIADMK schismed. The Congress (I) government in New Delhi led by Rajiv Gandhi used the occasion to vie for government in Tamil Nadu by mounting one of the most expensive and apparently well-orchestrated political campaigns in India's electoral history. It failed miserably. In the elections of 1989, the DMK was returned to power after thirteen years in opposition. In 1991, the DMK was succeeded in government by the AIADMK, under the leadership of MGR's most famous protégée and a formidable politician in her own right, Jayalalitha.

Tamil Nadu is probably the Indian Union's best established nation-province. In its political arenas, the major contestants, government and opposition, are the parties of Tamil provincialism: the factions of the erstwhile Dravidian movement. These parties exist nowhere outside of Tamil Nadu. Except as representatives – in parliament, among other places – of Tamil interests in the Indian Union and even abroad: in the Union's relations with Sri Lanka, for example. The Tamil parties *negotiate* with the government in New Delhi. They must. They are no longer secessionist. Tamil Nadu is fixed as a state of the Indian Union. There is no serious inclination among Tamils to go elsewhere. Really, there is nowhere better to go. The Indian states are financially and economically dependent on the Union. The Union is their constitutional superior: and if push came to shove, that superiority could and would be readily enforced from New Delhi. But the political party that ruled from New Delhi for thirty-nine of the first forty-four years of India's independence and rules now, precariously, but with increasing sure-footedness, exists only on the margin of Tamil Nadu's domestic politics: a has-been, spoiler, also-ran, makeweight, bitplayer.

In Punjab, too, these have become Congress (I)'s roles, notwithstanding its "victory" in the state elections of 1992. These were widely boycotted by Sikh voters; and a solidification, however temporary, of the Sikh movement seems to have been the major effect of these elections. The party whose prime minister in 1984 ordered the Indian Army to besiege Amritsar's Golden Temple, the Sikh's holiest of holy places, that Congress (I) is still anathema to most Sikhs or they risk – at the very least – being anathematized for supporting it. The Sikh movement and its political party, the Akali Dal (the party of the Godly), also products of the years between the world wars, are even more fragmented than the erstwhile

Dravidian movement. Various factions of the Akali Dal have come and gone, waxed and waned in their apparent popularity among Sikhs and in the favor and patronage of governments in New Delhi. There have been rounds and rounds of negotiations, even a short-lived "accord" between Prime Minister Rajiv Gandhi and the leading Akali faction of that day, but there has been no settlement. And in its absence, a handful of Sikh desperadoes and their supporters continue to pursue the murderous fantasy of a Sikh nation-state, independent of India. But there will be no such "Khalistan." The Government of India has both the determination and more than enough coercive power to insure that it will not be; and among Sikhs, in general, one of the most bourgeois communities in India, there is no great enthusiasm for "Khalistan."

What seems to enjoy considerable support among Sikhs is the demand for an unambiguous Sikh-majority nation-province in the Indian Union that would be capable of protecting the *panth* (faith) and the worldly interests of the *khalsa* (community). A leitmotiv in Sikh history has been the efforts of leading members of the community to emplace political barriers to the demonstrated capacities of Hinduism to be religiously absorbent, to their fear that it threatens Sikhism with reabsorption – either inherently or by design.

At the temple town of Anandpur Sahib in 1973, the Akali Dal called upon the Union government to limit its powers constitutionally to India's defense, foreign relations, interstate communications and transportation and the provision of its currency. All other government powers would be allocated to the states. In effect, the Anandpur Sahib Resolution demanded a *constitutional* framework for a multi-nation state of nation-provinces. Akali Dal politicians regard its terms as negotiable. The Indian government rejects it as such, but has come to regard as negotiable a *political* framework for a Sikh majority nation-province. Insofar as it has any political relevance, other than to the factional warfare among Sikh politicians, the terrible violence that erupts from time to time in Punjab serves the process of negotiations by other means – to paraphrase Clausewitz' wry description of war. In these negotiations Sikh parties, however fragmented and at war with one another, are for Sikhs the parties of the first part: us. The party of the *Dilli durbar* (the regime in Delhi) – as it was under the Sikh-oppressing Mughals – is the party of the second part: them.

And so the Congress (I) seemed to be becoming in other states in India during the 1980s. Indications of nation-provincialism multiplied. Most spectacularly in Andhra Pradesh. There in 1983, in spite of "Indiramma's" (mother Indira's) relentless personal campaigning and her best efforts to mobilize government and party resources to win the state elections, her Congress (I) was defeated almost single-handedly by one Nandamuri Taraka Rama Rao. "NTR," to his fans, is the all-time super-star of the Telegu silver screen. Like MGR, he personifies the provincial ethos in its most popular medium. It is in this way, and not only in India, that movie stars are not merely actors and actresses who portray heroes and heroines, but heroic performers in their own rights.

Before 1983, NTR had never appeared in an election. To carry him to victory he fashioned *en route* and largely from his fan clubs a political party which is called Telegu Desam: the Telegu nation. It is the self-proclaimed defender of the "3,000 year old history of the Telegu people," and it demands provincial autonomy in terms that are not markedly different from those of the Anandpur Sahib Resolution. Alas, NTR proved to be less adept and creditable as a politician than he is as an actor; and in 1989, the voters of Andhra Pradesh voted his Telegu Desam out of power. But its legacy of Telegu nation-provincialism survives the Telegu Desam's demise; and if NTR's Congress (I) successors fail to cultivate it, they are unlikely to remain in office for long. The lesson to be learned is from Maharashtra. The most noteworthy Congress (I) successes in the 1990 state legislative assembly and the 1991 parliamentary elections were there, where the party is led by a bona fide son of the soil with deep roots in Marathi provincialism.

The Asom Gana Parishad (Assam people's organization) is unabashedly a party of "Assam for the Assamese." It was voted into power in 1985. The *parishad* is led by former student activists who throughout the 1980s agitated against the presence of too many Bengalis in Assam, in general; and in particular, against the presence of illegal migrants from Bangladesh on Assam's electoral roles and the reluctance of the Union government to have them purged. Bengalis are the Congress (I)'s vote bank in Assam. They had voted Mrs Gandhi's man into power in 1983, in an election that she was determined to win – apparently, at any cost. Those elections, boycotted by a majority of Assamese voters and accompanied by police and mob violence, culminated in one of the grisliest massacres of independent India's history: of Bengali Muslims, mostly women and children, by a gang of Assamese tribesmen. Today, the *parishad* has been outflanked in the cause of Assamese provincialism by an armed secessionist movement of Assamese Hindus, the United Liberation Front of Assam (ULFA), which has been troublesome enough to merit the intervention of the Indian army, the dismissal of the *parishad*'s state government by the center, under its constitutional power to do so, and the imposition of its administration. A Congress (I) state government now rules in Assam. But Assamese provincialism continues to roil and in its turbulence there is yet another, unrelated ethnic demand: of armed Bodo tribesmen for their own "Bodoland" state of the Union.

Founded by the legendary Lion of Kashmir, Sheikh Mohammad Abdullah, the National Conference was the party of Kashmir's Muslims. Though communal in its membership, the Conference was secular in its ideology. And from Indira Gandhi's installation of Sheikh Abdullah as Jammu and Kashmir's chief minister in 1975, the Conference or a faction thereof more or less enjoyed the confidence of the Congress (I) and depended on its support. During the 1980s these factions were joined as major contenders in Kashmir's political arena by groups that are ideologically Islamic and/or secessionist. Competition among them is having the effects of distancing Kashmiri politics from those of the (Hindu) *durbar* in *Dilli*. The Congress (I) has been pushed to the margin of Kashmiri politics, and these have become increasingly communitarian, provincial, violent and secessionist. There is little doubt but that the current secessionist movement in Kashmir will fail as its counterpart in Punjab has all but failed, and for at least this same reason: the Indian government will not allow it to succeed. But there is this possibility that Kashmir's Muslims will take the Sikh's Punjab as their precedent for demanding a nation-province based on religious community.

The Mizos have a provincial party as do the Nagas and some other tribal groups. These are, at least, potentially the parties of nation-provinces. The Gorkhaland National Liberation Front (GNLF) is potentially the party of the "Gorkhaland" for which it agitated during the 1980s. Gorkhaland would be carved from Darjeeling district of West Bengal and neighboring states, particularly Sikkim, with substantial Nepali-speaking populations.

Not only provincial parties, parties of their particular ethnic group, but established, multi-state parties, as well, have accommodated themselves and promoted the drift to nation-provincialism in India. Of India's two communist parties which take the "parliamentary path," the larger and more successful is the Communist Party of India – Marxist (CPI-M). It is "the DMK of West Bengal," quipped

Arun Shourie, one of India's leading journalists.[2] And only some-what less is it the DMK of Kerala. The CPI-M prides itself on being a national party of India with a well-articulated and debated Marxist ideology and relevant policies appropriate to India and to its position in the world. Yet the party is a serious contender for power, and has held power only in West Bengal and Kerala. Most of its members come from these states. In them, its leaders have been not only widely respected members of their party, but politicians with deep roots in Malayalam and Bengali provincialism, profound understanding of them and solicitude for them. The provincializing of the CPI-M worries party ideologues, but in West Bengal and Kerala it is the open secret of its success.

Karnataka and, particularly its metropolis, Bangalore, have a large population whose mother tongues are other than Kannada, the state's "principal language." These non-Kannadigas for various reasons enjoyed the solicitude of the state's former Congress (I) governments, and that solicitude was part of the Congress (I)'s undoing. It was defeated in 1983 by a small multi-state party, then the *Janata*, whose winning campaign promise was to make Kannada the sole first language in Karnataka's educational syllabus and its only language for "official transactions." Karnataka returned to the Congress (I) fold in 1989; but whatever its government, it is now unlikely to be anything less than a champion of Kannadiga provincialism.

Finally, and again, there is Devi Lal: now discredited, but by his avarice and not his ideology. In his successful campaign of 1988 to become a non-Congress chief minister of Haryana and to participate in 1989, however opportunistically and erratically, in the leadership of a National Front opposition to the Congress (I), Devi Lal bested it in its bailiwick: the Hindi-speaking north. All Congress and Congress (I) prime ministers had come from there. Most of their votes had come from there. Delhi, their capital, is an enclave in Haryana. But the sentiments of nation-provincialism to which Devi Lal pitched his successful appeals are based not on affinity of language and not even of ethnicity. They were based on folkishness. The citizens of Devi Lal's nation-province are the sons and daughters of its soil: not the plutocrats and politicians and bureaucrats of Delhi who work in air-conditioned offices and go home to foreign wives and keep their money in Swiss banks and cannot tell a paddy field from a field of wheat. Folkishness is the underlying ideology of the parties which in the 1989 and 1990 elections routed the Congress

(I) in the Hindi states. One of the first acts of the non-Congress (I) government of the Nehru–Gandhi dynasty's home state, Uttar Pradesh, was to declare that all official communications in it would be *only* in Hindi, the language of the folk. Rajiv Gandhi's first language was English. An election joke was that Rajiv was not exactly a foreigner but rather a resident NRI (non-resident Indian). In 1991, the party elected to govern Uttar Pradesh was the Bharatiya Janata Party (BJP): the party of Hinduism, the religion of the folk, their assertion of folkishness.

Given the long-lived strength and diversity of India's ethnicities and their access to parliamentary democracy and the possibilities of capitalist economic development, group demands of one sort or another for homeland-states in the Indian Union and their transition one way or another to nation-provinces were probably inevitable. And will probably continue to be. Indira Gandhi's contribution to these processes was, I think, to hasten them and separate them from the Congress (I).

Mrs. Gandhi's first political victory was over the Congress's provincial bosses. She replaced them and their protégés at chief ministers and PCC presidents with placemen of her own in the late 1960s and 1970s. She did not want strong provincial politicians at the heads of strong state Congress (I)s. The politicians who rose to high office in the state branches of her party and their ministries were those and only those who enjoyed "madam's" favor: *durbaris* (courtiers) whose roots were in her court rather than in their provinces. Sycophancy and opportunism were commonplace among them; competence, probity and popular esteem were rare.

They came and went in factions, and always at Mrs. Gandhi's pleasure. In the two years before NTR's 1983 election victory, for example, Andhra Pradesh's chief ministership was held by no less than four of Mrs. Gandhi's *chamchas* (tools; literally spoons) and almost 180 ministers had come and gone, come again and gone again. In less than three years before the elections, the Andhra Pradesh Congress (I) Committee had five presidents, all chosen by the prime minister. In such a state party, no more than a satrapy of the *Dilli Durbar*, there was no hero for Telegu provincialism, no torch-bearer. He was to be found instead, larger than life and however flickeringly, on the Telegu silver screen.

A year or so after NTR took office, Mrs. Gandhi tried to topple his government. Her tolerance for provincial heroes who were not Congressmen was no greater than her willingness to have them in her party. She and her son tried with combinations of political skullduggery, government resources and constitutional authority to unseat or otherwise deny power to virtually every non-Congress (I) state government that they encountered. The immediate results of these attempts in the 1980s were usually embarrassing defeats for the prime minister: in Andhra Pradesh, Punjab, Kashmir, Assam, Tamil Nadu. To put down provincial roots, nowadays, is probably requisite for any parties that aspire to rule in the states. And whichever party rules from Delhi, it will probably have to evolve new, appropriate *modi vivendi* between the multi-nation Indian Union and its nation-provinces, in being or becoming. The quasi-federalism of the Indian constitution, much less Mrs. Gandhi's centralism, are unlikely to do much longer.

Bourgeois revolution

What has all this, the growth of nation-provincialism, to do with bourgeois revolution in India? The development *together* of capitalism and parliamentary democracy *in India's provinces* has been particularly beneficial to their middle classes and particularly conducive to provincial embourgeoisement, i.e., to the development and growth of middle classes in the provinces and most dramatically, their cultivating middle classes. Bourgeois revolution in provincial India has both a causal and effective relationship to the development of nation-provincialism. The provincial middle classes supported the creation of ''linguistic states'' in anticipation, correctly, of being its beneficiaries. States of their own enable provincial middle classes to legislate monopolies on the use of their languages for public business, for example, or to facilitate the aggregation of the interests of their *jatis* or *jati*-subgroups by concentrating their numbers in the same provincial parliamentary system or systems. In their transition from ''linguistic states'' to nation-provinces, a moving force – apart from but connected to party politics and the inertia of ethnicity, the drift to folkishness – has been the thrust of the provincial middle classes, and particularly, its new entrants and aspirants, to vest their interests, mark their turf, e.g., in the Karnataka and Uttar Pradesh governments' reassertions and extensions in the 1980s of Kannada and Hindi as their ''official languages.''

''Nationalism and subnationalism'' in India have *not* developed ''at the expense of each other,'' as the Dar Commission feared. Although there certainly has been some expense on both sides.

India's nation-provinces and India as a multi-nation state have for the most part developed together and symbiotically. In general, by agreeing to establish ethnic homeland-states, the Indian government may have discouraged secessionism; and it certainly stabilized the Union by acceding to demands that were popular, not only with middle classes, and demonstrably disruptive. Over the years, as these homeland-states have been taking on the characteristics of nation-provinces, the Union government has simultaneously encouraged and contributed to the construction of a *national* economic and political infrastructure that is of increasingly vital relevance to provincial middle classes.

In other words, bourgeois revolution in the provinces proceeds in dependency on their incorporation in the Indian Union. In some way of summary and review of part I and in some way of addition to it, we pursue this argument in sectors: agriculture, education and business.

Green revolution technology, to which I have already alluded and credited with some of India's agricultural development, was introduced in the late 1960s. Basically it is the application of high inputs of chemical fertilizers, pesticides and irrigation waters to specially developed, high-yielding varieties of seeds. The results have been high per-hectare outputs. The area planted with high-yielding varieties of seeds has increased steadily: quadrupling since 1970 for all food grains taken together. Nowadays, more than four-fifths of its wheat and three-fifths of its rice, India's two largest crops, are produced under green revolution technology.

It is a technology for commercial agriculture. It has developed along with lending agencies and physical and administrative marketing facilities. The green revolution has become, in effect, not merely the technology but the strategy for the development of commercial agriculture in India. The economy of bourgeois revolution in the Indian countryside is commercial agriculture. Again, its principal, though by no means, sole beneficiaries are the upper quintile of farm households. By contributing to the increase in productivity of small holdings, the green revolution has also whetted the aspirations for embourgeoisement and facilitated it among farm households below the upper quintile.

To India's growing number of green revolution farmers, their increased production would, of course, be useless to them without markets in which to sell it. Increasingly, their markets have become part of a national market. The Indian Union is their national market.

The Government of India is their guarantor of privileged access to the Indian market and its regulator, the subsidizer of the prices they pay for chemical fertilizer and the supporter through its procurement programs of the prices they receive for their produce. It is not difficult to read the Anandpur Sahib Resolution as the charter of India's most successful farmers: demanding *laissez-faire* on the one hand, enjoining the Union government from interference in their provincial affairs; but on the other, calling for the Union's continued and concentrated facilitation of their national and international commerce in agricultural produce.

The rural middle classes need to sell their produce; and second only to this, they want to educate their children, particularly their sons. Educated sons, like our hypothetical medical doctors, produce prestige and remittance income for farm households. Educated daughters ally the household to well-employed, prestigious and useful in-laws. The education that best serves these purposes is a university education. The relationship in India between university education and university-educated employment is not dissimilar to that between agricultural production and marketing: a relationship of symbiosis, in which the states produce the graduates and the Union provides them with a national market for their university-acquired skills.

The number of university students in India has increased from about 360,000 in 1950–51 to about 3.6 million (one-third of them women) in 1985–86: a ten-fold increase compared to an increase of less than three-fold in the general population. This percentage increase in university enrolments also exceeded the increase in primary and secondary school enrolments. Per literate members of their populations, the number of universities in India and enrolments in them are about equal to what they are in Britain.

Of India's 178 universities in 1988, only nine were governed and directly funded under laws of the national parliament. All the others are state universities. In the best of these, the best colleges, departments, institutes and so forth are comparable to the best anywhere. Unfortunately, however, they are exceptions. The rule is a poor to mediocre standard of education, often further vitiated by improper and meddlesome interference from politicians and bureaucrats, administrative incompetence, nepotism, caste-ism, communalism and corruption. If Indian state universities are not celebrated for their educational standards, however, they are nonetheless noteworthy for their contributions to contemporary Indian society.

They have broken the monopoly on university-educated employment that was enjoyed under the British *Raj* by a tiny, largely self-perpetuating, largely urban elite of English-language proficients. In British India, English was not only the sole medium of university instruction, English-language proficiency was the *sine qua non* of career advancement: from university matriculation to Indian Civil Service promotion. The state universities of independent India have not so much put an end to all this, but rather pushed it to the top of a national career ladder which, at the same time, they have pulled downward into the realm of the largely Indian-languages proficient provincial middle classes.

Other than into professional courses, e.g., medicine or engineering, at some state universities, university admission is not particularly difficult for ordinary state high school graduates who have completed a two-year university preparatory course. In the Hindi-speaking states most undergraduate education, particularly in non-professional courses, is in Hindi. In the universities of most other states, undergraduates in non-professional courses, at least, can study in their state's language in preference to English. In university courses where English is the formal language of instruction, a reading knowledge of it relevant to the course is necessary; but otherwise English frequently mixes for instructional purposes, informally, in greater or lesser measure, with the state's language. In sum, university education is available to middle-class village and town households' children who have virtually no English or only some English as a second language. Concomitantly, the states have made *not* English but their languages the official languages of university-educated employment in their bureaucracies and public-sector enterprises. In India, the public sector employs about twice the number of people employed by the organized private sector; and state governments and their public sector enterprises employ almost twice the number of people employed by the Union government (including the military) and its public sector enterprises.

State university graduates may, of course, seek and possibly find rewarding and remunerative employment in their own states and in their own state language. But they need not. By virtue of their Indian citizenship, they have privileged access to an India-wide university-educated employment market. In order to enter and compete in it, however, state university graduates must themselves enter into the symbiotic relationship between the states and the Indian Union. They cannot in their working lives, at least, remain provincial. They must become Indians. They must be able to work in languages of India other than those of their states.

In particular, they must be able to work in either or both of the Indian Union's official languages: Hindi and English. The Hindi-speaking states – of which the Union capital is, after all, but a cut-out – have so assiduously cultivated Hindi as their state language as to have the effect of closing to job aspirants who do not have some proficiency in Hindi, at least as a second language, about one-third of the opportunities for university-educated employment in India. More than one-third of India is governed by states whose official language is Hindi. This has been the primary incentive to increased Hindi-language learning all over India: not the constitutional provision that makes it the Union's first official language nor any revision of the ideological or regional objections to it being so.

As I noted earlier, the first official language *de facto* of the Indian Union, certainly at its higher public and private reaches, is still English. It is still the language of India's university-educated upper middle classes. But it does not exclude as it once did. Nowadays, there is a ladder down, and its bottom rung for provincials who are bright, lucky, enterprising, ambitious, well-connected is an undergraduate degree from a state university. They learn English on the way up. Their skills are marketable nationally; and with a postgraduate degree from the University of Delhi, for example, and proficiency in English, internationally.

Small business is particularly dependent on patronage from the states and state politicians, and the patronized are typically from their states' urban middle classes. Their market for almost 95 percent of their goods is the Indian Union. Indian government funding and policies, e.g., of procurement, have encouraged small business, certainly, and New Delhi has facilitated its exports. But the principal encouragement to small-scale industrial entrepreneurs is privileged access to India's vast and apparently insatiable domestic market.

In sum, then, congruence has characterized bourgeois revolutions at India's center and in its provinces. With leads and lags, to be sure, capitalism and parliamentary democracy have developed *together* in India, and *together* in national and provincial India in such ways as to complement and supplement each other. Capitalist agriculture which developed under the patronage of parliamentary democracy in the states (albeit with New Delhi's encouragement) increasingly turns for its further development to parliamentary democracy at the center. Parliamentary democracy at the center serves the aspirations of provincial university graduates and entre- preneurs. My guess is that the multi-nation Indian Union is in no danger of being balkanized by its nation-provinces as long as it meets the demands of India's middle classes in ways in which its nation-provinces cannot.

The explosions of state-destroying ethnicity in eastern Europe from the late 1980s provide us, perhaps, with occasions to reflect on the considerable success of bourgeois democracy in integrating India's ethnicities. But while bourgeois revolution has been a binding force in the Indian Union, there have been unravelling forces, also. Of these, I can think of two. Neither are current dangers to the Union's territorial integrity, though they may become so, but rather to its humane and efficient functioning.

First, the apparent unwillingness of governments in New Delhi, of whatever party, to acknowledge, to face up to the fact that they rule a multi-nation state of nation-provinces and to act accordingly, politically and constitutionally, and in a fashion less *ad hoc* and more comprehensive. The Congress (I) under the Gandhis acted contrarily. Its persistent attempts to subvert, one way or another, the regimes of provincial parties did more to discredit the Union government and increase disruptive and defensive provincialism than to recapture the states as satrapies of the *Dilli durbar.* Under the regimes of the Gandhis, mother and son, the danger to India's efficient and humane functioning was less in what used to be called the ''fissiparous tendencies'' of provincialism than in the ''relentless centralization and ruthless, unprincipled intervention''[3] into state politics by the Congress (I).

India is vast and diverse beyond the dreams of the most ardent centralizer. It never has been and it cannot now be ruled entirely or even mostly from its center. A redivision of constitutional powers between the Union and the states on the lines of the Anandpur Sahib Resolution is unlikely to occur. But as a rational response to the growing force of nation-provincialism, the Union government ought to give some serious thought to increasing the autonomy of the states. The appropriate commission is, of course, in place. But its contributions to accommodating the Union to nation-provincial- ism are yet to be made. My guess is that this will be done, as a consequence of democratic elections, and sooner rather than later.

Second, the apparent lack of any way without violence for ethnic groups which do not now have homeland-states to put forward serious demands for them. So numerous and diverse are Indian ethnic and subethnic groups, that the task of reconciling all of their demands, for homeland-states and otherwise, is likely to be unending. In recent memory there have been unfulfilled demands for states of their own from groups in the hill districts of Uttar Pradesh, the Nagpur-Vidarbha region of western Maharashtra, the Chhattisgarh area of western Madhya Pradesh and the coastal districts of Andhra Pradesh.

After lying dormant for more than a decade, the movement among tribal people of the Chota Nagpur area of southern Bihar and western West Bengal for a "Jharkhand" state of their own was revived in the late 1970s and is still alive. The demand of Nepali-speakers in the 1980s for a "Gorkhaland" state was accompanied with considerable violence. The armed insurgency of Mizo tribesmen in the northeast was ended with the establishment of Mizoram as a state of the Union and the installation of the insurgents' commander-in-chief as the state's chief minister. Whether or not the Bodos will get their "Bodoland" is anyone's guess.

Groups which have homeland-states, demanded an enhancement of their powers in the 1980s. Again, Sikhs have demanded, in effect, for their *Punjabi Suba*, power to protect and promote the interests of the *panth* (faith) and the *khalsa* (community). They want a Sikh state in a constitutionally secular Indian Union! That demand has been virtually obscured in bloodshed. Tribal people have demanded for their homeland-states the power to use reservations for scheduled tribes to the extent of practically disenfranchising and disqualifying for public employment non-tribal residents of these states. In an Indian Union whose constitution provides for a single Indian citizenship and the right of citizens to reside anywhere in the Union!

At issue are *not* the demands regarding homeland-states. I assume that these and similar demands from ethnic groups will always be part of the Indian Union's environment; like its monsoonal climate: not a problem to be solved, but only to be managed with more or less success. Secessionist demands, currently in Punjab, Kashmir and Assam, will be suppressed by armed force, if necessary, wherever they arise and for as long as it takes; but the government will be prepared to negotiate with repentant secessionists and even with those who have only stacked their arms. At issue is the lack of a Union management policy to recognize as serious those ethnic group demands for homeland-states that are not put forward violently or before they are put forward violently and/or as secessionist demands. As it is now, ethnic groups can expect their demands to be taken seriously only if they are put forward violently. The government, of course, responds in kind. Ethnic groups, even some that are apparently secessionist, use violence not to win their battles, that would be impossible, but to establish their negotiating positions. They want a negotiated settlement. If the government can suppress the violence at an acceptable political cost – which, of course, varies from case to case – and thereby nobble the demand, it will. If it can't, it negotiates. The demands of emergent ethnic groups are almost always troublesome: not least because they invariably impinge on the interests of settled ethnic groups.

The government's acceptance, in fact, of the principle that serious demands are by definition violent has had costly consequences: in property ruined and lives damaged and destroyed. There is the further danger, so well illustrated by the carnage in Punjab, of these costs being multiplied in violence that perpetuates itself purposelessly, by its own momentum: violence rationally related neither to negotiations nor even irrationally to winning some battle, but related only to the intra- and inter-group dynamics of "the boys" and their mentors.

Part II

Change from above

There are six essays in part II. Underlying most of them and related, however tangentially, to all is an argument that I advanced in my introduction.

Bourgeois revolution in Indian society was initiated in its experiences of British imperialism and domesticated, particularly, by the Indian National Congress which evolved in response to British imperialism, became an India-wide, mass nationalist movement under the leadership of Mahatma Gandhi and finally succeeded the *Raj* in 1947. That is the underlying argument of the first two sections of chapter 5. Because of its relevance here and to my earlier discussions of subcontinental Islam, I have added a section on Muslim separatism.

The argument that underlies the first two sections of chapter 6 is this: through its policies of economic and political development since independence, the Indian Union has promoted and institutionalized the growth in tandem of capitalism and parliamentary democracy, and this growth accelerated from the mid-1970s. I have attached to chapter 6 a section about India's international politics.

Following both a suggestion of Barrington Moore, Jr. and what seems to me self-evident, I accept the following proposition: a major contribution, though not the determinant, of bourgeois revolution's development in India was the Indian National Congress's pre-independence alliance of English-educated professional people, landed peasants who were to become cultivating small holders, and, with some reluctance until the late 1930s, modern industrial entrepreneurs. Certainly, there were other contributions to bourgeois revolution in India, without which it might well have aborted or died long before the Indian Union's forty-fifth birthday. Characteristics of British imperialism, e.g., its bureaucratization, Gandhi's *satyagraha* strategy of conflict and conflict resolution, Jawaharlal Nehru's commitments to parliamentary democracy and a planned and "mixed" economy, the swift and virtually bloodless integration of the princely states into the Union, Congress's post-

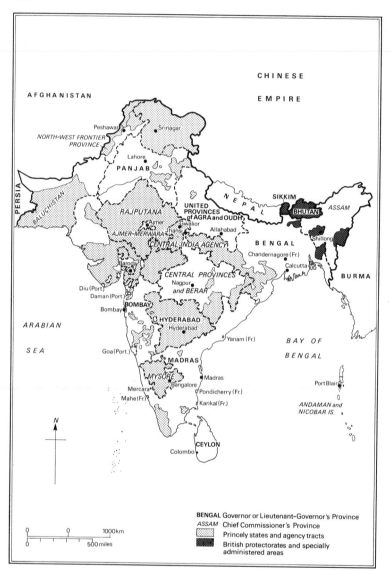

3. The British empire in India *c.* 1900

independence one-party dominance, are some of these contributions.

Britain's "transfer of power" – an apt expression – to the Indian Union did not disarray the Congress's alliance of middle classes; and these middle classes, in size and diversity, have increased dramatically since 1947 and come to political predominance, inside the Congress and out. It is not surprising, then, that India's middle classes should be the primary beneficiaries of the development together of capitalism and parliamentary democracy and their spin-offs, e.g., Indian-language medium state universities, *panchayati raj*, an import-substitution strategy of industrial development.

My use of the term "classes" here is consistent with my earlier use, in chapter 3: groups which share a similar "market situation," whether or not they are conscious of it. The taxonomy is mine not theirs; and my use of the plural – as in modern business *classes* – is meant to indicate that they are both localized and primordially diverse. *My* middle *classes*, again, are those groups whose families and incomes are derived from employment in the educated professions, including politics, higher salaried positions in modern commerce and industry and family-farm based commercial agriculture.

It is to these classes that I have now addressed most of my discussion in the essays that follow: in form, for the sake of economy, expository order, congruence with my argument and because they are essays rather than summary tours of the horizon; and in substance, because I believe that India's development is best understood, not entirely but mostly, as the product of, by and for its middle classes.

5

British imperialism, Indian nationalism and Muslim separatism

To argue that bourgeois revolution in India was the consequence of British imperialism and Indian nationalism is really one argument of related parts, certainly from the last decades of the nineteenth century. From then and for the next half century or so until India's independence, its history unfolded largely in response to the intricate interplay between and within the forces of imperialism and nationalism (see table 5). One consequence, in part, of the exchange, now marked by Pakistan and Bangladesh on the map of the subcontinent and on the consciousness of its inhabitants, was Muslim separatism.

British imperialism (see map 3)

Nowadays, students of modern Indian history are routinely cautioned against regarding the British imperial enterprise in India as a monolith. And indeed it was not a monolith. There was Her Majesty's Government in London under whose ultimate authority India was governed; but of whose concerns, governing India was only one, and rarely a major one. The secretary of state for India was the concerned minister; but, of course, his concerns had to contend with those of other ministers and correspond with the interests, electoral and otherwise, of the government.

There was a British Government of India, in Calcutta until 1911 when it shifted to Delhi. It was headed by a titled British politician, the viceroy and governor-general. Although he was in organizational theory the secretary of state's man in India, in practice, relationships between the two men and their governments were negotiated. The British government in India was run by bureaucrats. The *Raj* was a bureaucratic empire. At the imperial and provincial levels of empire and between them, between bureaucrats who were department heads and bureaucrats in the districts, there were competing concerns, conflicting interests, divergent views, personal animosities. Some-

131

Table 5. *Major political events in the related histories of British imperialism and Indian nationalism, late nineteenth and twentieth centuries*

1858	The Mutiny defeated, imperial rule is directly assumed by the British government; and by the Queen's proclamation, Indians are promised impartial admittance to the empire's governing bureaucracies.
1869	The opening of the Suez Canal facilitates British rule in India and commerce between the subcontinent and Britain.
1875	Two portentous events in Hindu–Muslim relations: the foundation of the major Hindu revivalist organization in northern India, the Arya Samaj; and Saiyid Ahmad Khan's establishment of his Muhammadan Anglo-Oriental College.
1883	Indian government's withdrawal of the Ilbert Bill is widely interpreted by the educated middle classes as a concession to Anglo-Indian racism.
1885	First meeting of the Indian National Congress: an interest group of the educated middle classes, primarily, and primarily Hindu.
1892	The Indian Council Act begins the history of participation of wise, wealthy and well-born Indians in central and provincial legislatures.
1905	Viceroy, Curzon, partitions Bengal into two separate provinces: Congress's first *cause célèbre* and the first major trauma in Hindu–Muslim relations under the *Raj*.
1906	All-India Muslim League founded by landlords and haute bourgeois.
1907	Tata Iron and Steel Company established at Jamshedpur.
1909	Morley–Minto Reforms expand considerably the representation of Indians in legislative assemblies, reserve a "weighted" number of constituencies for Muslims and establish the principle of separate communal representation.
1911	The partition of Bengal is annulled.
1916	The "Lucknow Pact" between the Congress and the Muslim League allows collaboration in the Non-Cooperation/Khilafat movements which gradually disintegrate during the early 1920s.
1919	Montagu–Chelmsford Reforms enable elected Indians to hold minor ministries in provincial governments, i.e., "dyarchy'; and invite corporate representation of princes in the Chamber of Princes. Jallianwallahbagh Massacre takes place in Amritsar.
1920	Mahatma Gandhi becomes the Congress supremo.
1923	Government of India sets tariffs to protect selected Indian industries – too little, too late.

Table 5. *(cont.)*

1928   British government sends Simon Commission to recommend
further constitutional reforms for India, but it has no Indian
members. In protest All-Parties Conference drafts a constitution
for India, but fails to resolve differences between Hindu and
Muslim middle classes.

1930   Gandhi initiates Civil Disobedience movement with Salt Satyagraha.

1932   In response to British government's "communal award"
providing separate representation for untouchables, Gandhi begins
"fast unto death," and ends it by agreeing to "Poona Pact"
compromise with B. R. Ambedkar.

1937   After elections held under the India Act of 1935, Congress forms
ministries in eight of eleven provinces. Muslim League polls
poorly among Muslims.

1939   Congress's provincial ministries resign in protest against the
viceroy's declaring India at war without consulting any Indian
politicians.

1940   Muslim League passes enigmatic "Pakistan Resolution."

1942   Congress rejects Cripps Mission's strong provinces/weak center
formula for post-war Indian government and calls for a mass civil
disobedience campaign to force Britain to "quit India." In reply,
all of Congress's "high command," including Gandhi and Nehru
are jailed. Considerable anti-British violence in India during the
war; and on its border, to fight the Indian Army, the Indian
National Army, organized by the Japanese and led by the Bengali
firebrand and former Congress president, Subhas Chandra Bose.

1944   "Bombay Plan" of leading Indian businesses for government-led
post-war industrialization.

1946   Muslim League sweeps the field of Muslim constituencies in
general elections; and thus, establishes itself and its leader
Mohammad Ali Jinnah as negotiators apparently equal to the
Congress in determining the subcontinent's future.
Cabinet Mission variation on strong provinces/weak center
formula is rejected by Congress.
Communal violence engulfs northern India.
Mutiny in the Indian navy and popular demonstrations against
treason trials of Indian National Army soldiers.
Newly elected Labour Party government led by Clement Attlee
sends Lord Louis Mountbatten as viceroy to negotiate an end to
the *Raj*.

1947   Indian independence and the partition of the subcontinent
between it and Pakistan.

times, decisions made at the top evaporated as they filtered down, and decisions made at the bottom percolated up as *faits accomplis*. There was a Political Department which exercised the Indian government's "paramountcy," i.e., its protectorate, over princely India, about one-third of the subcontinent: in effect, another, related, parallel imperium. There was the Indian army which was part of both the *Raj* and the British military establishment. There were British companies in India and companies in Britain with major business interests in India. There were British planters. There were churchmen and missionaries. There were British families.

While not a monolith, the British empire was nonetheless a purposive undertaking. It was a British state enterprise which used Indian resources to serve British economic and political interests. That was not all that it did, certainly. But that was its *raison d'être*. That it served British interests well, there is little doubt. The doubts, expressed with increasing persuasiveness in the revisions of economic historians, are about the disservices of the British *Raj* to Indian interests, about the "exploitation" of the subcontinent by British imperialism.

India best served British interests as an approximation of a "colonial open economy,"[1] of whose urban, industrial aspects we are most concerned with here and as the source of an army and the resources which sustained it.

On terms largely dictated by British governments, India became from the nineteenth century a major supplier of raw materials to British factories and a major market for the manufactured products of those factories. India was also a major market for British investments of capital: particularly in railways, mining and such major export industries as tea and jute production. These enterprises were largely British owned and managed, and British financial investments in Indian enterprises were almost entirely in them. Their major financial arrangements were managed by British banks. Rates of exchange, between rupees and pounds, were determined by British authorities to British advantage. British ships carried most of India's exports and imports. On these, tariffs and other charges were determined by British governments. As a major purchaser of British manufactured goods and a major supplier of textile goods and raw materials to other parts of the world, India from the late nineteenth century enabled Britain:

to make good between two-fifths and one-third of her deficit with other industrialized nations, and to continue to perform as an economy with a world-wide balance of payments surplus long after her trading position had declined.[2]

The British Indian army protected India by suppressing domestic "unrest" and was otherwise used to fight Britain's battles all over the world: in the Crimea, Afghanistan, Africa, China, Persia, Turkey, Southeast Asia, North Africa, Europe. In peacetime, the costs of the Indian army's maintenance were borne almost entirely out of Indian revenues; and these paid, directly and indirectly, for most of the army's expenses in wartime. Ordinarily, the Indian army accounted for about 40 percent of the Government of India's budget: by far its largest single item. Would Britain have been a great power from the middle of the nineteenth century through the early decades of the twentieth without an Indian army sustained by Indian revenues? It seems unlikely. The Indian army fielded a million and a half troops during the First World War and two and a half million during the Second. Of such value was the Indian army to Britain that even from 1917 when British governments began talking about "dominion status" for India and greater control for the (British) Indian government over its tariff and monetary policies, the plan for the Indian army was to bring it under the direct control of the Imperial General Staff.

These services to Britain's interests performed by its Indian empire imply costs to it, certainly. But economic historians now question whether these implications have been accurately drawn and whether and in what ways British "exploitation" of the subcontinent actually disserviced Indian interests. So, for example, in spite of British unwillingness to protect it with tariffs, a cotton textile industry developed in nineteenth century India to become one of the world's largest, and it was overwhelmingly owned and operated by Indians. It seems unlikely, as the demonology of imperialism would have it, that imports of British cloth "deindustrialized" India and devastated Indian handloom weavers; and insofar as they were devastated by power looms, it is more likely that these were owned by Indian producers of coarse cloth.[3] In spite of a general British policy in the First World War of discouraging Indian industrialization, more than a decade before the war the Parsi entrepreneur J. N. Tata received "extensive official assitance" in his efforts to establish the Tata Iron and Steel Company. Its shareholders were almost all Indian, and its mill at Jamshedpur in Bihar would grow under imperial patronage to become one of the largest steel works in Asia.[4] In spite of British governments' insistence on collecting their "home charges" from

India – the cost to it, in pounds, of servicing its public debt to Britain and enjoying Britain's military protection and the administration of its bureaucrats – the extent of this "drain" on India's resources has probably been exaggerated.[5]

To better understand India's introduction to economic modernity under the British *Raj*, some shift in emphasis may be helpful: *away* from what the *Raj was*, an "exploitive" imperial regime, and *toward* what it *was not*. It *was not* a national government. The shift does not mitigate, except incidentally, the British imperial government's defects as an industrializer of India, but rather emphasizes imperialism's inherent, structural weakness as a system for the economic development of its colonies. However keen on India's industrial development – particularly after the First World War, dedicated to the service of Indian interests, farsighted and intelligent they may have been, and any number of them were, British India's officers were ultimately the servants of a foreign country's government: the representatives of a government in India that was indirectly responsive to a British electorate. As such they were disabled from the vigorous pursuit of any industrialization strategy whose primary concern was India's "national interests," and which demanded in their service some sacrifices from sectorial and provincial interests. Incapable of singular purpose and deficient in legitimacy, the British government of India could not have done what the Japanese government of Japan did from the late nineteenth century; nor, certainly, could it have pursued a consistent import-substitution strategy of industrialization as had the Indian government of India from the latter half of the twentieth century until 1991.

Under the *Raj*, India industrialized in bits and pieces, in "enclaves"[6] of industrialization in an unindustrialized subcontinent. So, not only were the Indian railways built to facilitate agriculture, commerce and troop mobility *rather* than industry, but their effects on furthering industrialization were limited because they purchased their locomotives and other complex machinery from Britain, and they employed Englishmen in their higher managerial and technical positions. India's highly developed cotton textile industry, too, bought its heavy machinery from Britain: it was not manufactured in India. India's foreign trade was mostly in the hands of British companies. Most foreign investments in India were arranged in London, and the development of share markets and a modern banking industry in India was thereby retarded. During the Great Depression of the 1930s, British authorities maintained an overvalued rupee: in British interests and to the consternation of Bombay's mill-owners. But these same British authorities were ever fearful of disaffecting these mill-owners by taxing them to support India's development. Where its own interests were not immediately concerned, imperial government, as many historians now contend, was timid. *Laissez-faire* was doubtlessly an ideology that rationalized the use of India's resources by Britain in its interests, but it was also an excuse for leaving well enough alone, for not rocking the Indian boat.

The cumulation of India's industrialized bits and pieces, of other enclaves of imperialism, e.g., an English language university system in (but barely of) a society whose population was overwhelmingly non-English speaking and illiterate, and the imperial framework in which the bits and pieces were cumulated were consequential for India's development. The institutional consequences were at least these: an administrative and political integration of the subcontinent that was unprecedented and sustained by subcontinental systems of law and administration, government-monopolized coercion and repression, the interplay of imperialist and nationalist politics, nascent capitalism in industry and agriculture, tertiary education and professional training, modern transportation and communications.

For our purposes, the cumulative and related effects of these consequences were that they initiated bourgeois revolution on the subcontinent and provided the foundations and some of the superstructure on which the Indian Union was to be built. British-initiated bourgeois revolution did not produce general welfare in India and may have reduced it. After more than a century and a half in Britain's possession, its erstwhile "jewel in the crown" was possibly the largest aggregate of impoverished, unhealthy and illiterate people in the world. But the *Raj* did produce Indian bourgeoisies. Modern educated and business middle classes developed under the British *Raj* and in response to it. Their development was the human aspect of the institutional consequences to India of British imperialism. In 1947, when the British *Raj* was succeeded by the Congress *raj*, these middle classes were its senior partners. The cultivating middle classes, too, were conceived as a consequence of bourgeois revolution's initiation in British India, but remained embryonic until land reforms of the 1950s in the states of the Indian Union. Nowadays, as I indicated earlier, no one doubts but that the cultivating middle classes have emerged. The *Raj*'s contribution to the shaping of modern Indian middle classes is the story of the rest of this section and it is organized accordingly.

The development of English-educated middle-classes in India paralleled and was in the first instance a consequence of the deposal and debilitation by the British of the warrior-landlord classes of post-Mughal India. During the decades before the Mutiny in 1857, the British ended the regimes of *rajas* and *nawabs* in over two-thirds of the subcontinent. Many of these Indian princes, their barons and courtiers retained their landholdings – albeit under a new form of land ownership, to be discussed below, their titles, power over their tenants and dependants and local influence. But they ceased being rulers, and became subjects of the British *Raj*.

After the Mutiny, the British government ended its policy of deposing princely regimes and aggrandizing their territories into British India. The princes, by and large, had served the British as "breakwaters in the storm" of 1857 and were to be encouraged to perform the same service in the event of storms to come and, in general, to serve as Britain's "subordinate allies" on the subcontinent. So, to those princes who were still sitting on their *gaddis* went British guarantees to this effect: that they and their heirs would be permitted to continue to rule their principalities as clients of the British government.

As British clients many of the princes prospered and the power of some princely *durbars* (regimes) increased in their domestic politics: *vis-à-vis* their nobilities, for example. But their prosperity and, particularly, their power, as ruling princes and members of a princely order, became increasingly dependent on their clienthood. In 1947, the British political system on whose patronage the princes depended was taken over by a bourgeois Congress government which wanted no princes as clients or otherwise. They were allowed to retain their titles and chattels and pensioned off with generous "privy purses." But their *durbars* were liquidated and their territories merged into the states of the Indian Union – all done in a year or so, with no great fuss and the show of armed force in only three instances.

The British government's imposing an alien, bureaucratic regime on its India and keeping it separate from an "Indian India" of 500-odd principalities pushed the subcontinent's warrior-landlord classes to the *Raj*'s political margin. It tried to pull them back post-Mutiny: to encourage the collaboration in imperial maintenance of India's "natural leaders," individually and collectively. Four "chiefs' colleges" were opened in the 1870s to educate sons of the aristocracy to *noblesse oblige* and imperial loyalty. A Statutory Civil Service was inaugurated to employ them and, later, an Imperial Cadet Corps was formed to stimulate them to manly pursuits and symbolize the viceroy's particular concern for the Indian aristocracy. Princes were invited to invest in the Indian railway system, hold Government of India securities, and maintain, in their otherwise ceremonial armies, crack units which could and would be used – under British command, of course – to defend the empire. Tied into the 1919 and 1935 packages of British "constitutional reforms" for India were provisions for incorporating a collective representation of the princes' interests into the structure of the *Raj*.

Whatever else it may have accomplished, this solicitude for India's "natural leaders" did not have the intended result of relieving the *Raj*'s daily dependence for its business on the English-educated middle classes of India. A handful of British bureaucrats spread over a vast, populous and exotic terrain had little choice, in the very nature of bureaucracy, but to depend for their regime (and take the political consequences of that dependence) on a much larger group of locally recruited and trained subordinate bureaucrats and professionals, e.g., lawyers and teachers, who provide bureaucracy's ancillary services. And who were overwhelmingly from middle rather than warrior-landlord classes.

They had to be Indians. Britain could not supply the empire with India's subordinate bureaucrats and professionals in their tens of thousands; and even if it could have, employing them would have been prohibitively costly and politically dubious. Indians of the *ancien régime*'s educated *jatis* and classes were readily available. They worked cheaply, India was not exotic and orientally inexplicable to them – they spoke the language, and their employment by and in the British *Raj* might have given them some interest in becoming its collaborators.

In the nineteenth century, India's English-educated middle classes came disproportionately from the places in which the British regime was earliest and best established: from the three coastal "presidency" towns of Calcutta, Bombay, Madras and their environs. They were mostly Hindus from twice-born *jatis* or *jatis* which aspired to that status, in which the skills of literacy and numeracy and their supporting values are cultivated. Portentously, there were Muslims, too: primarily in the cities of the Gangetic Plain, from families that had served or claimed to have served Muslim courts. The families of the educated middle classes, Hindu and Muslim, tended to be relatively well-to-do rather than rich: families that wanted careers for their sons and were willing, often at some sacrifice, to pay for their education. From the latter half of the nineteenth century, their formal education was in English and they were most likely to be educated at a university that had been established in India by the British to train subordinate bureaucrats and professionals.

The Indian National Congress was founded in 1885 largely as an interest group of the English-educated middle classes. Increasingly aware of the empire's dependence on their services, the English-educated middle classes used the Congress to put forward – accompanied, to be sure, with declarations of unswerving loyalty to Her Majesty – two related sets of demands: for their employment in *superior* bureaucracies and bureaucratic positions and their representation on deliberative, quasi legislative bodies at the empire's center and in its provinces and cities.

For the British, meeting these demands *to some extent* would have been only additional costs of using India's resources. *To some extent*, the imperial enterprise would have been able to absorb these additional costs. They would have been *to some extent* investments in Indian human capital that could have increased the dividends earned by British interests. But to what extent? That was the question. I can only indicate the answer: *not* to the extent that these additional costs, as estimated by the captains of empire, would have impinged upon India's rule by British officers.

With regard to their employment as superior bureaucrats, the educated middle classes of India might have hoped, mistakenly but not for long, for the fulfillment of the promise in Queen Victoria's post-Mutiny proclamation of 1858:

so far as may be, our subjects of whatever race or creed, [shall] be freely and impartially admitted to offices in our services, the duties of which they may be qualified by their education, ability and integrity duly to discharge.[7]

That promise was never fulfilled. Given the underlying purpose and structure of the British superior bureaucracy in India, it probably could not have been fulfilled. From the middle of the nineteenth century, the rationale for it not being fulfilled was, increasingly, racist.

The purpose of the superior bureaucracy in India was not simply to govern it, but to govern it in British interests: to facilitate Britain's use of India's resources. Now, if after 1858, Indians had been impartially admitted to the elite Indian Civil Service (ICS) and impartially employed by it, it seems likely that this governing bureaucracy would have – sooner rather than later – drawn the large majority of its officers from the subcontinent's English-educated middle classes. Could they have been relied on to govern India in Britain's interests? The captains of empire thought not. The English-educated middle classes, for example, had through their Congress, from its earliest meetings, objected in India's interests to one of the empire's crucial services to British interests: the use of Indian manpower to fight Britain's wars and of Indian revenues to pay for them.

But the Indian English-educated middle classes were not simply men who had Indian interests. Nor were they simply men of Indian cultures who could not or would not become through their education "English in taste, in opinion, in morals and intellect": the naive imaginings of Thomas Babington Macauley in 1835 to the contrary. The educated middle classes were men of Indian *races*. All different: the feline Bengali, the non-Aryan Tamil, the martial Punjabi. And all *inherently* inferior to the British in their capacity to rule according to "law and system," i.e., bureaucratically. Bureaucracy was a genius of Europeans. In the last quarter of the nineteenth century, one of the empire's guardians, scholar and hierarch, Sir Alfred C. Lyall considered seriously the affirmation of Joseph Arthur de Gobineau, an originator of modern European racism, that "the civilization of Europe has never taken and will never take root among the old races of Asia."[8] Self-evidently superior to the civilizations of India, in general, and particularly, in its capacity for systematic government, European civilization could take root only on the subcontinent in that new race of Asia: the Anglo-Indians.

The Anglo-Indians were the core of British society in India. The barrier that protected them from India was racism. At the basic level of self-protection: more Indians in Her Majesty's superior services were readily translatable into fewer positions in India for the sons and nephews of Anglo-Indian families and fewer prospective husbands for their daughters and nieces. Of more general imperial concern, what effects would such translations have on Anglo-Indian rule in India? The Anglo-Indians were a ruling aristocracy of (largely middle class) British families in India. No less, they were a community of British families. They were not a landed aristocracy. They were an aristocratic meritocracy which ruled from its positions of superior employment in the bureaucratic empire, and informally but no less, from its place as an aristocratic community. The Anglo-Indians spoke each other's language, joined in each other's secrets, shared each other's stereotypes of Indians and fears of India, tipped each other off, helped each out, talked to each other as equals, let their hair down in each other's company, didn't let the side down in the company of Indians, dined in each other's bungalows, married each other's children, had affairs with each other's spouses, referred to the same distant island as "home," were each other's kind, "us." The *daftar* (office) and the club were connecting rooms in the same house of British imperialism.

From the latter half of the nineteenth century, access to both were impeded for Indians by the general acceptance in Anglo-Indian society of modern, "scientific" racism as a social ideology of the empire. It was a self-serving ideology, to be sure; but no more so than most. Like most modern ideologies, it gave "scientific" sanction to the self-interest of those who adopted it. So, because it was uninformed by "science," Queen Victoria's promise to India's educated middle classes could not be kept, ought not to be kept. Uninformed by the research of physical anthropology and social evolutionism, Her Majesty could not have known that Indians were racially unsuited to be admitted "freely and impartially" to the empire's superior service. Informed by "science," her ministers, their successors and her Anglo-Indian aristocracy would have to negate her promise in the interests of her empire.

Examinations for the ICS were so structured as to make it exceedingly difficult for any young man to take and pass them if he did not have: a first-language competency in English, an English "public school" and university education and a residence in Britain. The Indian group that was most successful in competing on their intellectual merits for places in the empire's bureaucracies and professions, the Bengali *bhadralok* (*jatis* which cultivate the skills of literacy and numeracy; literally: gentlefolk) became an imperial object of scorn and ridicule. "Babus," Kiplings, *banderlog* (monkey people), "competition-wallahs," a "half-civilized *avocasserie*, that bane of all British India," Lyall called them, who excelled at swotting up for examination, but lacked both the depth of knowledge and the soundness of character that distinguished British officers.

A landmark in the development of nationalism among the English-educated middle classes was the successful campaign by the Anglo-Indian community in 1883 to pressure the viceroy to withdraw what was known as the Ilbert Bill. The bill would have made Europeans in India equally subject to trial as were Indians in India by British district court judges who happened to be Indians. Membership in the best clubs of British India was for *Europeans only*. The Anglo-Indian community tabooed marriages between Europeans and Indians and closed its doors to their offspring.

In sum, for the British, racism served the end of securing the empire under Anglo-Indian rule. It did this by denying to the Indian English-educated middle classes the prerequisite racial merit for membership in a European superior meritocracy and the fundamental human equality that Anglo-Indians recognized in those of their own. To the Indian English-educated middle classes, racism was the added insult to the injury of professional discrimination. Both were felt more keenly as educated unemployment grew from the twentieth century. That both the insult and the injury were strikingly similar to that meted out for centuries to low and untouchable *jatis* by the twice-born *jatis* from which the English-educated middle classes largely came, was doubtlessly appreciated more among them for its irony than as a consolation.

With regard to the English-educated middle classes' other major demand, for representation on various legislative councils: the question for the British was, again, *to what extent* could such a demand have been absorbed into the cost structure of their enterprise. *To some extent*, the demand could be put to its political use, to the service of British interests by the imperial government. After the Mutiny, the British began to use Indian haute bourgeoisie as municipal councilors. The anticipated benefits, to the British, from Indian participation on such councils were these: they would raise municipal revenues and in the process relieve the British government of some of the onus of collecting taxes, provide a source of political information for British officers and help to recruit collaborators by making the prestige and boodle of municipal administration available to local notables.

During the remaining decades of British rule in India, and largely in reaction to demands of the English-educated middle classes, the imperial government allowed more and more Indian representation at higher and higher political levels: from municipal corporations to provincial legislatures to governor-generals' councils. From the early decades of the twentieth century and, certainly, from the time of the First World War's political ferment in India and Mahatma Gandhi's rise to power in the Congress, the English-educated middle classes could no longer be safely (however accurately) dismissed as a "microscopic minority." Their so-called nationalist movements were self-serving and essentially inauthentic, to be sure; but troublesome nonetheless, and increasingly so.

Originally appointed by the British Government of India, Indian members of provincial representative councils were from 1909 elected by Indian constituencies. The franchise in British India was always subject to economic and educational qualifications, but these became less and less restrictive over the decades and the proportions of Indians entitled to vote increased. Their elected representatives were granted more and more legislative and governmental power under a succession of British laws. From 1917 British politicians began to talk about responsible government and eventual self-rule in India.

Was that really the eventuality, the inevitable course of British Indian constitutional reforms, ended forever by the Second World War? Some historians have tended to think so, but Indian politicians at the time were more sceptical. In the course of constitutional reforms, they discerned – I think, correctly – a persistent British unwillingness to part with the substance of power. Periodically, the British government delivered packages of constitutional reforms in which ostensible concessions to nationalist aspirations were wrapped together with insidious schemes to protect British power from what it conceded.

We can identify the schemes, simply, as *divide and rule*, and *retain the prerogative*. Both were present in the India Act of 1935. It is instructive to consider it. The 1935 act provides a tally at endgame of the costs that Britain was willing to incur, the extent to which it was willing to go, to mollify the Indian middle classes. The 1935 act and the elections held under it in 1937 represent, in effect, Britain's last chance to negotiate a continuation of empire by conceding to Indian middle class demands for self-government. The extent of the concessions was great enough to outrage died-in-the-wool imperialists like Winston Churchill. It was endgame, nonetheless. With Churchill's government after 1939, and Attlee's, the Indian middle classes were willing to negotiate only a termination of empire. The 1935 act and the elections held under it in 1937 were landmarks in the course of bourgeois revolution in India.

The centerpiece of the 1935 act was responsible parliamentary self-government in the provinces of British India. Popular elections were to be held. From among the elected, British governors were to choose ministries which enjoyed the confidence of a majority in the legislatures. This was a considerable advance over the omnibus India Act of 1919. Under its ill-fated system of "dyarchy," some minor portfolios had been "transferred" to elected Indian politicians who served as the governor's ministers: at his pleasure and often under the *de facto* supervision of their ICS department secretaries. Under the authority of the 1919 act about 3 percent of the Indian population had been enfranchised. This percentage was increased about five-fold under the authority of the 1935 act. Under neither act, however, was the electorate to vote in general, geographical constituencies. The constituencies were, in effect, communal and "special interest." Muslims, Sikhs, Eurasians, Indian Christians and Europeans had their separate constituencies: most of which in most provinces elected numbers of representatives that were "weighted," i.e., in positive disproportion to the communities' numbers in the electorate. The British government's "communal award" of 1932, as I noted earlier, would have introduced yet another separate electorate, for untouchables, had Gandhi not opposed it by embarking on a "fast unto death." The "special interest" constituencies were for commerce and industry, universities, landlords and organized labor.

"General constituencies" in these elections were, in effect, Hindu constituencies. In general, they elected numbers of representatives in negative disproportion to the number of Hindus in the electorate. More, the provision of separate electorates and weighted representation to non-Hindu religious communities, in particular, invested them with political interests secured by British power: interests in keeping their political lots apart from the Congress's and from those of its dominant Hindu middle classes. The British position was that they were only protecting minorities in response to their demands for protection – from Hindus. Congressmen believed that the British were playing the "communal card" to divide and rule: readily acceding to minority demands because it suited British interests to do so, trying to reduce the Congress to an organization of some twice-born and touchable Hindus, discrediting Indian nationalism, proliferating and politicizing communal divisions within the Indian middle classes in order to oppose them one to another and fragment their opposition to British rule. In a subcontinent of myriad ethnic diversities, it was a card that could be played over and over again.

It didn't win in the 1937 elections, however. Congress did. It was able to form ministries in eight of British India's eleven provinces. But it withheld them from taking office until it received assurance, "for what it was worth," from the British government that the powers conferred on provincial governors by the 1935 act would be "restricted to the narrowest limits possible."[9] Under the 1935 act, provincial governors had the power to enact legislation entirely on their own authority, without the advice of their ministers and without the approval of their legislatures. Over expenditures from their provincial budgets, governors had almost complete control. By refusing their assent, governors could nullify with finality any bill passed by their legislatures. Governors had the power to prorogue their legislatures and dissolve their lower houses.

Over and above the powers of provincial governors were the powers of the governor-general. And these, for all intents and purposes, were unreformed and absolute. He was responsible only to the government in London. There was a scheme in the 1935 act for a bicameral central legislature. It and its ministers would have been completely subservient to the imperial viceroy. But it never came into being. The failed scheme was called "federation." In effect, it was meant to "federate" the Indian princes, Britain's most loyal and dependent collaborators, into the structure of empire by giving them collective representation in its legislature. A Chamber of Princes had been tied into the 1919 package of constitutional reforms. Though only consultative, the Chamber had embodied for the first time a British invitation to the princes to act collectively in support of their privileges in the empire that provided them. "Federation" was the second invitation.

It provided for a weighted princely contribution to imperial legislation. Although the population of the princely states was about one-quarter of the empire's, the princes, *not their subjects*, were empowered by the act to appoint one-third of the representatives to one of the central legislature's houses and two-fifths of the representatives to the other. Even greater would have been "federation's" qualitative overrepresentation of princely interests. To the India of 1935, the princes' contributions had been marginal. Congress opposed "federation," of course. And the princes, for a variety of reasons, not least their shortsightedness, balked at "federating."

So, at the center of empire in the years after 1935, the British played their "princely card." But it lost. It was never a winning card. "Federation" failed, as did every other British attempt to use the princes, individually or collectively, to diminish either the political importance of the English-educated middle classes in British India or the empire's dependence on them to staff and operate its bureaucracies and ancillary professional services. Like the "communal card," the "princely card" diminished the credibility of their British players and British constitutional reforms.

The most succinct contemporary evaluation, indirectly and in spirit and deed, of the 1935 Indian Act and the elections held under it in 1937 was provided by the viceroy, Linlithgow, in 1939. He simply ignored them, and acting entirely on his own authority and without even pretending to consult Indian representatives, declared India to be at war. Immediately, the only substantial land force under British colors was the Indian army. In the cause of imperial defense, constitutional reforms were postponable, at least, to another day. But not for the Indian National Congress. Its "high command" ordered Congress's provincial ministries to resign in protest, and they did. At the cost of turning India's provincial government over to its politicians, Britain's last serious attempt to hold India to the empire failed.

For India, however, the 1935 act and, particularly, the elections of 1937 were of great consequence to the advancement of bourgeois revolution. The basic Congress alliance – between urban, educated professionals and peasants, mostly middling to better-off – held and triumphed at the polls. For reasons that I have yet to discuss, the reluctance of industrialists and "merchant princes" to join the Congress alliance diminished considerably through the 1930s, and they became – as they continue to be – Congress's financial angels and the recipients of its *quid pro quo*. The 1937 elections were the precursor of parliamentary democracy in India; and more than any other, the triumphant party of India's democracy-to-be enjoyed the patronage and support of India's great capitalists.

From 1937, Congress became what it was to become: a moderate, reformist party that played to the accompaniment of radical, leftist rhetoric. Its most popular rhetorician, Jawaharlal Nehru, made his debut as Congress's prize vote-getter in 1937, and remained so for the next twenty-five years. Congress began its career as a party of vote-getting in 1937: "a political environment," as Judith M. Brown calls it,[10] to which all who were interested in the exercise of power or its rewards or its protection gravitated: upper *jati* local politicians, dominant *jati* faction leaders, untouchables, ideologues of almost all varieties, millowners, trade union leaders, intellectuals. Increasingly, Congress came to depend for its sustenance on landed peasants at its base and *crorepatis* (millionaires) at its summit. In consequence, moderation in all things, save rhetoric, but including attention to the plight of the landless and the urban working classes, became

Congress's *modus operandi*. In a word, the "Congress system" which guided India to parliamentary democracy and held it there for two decades, and to some extent still, made its electoral debut in 1937. The 1937 elections were also a landmark in Congress's failure to carry bourgeois revolution to the subcontinent's borders. That failure did not certainly make the 1947 partition of the subcontinent inevitable, nor the creation of Pakistan, nor the stillbirth of bourgeois revolution there, but it increased the possibility of these things happening. Insofar as there was an India-wide political organization of Muslims in the 1930s, it was the Muslim League. It was, in comparison to the Congress, poorly organized and lacking in grass roots support. It did very badly in the 1937 elections: winning only 5 percent of the votes and less than a quarter of the seats in constituencies reserved for Muslims. And thus, opening to ridicule the League's claim to be "the only authoritative and representative political organization of Musulmans in India."[11]

But in its bid for Muslim votes throughout India, Congress did even worse than the League. Only in Muslim-majority provinces – Bengal, Punjab and Sind – was Congress badly defeated. In victory and in apparent vindication of its secular nationalism, Congress in the United Provinces defeated itself in Muslim opinion: it reneged on its pre-election commitment to take into its ministry League leaders. For the League and its growing audience here was evidence yet again of the central contention of Muslim nationalism on the subcontinent: a Congress *raj* would be a Hindu *raj*.

Spreading out from the United Provinces, the League began in earnest the campaign after 1937 that it should have begun before: vote-getting, mobilizing support for the League among Muslim villagers. It was, however, a campaign of mobilization largely by propaganda that appealed directly to the religious and communitarian sentiments of ordinary Muslims. *Islam was in danger!* Political time was short in 1937. By and large, the League did not campaign to enlist peasants into its alliance. It was and remained an alliance of urban, educated professionals, landlords and a few industrialists. It was to become the League's legacy from 1937 to the non-development of parliamentary democracy in Pakistan. Under Legaue auspices, reports were prepared after the 1937 elections which accused Congress ministries of being explicitly Hindu in their style and in their substance insensitive to Muslim sentiments and interests. In 1939, the League's *Quaid-i-Azam*, its great leader, Mohammad Ali Jinnah, called upon Muslims to celebrate as

Deliverance Day the resignations of Congress's provincial ministries. A year later, at Lahore, the League passed its enigmatic and portentous "Pakistan Resolution," about which I will have more to say below.

By refusing to "federate" under the 1935 act, and thereby establish their corporate presence as Britain's loyal ally at the center of its Indian empire, the princes' left unbuilt what might have been an obstacle to bourgeois revolution. "Federation," by increasing the princes' bargaining power with Congress's "high command," might have helped to impede the growth in the princely states of local Congress organizations-in-disguise, *praja mandals* (popular groups). *Jati* and communal ties crossed the borders between princely states and their neighboring Congress-ruled provinces, and so, particularly after 1937, did the whetted ambitions of Pradesh Congress Committee politicians.

More broadly, the nonoccurrence of "federation" might have helped to frustrate the possible development of an Indian variant of the late-nineteenth-century marriage of iron and rye in Germany: Moore's archetypical anti-democratic alliance of a rising group of industrialists with an established landed aristocracy in a country where the majority of people are peasants. Certainly, with imperial sponsorship, such an alliance in India was at least possible. Though ultimately unsuccessful, the British were interested in conciliating India's industrialists, not least to close their coffers to the Congress. India's great industrialists were better known for their fear of labor "unrest" and the Congress left, than for their fondness for parliamentary democracy. In the 1930s, there was an increase, "not altogether negligible," of industrial investment in the princely states, where there were no trade unions and hardly any labor legislation; and princely investments in Indian industry in British provinces were probably "constant and significant."[12] In Rajasthan, certainly, there were close familial and business connections between local and expatriate business families and the families of Rajput noblemen and princes, e.g., between the Birlas and the Jaipur princely family.[13]

Finally, the 1935 act provided the basic framework on which India's democratic constitution of fifteen years later would be constructed.

Like the English-educated middle classes, the modern business middle classes of British India were composed largely of modernized rather than new men. There had been Indian traders, bankers and brokers who facilitated trade throughout the subcontinent and beyond for more than a millennium before the British East India Company established its "factories." As the English-educated middle classes were largely of families and *jatis* which cultivated the skills of literacy and numeracy, the modern business classes were largely of families and *jatis* which cultivated the skills of commerce. Even more than the educated middle classes, the business middle classes were Hindu. Exceptions, more notable for their success than their numbers were business families of Jains and Parsis: followers of an ancient and well-articulated variation of Hinduism and descendants of Zoroastrian migrants from Persia. There were some Muslim quasi *jatis* in Gujarat, Sind and Kashmir whose families cultivated the skills of commerce. But apart from these, Muslims in commerce were few and far between, except as petty traders.

The Indian business classes began their modernization in the seaport "presidency" towns of British India. Some business families were locals. Many were migrants. Most notably, Gujarati traders migrated down the coast of the Arabian Sea to Bombay and Marwari traders travelled from Rajasthan across the subcontinent to Calcutta. Typically, they began their modern careers by performing a variety of comprador services for British businesses in India: money changing, labor contracting, arranging for the supply of Indian raw materials and the distribution of British manufactured goods.

Their heirs were to become India's great families of industrialists and "merchant princes." In Claude Markovits' group portrait of them in the 1930s, on the eve of their country's independence, they appear as men confident in their business and hesitant in their politics.[14] If they suffered economically, it was not from having too little, but rather from having not enough. Their political dilemma was, on the one side, a known imperial regime in which the safety of their enterprises was apparently assured but their opportunities limited; on the other, an unknown Indian national state in which their opportunities would be less limited – far less, perhaps – but only if the safety of their enterprises could be assured.

India's major manufacturing industry, and one of the world's largest, cotton textiles, was owned and managed almost entirely by Indian investors and entrepreneurs. Bombay was their capital; and Ahmedabad, their second city. Across the subcontinent, in Calcutta, the British business capital of India, Indian firms had entered successfully into the erstwhile European monopolies of jute manufacturing and external trade during the First World War's boom time for Indian industry. Existing Indian industries profited from the import-substitution that wartime shortages imposed on the subcontinent; and other industries, e.g., munitions and cement, had their beginnings. At Jamshedpur in Bihar, there was more than the beginning of an Indian steel industry. In the railways, there was the potential for Indian heavy manufacturing.

Through combinations of circumstances and efforts, Indian industry had grown in spite of the unwillingness of the British government to protect it; notwithstanding its commitment to a policy of ''free trade'' which had, in effect, maintained in India a minimally industrialized variation of a colonial open economy dominated by British interests. After the war that changed. Henceforth, the British Government of India was to be allowed to impose tariffs to protect Indian industry. Events external to India, primarily the relative decline of British naval power during the war, had convinced London that in defense of the empire, its Barracks in the East would need the logistical support of an Indian workshop. Indian events, particularly the quickening of nationalist activity before and during the war, and Gandhi's elevation to the Congress's *gaddi* in 1920 and its call for *swaraj* (literally, self-rule), inclined the British to conciliate Indian industrialists. Their unheeded calls for protective tariffs were long-standing, persistent and wound into the mythology of imperial ''exploitation.'' Between the Mahatma and two of India's major business groups, Gujarati *banias* (*jatis* whose traditional business is business) and Marwaris (expatriate Rajasthani *banias*) there were *jati* and Hindu affinities, at least, and increased access to their purses would have been (and was) of considerable benefit to the Congress.

In the end, the offer of protective tariffs and even the tariffs themselves, which were in some cases substantial – in addition, of course, to imperial assuredness – were insufficient to reconcile Indian industrialists to the *Raj*'s perpetuation. We may understand their insufficiency, as, I think, Indian industrialists came to understand it: by reference, again, to what the *Raj* that legislated the tariffs *was not*. It was *not* a national state with a government of its own to which millionaires have the privileged access that money buys. At best, the Government of India was a semi-autonomous branch of a foreign government. In its interests, the constitutional reforms of 1935 *did not* transfer India's finances from the viceroy's control; and despite the protests of Indian industrialists throughout the 1930s, an overvalued rupee was retained because it was in British interests to retain it. The Government of India preferred Indian industrialists to negotiate their tariff protection within the framework of "imperial preferences" and to take their consequences. For protection against the importation of Japanese cloth, for example, Bombay had to come to terms with Lancashire to the disadvantage of Ahmedabad. To circumvent India's new tariff barriers, British firms opened subsidiaries on the subcontinent. A British-owned Lever Bros. subsidiary replaced an Indian-owned company as India's leading soap manufacturer. In general, that competition was unwelcome to Indian businessmen. And in particular, they could reasonably anticipate from their own experiences that British business managers in India would enjoy, if not the outright favor, at least the sympathetic ties of countrymen with British officers who enforced the *Raj*'s rules and did its purchasing. The board room of British firms, after all, adjoined the club and the *daftar*, too.

Indian businessmen with imperial interests were distressed by Burma's separation from the Indian empire in 1935, and by the apparent disinclination of British officers in Africa to protect, as they had in the past, Indian business interests there from local hostility and competition. Indian businessmen who wanted a share of India's coastal shipping were distressed by the unwillingness of the Indian government to support their ambitions. Indian businessmen, in general, were distressed by Sir James Grigg, who was the Government of India's Finance Member from 1934 to 1939. It was not only this British bureaucrat's outspoken advocacy of agriculture's primacy in India's economy and *laissez-faire* in its industrial economy, nor his particular hostility to leading Indian businessmen and his insensitivity to their concerns in general, that distressed them. It was his personification of their powerlessness.

In the 1930s, India's industrialists probably had no clear consciousness of themselves as a modern business class, no shared vision of their country as an industrialized nation, no ideological or programmatic unity and many competing interests: between the cotton mill-owners of Bombay and Ahmedabad, between Congress sympathizers and empire loyalists, between Marwaris and Gujaratis, between Tatas and Birlas, between trade associations, between factions within trade associations, between *banias* of different families, and so forth. They did, however, share a "market situation" as modern business classes, and there was a set of stimuli to which they could, and would share a negative response: their powerlessness under the *Raj* to make or take their opportunities. The elements of their "common situation," according to Markovits were:

their integration within the framework of a colonial economy over which they had no control but which still offered them some scope for expansion, and . . . their radical separation from political power.[15]

Their situation in the *Raj* pushed them toward the Congress. Congress conservatives, at least, most notably Gandhi and Sardar Vallabhbhai Patel, pulled the modern business classes toward them. But there were crosscurrents. For some, most notably the Tatas, the Government of India's railways were major customers. Some were ideologically attached to the empire. Almost all were frightened by the apparent growth and growing prominence within the Congress of its left wing, its proponents of socialism; and particularly, the prominence among those of Gandhi's anointed and the Congress's rising star, Jawaharlal Nehru. Businessmen were distressed by the emphasis on rural reform in the Congress's pronouncements, a consequence of Gandhian ideology and the Congress's developing alliances with landed peasantries. Congress's "civil disobedience" was a form of opposition that worried businessmen. It was immediately disruptive, and in the long run, perhaps corrosive of the law and order which protected property and on which the conduct of business depended.

Over these crosscurrents, push and pull finally brought the modern business classes to Congress *in power*. In provincial power, from 1937 to 1939, Congress governments were moderate and reformist: financially responsible, defensive of bureaucratic order, protective of property in the countryside, discouraging of labor union militance and strikes in the cities, responsive to the money-power of industrialists and sympathetic to their interests, purchasers of *swadeshi* (Indian manufactured) goods. In their moderation, Congress's provincial governments were supported not only by big business friends of its "high command," but by Jawaharlal Nehru. More, if one discounted Nehru's left-wing rhetoric, and one could, he was no enemy of Indian business. In contrast to Gandhi and other Congress conservatives, Nehru was an unequivocal advocate of Indian industrialization. A leading light of Congress's National Planning Committee, founded in 1938, Nehru shared with Indian industrialists their enthusiasm for planned industrialization.

Here was the point of convergence between the Congress and modern big business, and the beginning of a mutually beneficial industrializing design. India could industrialize and Indian industrialists could make their opportunities only with the active assistance of a national state, and a national state governed by Congress would industrialize with the active assistance of India's modern business classes. The safety of their enterprises would be assured in a Congress *raj*. In 1944, the Bombay Plan, signed by almost every major Indian industrialist, was their proposal for the development of an industrial economy in India through the cooperation of Indian government and Indian big business. During the 1930's depression, Indian industry had grown, if not at the expense of its British competitors, in relation to them, certainly. The Second World War was another boom time for Indian industry. By 1944, the Tatas and the Birlas, the Singhanias and the Goenkas, had outgrown the *Raj*.

The cultivating middle classes would grow primarily from the seeds of capitalist land ownership, sown over the subcontinent by various British "settlement" schemes. But the growth would reach maturity only after the British had gone, and we will discuss the cultivating middle classes in detail and pull together our scattered observations about them in chapter 6. Here, only a few statements about their incubation.

To facilitate and enhance its collections of land revenue, the British government at various times and places in India "settled" land ownership on families which were in some way involved with cultivation. The earliest, most infamous and ruinous, settlements were on the so-called *zamindars* of northeastern India. They had been for the most part, revenue-collecting intermediaries. They were made land owners by imperial fiat. In other parts of India, British Indian governments settled land ownership on families of chief cultivators, usually, or groups of such families. All settlements, however, departed from the usual Indian conception of landholding in this crucial regard: under British law, agricultural land became property that was *owned*. A commodity. It could be sold or otherwise alienated. It could be mortgaged and legally forfeited to the mortgagor in default of mortgage payments. It could be taken from its owner by government for non-payment of taxes and sold at auction.

In class terms, the settlements were noteworthy for producing noncultivating landlords and landowning cultivators. Of these, the landlords were far more important in British India. Some of India's richest and most powerful families were landlords. The British courted landlords as the countryside's "natural leaders" and as counterbalances to the middle classes. At the same time, because under the British dispensation land was something whose ownership could be lost, and often was, the social composition of landlord classes become more varied. Simply, families of warrior and *gens de la robe* landlords lost portions of their holdings to English-educated and modern business middle class families which invested their money in land and became absentee, rentier-landlords. Appropriately, their organization, the Indian National Congress, was not notable for its concern with the plight of India's peasantries (or industrial workforces) until it started to become a mass, nationalist movement in the twentieth century, particularly under the leadership of Mahatma Gandhi.

The legality of land ownership in British India also created families of landowning cultivators. They were, thus, sharply differentiated, as they had not been before, from families of landless cultivators. That differentiation has been retained and elaborated by state governments in the Indian Union, and it has become crucial to those class relationships that determine the realities of agriculture and village development in the Indian Union. In a word, by turning agricultural land into private property, the British laid the foundation for capitalism in agriculture, India's major industry, and for class relationships appropriate to it.

But under the *Raj* capitalism and parliamentary democracy *did not* develop together in the Indian countryside. The latter lagged. Before they had their state legislative assemblies and *panchayati raj* institutions, for example, families of landowning cultivators were still landed peasants: subject cultivators, albeit some well-to-do. They were, of course, subject of an imperial *raj* of foreign noncultivators. But even in their opposition to imperialism, and in spite of their *kisan sabhas* (farmers' organizations) and *jati* organizations, they were the peasant armies of *rajs*-in-becoming, their subordinate allies, the subjects of nationalist movements whose "high commands" were of Indian non-cultivators.

Mahatma Gandhi and Indian nationalism

Mahatma Gandhi, London-trained barrister-cum-Hindu saint–politician, domesticated India's bourgeois revolution. In no small part, he did this by attaching to his charisma a strategy of conflict and conflict resolution with the *Raj* which: first, fostered within the Congress the basic tripartite alliance that facilitated or allowed the development together of capitalism and parliamentary democracy and, second, preserved for the Congress's use those institutions of British India in which this development had begun and would continue. Significantly, perhaps critically, Gandhi's domestication of bourgeois revolution was in an idiom that resonated in and to his vast following of ordinary Indians, or at least, of their Hindu majority.

Gandhi became the Congress's supremo in 1920. He directed its final pre-independence transformation from an interest group of the English-educated middle classes to a nationalist movement. Over two and a half decades, his supremacy in the Congress was from time to time obliquely or directly challenged. From time to time he left the center of the political stage: of his own volition, to strategic withdrawal or social work; involuntarily (but not always inconveniently) to jail. But by compromising with his challengers or besting them, and by knowing intuitively how, when and with what to re-enter, Gandhi continued to dominate Congress affairs; until not he, but his trusted lieutenants, Jawaharlal Nehru and Vallabhbhai Patel, finally negotiated India's independence with its last viceroy, Mountbatten. So, for all but the last few years of India's final quarter century as a British possession, Gandhi reigned over India's dominant nationalist movement. He also articulated and personified Gandhianism, the dominant ideology of Congress and of Indian nationalism.

Certainly, there were other movements, other organizations and other ideologies. There was the Hindu Mahasabha and its belief that with *swaraj* (self-government) India should become *Bharat*: a Hindu nation of which non-Hindus, particularly Muslims, would be citizens on Hindu sufferance. There was the Muslim League and a Muslim nationalism that denied any common nationhood with Hindus. There was an untouchable movement led by Ambedkar which denied that touchable Hindus – however well intentioned, like Gandhi – were related to untouchables in any way other than on an ascending scale of hatred and a descending scale of contempt. The Dravidian movement in Tamil Nadu wanted its own state, apart from an Indian Union ruled by north Indian *brahmans*, like Nehru. There were communists who shared Gandhi's solicitude for the poor and his belief that their misery was a consequence of Britain's capitalist imperialism; but the remedies they offered were as repugnant to him as were his remedies obscurantist to them. There were, particularly during the latter decades of British rule, localized and more or less self-generated rebellions of poor peasants and tribals: "subalterns" as they have come to be called.[16] They marched under the banners of *jati*, tribe, religion, a new millennium, Gandhianism. They produced their own leaders or took their leadership from outsiders – some of whom were free-lancers, others more or less affiliated to outside organizations and ideologies.

But so central to Indian politics before independence were the Congress, Gandhi and Gandhianism, that all these other movements and organizations and ideologies had ultimately to come to terms, or be forced to terms with them. They are, appropriately, the focus of this brief discussion of the Indian nationalist movement. In particular, I want to pinpoint the consequences of Gandhianism and its central tenet *satyagraha* for bourgeois revolution in India.

For *satyagraha*, non-violent noncooperation is the usual English translation. It is not at all literal, neither is it satisfactory. But to begin the discussion, it will do. It was the ideology of a charismatic politician. Now, the ideologies of charismatic politicians may not be very important in the apparently literal meaning of their words. Charismatic leaders often personify as well as articulate their ideologies; and like Gandhi, their ideological articulation may be unsystematic and sometimes inconsistent. But charismatic leaders invariably come with ideologies, or messages which their disciples and successors articulate into ideologies. It is difficult to imagine a mute Christ. He came with a message. In essence, He may have been the message, but He had to say it out in words. The words may be ignored in practice, distorted, misused; but they are still important in a symbolic way as a bond between the charismatic leader and his followers. Followers who accept their leader's charisma can claim to be faithful to his or her ideology.

The faithful appropriate their leader's charisma and ideology as their resources. Resources are only things that can be used: publicly, privately; selfishly, selflessly; intelligently, foolishly; honestly, dishonestly; constructively, destructively; and so on, and so forth. Amongst users of these resources, there are likely to be great differences in why, when, where, how and for what purposes they are used. One need only reflect on the myriad uses to which Christians have put Christ and Christianity over the ages.

Amongst those politicians in the inner circle of Gandhi's lieutenants, men like Nehru and Sardar Patel who drew their political sustenance from him, there was not one who accepted the Mahatma's gospel that non-violence was a moral absolute in politics, or his belief that after *swaraj* the Congress should become a social service organization and that there should be a devolution of political authority and industrial production to India's villages. There were local and provincial politicians who identified themselves as Congressmen and Gandhians, thereby gaining access to Congress's material, organizational and reputational resources. These they used to fight their local and provincial battles, which sometimes had little or nothing to do with Indian nationalism.

Cotton-mill owners supported the Congress, although Gandhi made the wearing of handloomed cloth a nationalist virtue. Mill workers turned to Gandhi and the Congress (though not exclusively) to support them in their industrial conflicts with mill owners. Touchable Hindu farmers used the resources of Congress to defy the empire's tax collectors. Gandhi gave untouchable landless laborers some hope of ending their exploitation by touchable Hindu farmers.

Kisan movements linked Gandhi's name to their local rebellions, although these were often violent. Non-violent *satyagrahis* went down under police batons shouting *"Mahatma Gandhi ki jai,"* although they may have had only the most rudimentary notions about what academics have defined and politicians celebrated as Gandhianism. At Congress's call and in Gandhi's name, but not without some calculation of profit and loss, merchants observed *hartal,* closed their shops. In their battles against Indian timber merchants and British forestry officers, tribesmen were known to don "Gandhi caps" as amulets to protect them from police bullets. A charismatic leader and his ideology can be used as resources by different and sometimes mutually antagonistic followers, for different and sometimes mutually antagonistic purposes. Such varied use is likely to produce consequences unintended by the leader, but nonetheless significant. In his "Story of the Grand Inquisitor," a chapter in *The Brothers Karamazov,* Dostoevski treats this phenomenon with literary genius.

So, however Gandhi intended *satyagraha* to be used and used it himself, our concern is with the consequences of its varied use as a resource. As a resource of Indian nationalism, in general, *satyagraha* was at once stategies of conflict, conflict resolution and reassurance to the Indian middle classes.

Gandhi "invented" *satyagraha* during his long apprenticeship between 1893 and 1914 as a leading Indian politician in South Africa. Like most of his political inventions, *satyagraha* was a product of Gandhi's genius for revaluing the commonplace. The commonplace here is a technique of conflict and conflict resolution that has enjoyed for ages both wide familiarity and social acceptability in India. It is called offering *dharna*. That party to a conflict who is too weak to fight with physical violence, economic coercion, harassing litigation and so forth, may fight by offering *dharna*. Typically, *dharna* will be offered as a fast on the doorstep of their antagonist by aggrieved tenants or disaffected workers. Unable to punish their antagonist, they punish themselves in order to give public witness to their conviction of the rightness of their case and the wrongness of their antagonist's. Their objective is to shame their antagonist into a reconsideration of their case. *Dharna* is only incidentally non-violent. It is the weapon of self-sacrifice for those whose weakness precludes them from using violence successfully. Congruent with Indian inegalitarianism, is a non-belief in Marquess of Queensbury rules: a belief that in conflict, as in all things, unequal people are unequal; and that the weapons of the weak cannot be the same as those of the strong.

Gandhi ideologically revalued *dharna* from a weapon of the weak to a weapon of the strong, from a weapon of those who have no choice to a weapon of those who make moral choices. The revaluing, too, was in familiar terms: *satya* and *ahimsa*. *Satyagraha* was Gandhi's neology. He compounded it from two nouns: truth and insistence. *Satya*, truth, is the crucial noun. A central tenet of Hinduism and its offshoots is that God is Truth. "*Ram ka nam satya hai, Hari ka nam satya hai*" is the familiar chant that accompanies Hindu funeral processions. Whether called by the epithets *Ram* or *Hari*, God's name is Truth. Sikhs greet each other with *Sat Shri Akal*. God is Truth. God is the essence, i.e., the truth, of all things. Through study, good works, devotion, we strive to realize the truth that is God. Those who succeed become powerful beyond human measure: repositories of holy power. The power ultimately to transcend not merely victory and defeat, but life and death.

The *satyagrahi*, the one who insists upon the truth, is a moral actor in conflict and a powerful one. Ironically, because Gandhi was in a long line of Hindu reformers who condemned the practice of wives immolating themselves on their husbands' funeral pyres, the *sati*, literally, the woman of truth, was probably the *satyagrahi*'s best known ideological model in the Indian countryside. In one extraordinary act of conscious self-sacrifice in realization of the Truth, that she has no life apart from her husband's, in one act of the most extraordinary moral and physical courage, the *sati* transcends life and death. That is the ideology, anyway. Like the *sati*'s and unlike the *dharna* offerer's, the *satyagrahi*'s self-sacrifice is meant to be a choice derived from great strength and productive of strength greater still.

Ahimsa or non-violence is a major ethical precept of Hinduism (also of Buddhism and Jainism). It enjoins the doing of injury to any sentient being, and particularly its killing. Vegetarianism is *ahimsa*'s most conspicuous application in practice. Otherwise, there is a disconcerting inhumane, ritualistic formality about it. Hindus who will not eat animals treat them with cruelty and abandon. Hindus who will eat animals treat the slaughterer as a pariah. Jain moneylenders who take ruinous interest from their debtors protect themselves from the responsibility of killing moths by enclosing their light globes in gauze sachets. One of *ahimsa*'s supporting beliefs is that non-violence is spiritually rewarding to those who practice it. In practice, this belief seems to dominate the precept: the best reason for not doing physical violence to others is that it will vitiate one's own *karma*. Even so, violence, in its grossest to its most subtle forms, is probably no more or less prevalent in Indian society than it is in any other.

Gandhi interpreted the concept of *ahimsa* in humane, moral terms: an injunction against violence in its myriad forms. He extended the injunction to conflict. Unlike the powerless villager who has no choice but to offer *dharna*, the *satyagrahi chooses ahimsa* because it is morally *and effectively* superior to *himsa* (violence). The *satyagrahi chooses* self-sacrifice and non-violence not merely to give witness to the rightness of his cause but to triumph in it.

We need not be concerned with such questions as who among Gandhi's *satyagrahis*, and how many of them, believed in *satyagraha* or even understood it as he meant it to be understood. For example, that it was morally different to *dharna*. *Satyagraha* was a resource: an ideological extension of the Mahatma. From the 1920s, there were any number of campaigns of protest which called *satyagrahas* by their organizers. A few were national or of national significance, like the Salt Satyagraha of 1930. Many were local. The best remembered were directed against the British government or British interests in India, but there were others against industrial exploitation and untouchability. Some were led by Gandhi or his lieutenants, others were disapproved or censured by him.

Our primary concern, again, is with *satyagraha's consequences*. It was a resource whose use mobilized for the nationalist movement a far greater number of Indians than had ever been mobilized before: at one time or another, men and women, in virtually every part of British India. *Satyagraha* facilitated the development of the Congress's basic tripartite alliance. It gave the alliance a strategy of conflict that made a moral and political virtue of its Indian-ness and its incapacity and fear of violent confrontation with imperialism: the force of order and overwhelming, after all.

As distinguished from its serving as stimuli to charisma-induced responses, *satyagraha* as a strategy of conflict served the middle classes. As to why this was so, I can only repeat the usual suggestions. Gandhi hated *adharma*, disorder, and while he may never have read Euripides, I suspect he knew intuitively that middle classes save states. His own conservative bias, and that of most of his lieutenants, and their unanimous desire to keep their nationalist struggle against the British from turning into a class struggle amongst Indians served to direct their mobilizing efforts at the middle. They were themselves men of the middle, disproportionately of the upper middle, and they had their own interests in property and propriety. Perhaps the Hindu revivalism inherent in *satyagraha* and its *mahatma* had their particular appeal at the middle of Hindu society. Society's middle often provides the most enthusiastic audience for movements that rediscover the folk and its virtues. It may be, as Eric Wolf suggests,[17] that peasants who are most amenable to mobilization come from the middle of rural society: rather than from the top where there is a vested interest in the *status quo* (as there was in India) or from the bottom where poverty and debility preclude any organized and sustained movement – only rebellion born of despair. The middle classes also make states.

Might it have been otherwise in India? Did Gandhianism, in effect, preempt the possibility of proletarian revolution in India. I doubt it. I doubt that proletarian revolution was any more possible in British India than it has been in the Indian Union. In the 1960s the hope if not the expectation of many Indian revolutionaries was that localized communist-led conflagrations in West Bengal and Andhra Pradesh would spread into "prairie fires" engulfing India. Instead the local fires reached the local fire breaks of *jati*, tribe, religious community, and so forth: and were readily and finally extinguished by armed force. In the 1920s and 1930s and earlier, to be sure, there were peasant rebellions and even revolutionary movements among peasants, but they were invariably localized and easily suppressed. Why should the "prairie fire" have burned then that did not burn later? Why should the primordial fire breaks in Indian rural societies that work now not have worked then? In India's cities before independence, the potential for proletarian revolution was even less than it was in the countryside. The industrial working class was tiny, and only a proportion of it was organized in unions that were revolutionary. The Communist Party was small, its strength in some labor unions and rural pockets, but neither it nor any other party offered creditable, national revolutionary leadership.

Unaffected by Gandhi's charisma, there were imperialists, Winston Churchill for one, who rejected *satyagraha* as a strategy of conflict resolution and regarded it only as a nasty form of political blackmail: pitting unarmed volunteers, many of them women, against armed police. But a more thoughtful British view was that *satyagraha* was part of a negotiating process. It was meant, of course, to increase the negotiating advantage of Congress, but there were advantages in it for the Government of India as well. Gandhi was a negotiator. He and his lieutenants sought *swaraj*, always, through a negotiated settlement with the British. When Congress mobilized tens of thousands of *satyagrahis*, its message to the British was *not* that it wanted to fight but that it wanted to negotiate and it negotiated on behalf of a mass movement for Indian independence.

It is true that *satyagraha* imposed some limits that might not otherwise have been there on the Government of India's ability to meet Indian nationalism with violent suppression. But I do not think that these limits disadvantaged the British. Dean Inge's observation that you cannot sit comfortably on a throne of bayonets, is well-known and generally true. More particularly, the Government of India had a home front to contend with. Across the wire on that front, were politicians, journalists, writers, scholars, churchmen and other public figures who consistently made speeches, asked questions in the House, filed reports, wrote articles and editorials, sent letters to *The Times*, preached sermons, and so forth which were critical, and often very knowledgeably so, of the ways in which Indians were treated by their British government.

There were occasions, certainly, and usually during "emergencies," when the Government of India suppressed nationalist agitation with a very heavy hand. On its heavy handedness, however, there were limitations imposed from Britain's free society, of which its Indophile minority was a very small but vocal, informed and well-placed part. *Satyagraha*, illuminated by Gandhi's aura and his considerable public relations skills, used those limitations in the cause of Indian nationalism. We need not be concerned here with arguments about the universal applicability or non-applicability of non-violent noncooperation to situations of conflict. *Satyagraha* was a strategy of *Indian* nationalism, and any good strategist makes use of his opponent's limitations. Like *dharna, satyagraha* assumes that those against whom it is directed are shameable. The British Government of India was shameable. For almost two centuries, it had been telling itself, its countrymen and the world, and, I think generally believing, that there was a moral purpose to British imperialism.

The most infamous single incident of British heavy handedness in suppressing Indian nationalism occurred in the Punjabi city of Amritsar in 1919. At a place in the city called Jallianwallahbagh, British troops opened fire on an assembly of unarmed civilians; and in the months that followed this horrible incident, the British provincial government compounded the horror by imposing humiliating punishments on the citizens of Amritsar. The Jallianwallahbagh massacre is *the* British atrocity in the epic history of the struggle for Indian independence. More than three hundred people were killed, and about treble that number were injured. An atrocity, to be sure. "Any man's death diminishes me." But a small atrocity, really, in a century which measures its atrocities; in which the murder of 300 innocents was less than a day's day-to-day work in some *lagar, gulag*, detention center, free-fire zone, killing field; in which the uncomprehending, tormented, tortured, murdered victims of atrocities are numbered in their tens of millions.

The British government appointed a special commission to inquire into the Amritsar atrocities and allowed a Congress committee to investigate them and publish its condemnatory findings. The British military officer who was responsible for the massacre, Brigadier General Reginald Dyer, from an Anglo-Indian family, of brewers, was forced to resign from the Indian army: although he enjoyed the support of the governor of Punjab and of vocal groups of his countrymen in Britain and India.

The limitations on the British government's freedom to use violence to suppress the nationalist movement were certainly greater than the limitations on the viceroy's freedom to negotiate with Gandhi. And the viceroy was not at a negotiating disadvantage. It was his government, after all, that had the power. The power that

Congress wanted and could only negotiate for. Of the government's great negotiating advantage, some measure can be taken from my discussion of the 1935 India Act. As a strategy of conflict resolution, *satyagraha* was basically an invitation to negotiate: pressed by the weaker party on the stronger, acceptable to the stronger because of its negotiating advantage and the advantages to it of negotiating with the Congress rather than relying on violence to suppress it. Or of suppressing Congress, only to deliver Indian nationalism to a leadership less disposed than Gandhi's to negotiate.

Relatedly and finally, *satyagraha* was a strategy of reassurance for the middle classes. Gandhi's Congress would not allow the struggle against British imperialism to be turned into a class war among Indians. *Satyagraha*, of course, proscribed violence: the *modus operandi*, by everyone's definition, of class war. To this general promise that *swaraj* would not be followed by the expropriation of property, Gandhi added more specific ideological and exemplary assurances.

Yes, his ideal was a classless society. But reassuringly, it was not to be reached by force; but rather by the propertied voluntarily converting themselves into trustees of their wealth, pressured if need be by the non-violent non-cooperation of the propertyless. The state would not interfere to bring about a classless society. "The violence of private ownership is less injurious than the violence of the state."[18] Classlessness in India would be a product of class cooperation rather than conflict. A product of negotiations between the haves and the have-nots. In the words of one critic: "Gandhi recognised and renounced in burning words the barbarities of capitalist exploitation, but could not transcend his essential bourgeois outlook."[19] And would not!

This outlook was reflected time and again in Gandhi's leadership of the Congress. He readily accepted the support of Indian industrialists. He was loath to extend Congress activity into the princely states. Among peasant families it was generally the landed whom Congress sought to recruit to its banner and who rallied to its banner, rather than merely responding to Gandhi's charisma. He would "fast unto death" rather than allow the possibility of landless untouchables attaining autonomous political power. Within the Congress organization the men who consistently supported Gandhi and whom he consistently supported were those who shared his faith in negotiated settlements and his bourgeois outlook. The only partial exception to this was Jawaharlal Nehru, but Gandhi knew that Nehru's allegiance was less to socialism than to a united Congress and Indian independence.

Neither Gandhi nor his *satyagrahis* freed India. But the ongoing process of negotiations – occasionally interrupted but never terminated – that *satyagraha* as a strategy of conflict set in train and kept on course, helped to ensure that Congress would inherit from the British the foundation and skeletal superstructure more or less intact on which a bourgeois democratic state could be built. The civil bureaucracies, police forces and military were passed over virtually intact. There were no purges. Industry and infrastructure for further industrialization, e.g., the railways, had been established and were intact. They were no expropriations. The political infrastructure – electorates, legislative assemblies, a legal system, ministries – on which a parliamentary democracy could be built was embryonic but intact. There were no serious second thoughts about the appropriateness of bourgeois democracy for India. There was no serious inclination to class conflict as a political strategy for Congress in post-independence India. In pre-independence India, *satyagraha* as enunciated and personified by Gandhi, his concomitant social and economic theories and political maneuverings within the Congress affirmed the desirability of class cooperation rather than class conflict as Congress's *modus operandi*. Without such an affirmation, it seems unlikely that Gandhi could have effected the alliance of middle classes that was the Congress nationalist movement and became the Congress Party. Without Gandhi it seems unlikely that Congress would have survived intact to become independent India's ruling party. Partition tore the Indian fabric at its edges, but otherwise left it intact. Gandhi, we know, did not want India to become a bourgeois democratic, capitalist, industrialized country; but he is rightly, if ironically, honored as the Father of the Nation.

Muslim separatism

With tragic consequences, the middle classes which Gandhi was least successful in bringing into his Congress movement for an *Indian* nation were those whose members were Muslim. The ugly divorce that separated the Indian empire into the republics of India and Pakistan in 1947 was largely the consequence of a half-century-old political triangle whose principals were the Indian National Congress, various groups of wise, wealthy and well-born Muslims and British officers of the imperial government. Like all triangles, this one had a context. Its genesis long antedated the beginnings of bourgeois revolution anywhere; and to its substance, British imperialism's contribution was significant, certainly, but not determinant.

"Islam has a fundamental political orientation . . . ," writes Ishtiaq Husain Qureshi. That was an element in the context. "The Muslim community is, ideally, an association of believers organized for the purpose of leading their lives in accordance with the teachings of their faith."[20] Yet another ideal! And while it too – in Indian history, certainly – affects rather than reflects reality, for Muslims it affects reality *because* it reflects it. It reflects reality particularly in and from the *shari'ah* and the history of Islam's brief and glorious golden age.

Islam is more than the *shari'ah*, but the *shari'ah* is fundamental to Islam. It is The Law: God's law, Islamic sacred law. It is based on the Qu'ran, God's revelations to the Prophet, and what are generally regarded by Muslims to be authentic compilations of the Prophet's words and deeds as they were recorded by his Companions fourteen centuries ago. Through exegeses on these texts, generations of Muslim legists have elaborated sophisticated systems of Islamic jurisprudence, legal training, juridical practices, comprehensive penal codes and bodies of law that are meant to govern every aspect of the lives of believers: the minutiae of their ablutions, their diet, their personal and family relations, their behavior to coreligionists and others, their commercial and financial dealings, their worship and rituals of worship, their obligations to their rulers, and their rulers' obligations to God. In a word, for Muslims the teachings of their faith are incorporated in sacred law. Their teachers are not clerics nor even theologians, as they are in different guises for Christians and Jews, but *'ulama*, legists: interpreters and pronouncers of God's law.

In the *shari'ah* and from it are reflected the theocratic ideal of Islam: a government which rules according to God's law and is instructed in its governance by men who are learned in God's law. Most Muslims believe, however, that the theocratic ideal of Islam was only realized before the *shari'ah* was elaborated: for the four decades from the first year of the Muslim era (622 AD) when, from Medina, first, the Prophet and then four of his Companions, the "pious *khalifahs*" (successors), in turn, ruled the faithful according to their intimate knowledge of God's law and conquered an empire for Islam. Islam emerges into history not as the belief of those who were martyred by pagan rulers but as the faith of warriors who through God's will conquered pagan rulers, smashed their idols – most memorably in Mecca – converted their subjects to Islam and ruled them according to sacred law.

But, from the end of this golden age, in India as elsewhere, the political reality for Muslims has been more or less the same separation of Church and State, with more or less the same variations in cordiality and ideological consensus between them, as Christians have experienced in Christendom. Nonetheless, the Islamic ideal persists of itself. The Christian injunction to "render ... unto Caesar the things which are Caesar's; and unto God the things that are God's" is blasphemous (however apposite) preaching to Muslims. The ideal persists in the *shari'ah* and its continuous use by *'ulama* to proclaim God's law, even to the chastening of kings. It persists in the hagiography of the Prophet and his Companions. It persisted at least symbolically – not everywhere, to be sure, nor at all times – in the survival until 1924 of the office of the Prophet's successor, the *khalifah*, wherever located in the Muslim world and however titular for most Muslims.

For Muslims the effect of the theocratic ideal on their political reality has been to produce a second-best. The ideal is a boundaryless and politically undefined Islamic polity. Second-best is a Muslim state. If we understand that "second" includes higher and lower levels of acceptability, as in the divisions and gradations of second class honors degrees, for example, second-best is how we might, in general, describe Muslim governments in India before they were succeeded by the British *Raj*. A Muslim government is a government of Muslim rulers. They may barely recognize any Islamic restraints on themselves; but they more or less foster Islamic worship and patronize Islamic institutions, cater particularly for the interests of their Muslim subjects and apply the *shari'ah* to the regulation of their personal and family affairs, at least.

Prima facie, second-best political systems for Muslims seemed to disappear on the subcontinent as Muslim governments were dismantled by the British East India Company in the century or so before the Mutiny. The Company *raj* was, of course, a government of Christian rulers whose allegiance was to a Christian monarch. They brought their own legal system with them. They were, in general, no less contemptuous of Islam's "fanaticism" than of Hinduism's "superstitiousness." Most of the Company's subjects in India, including most of its collaborators and compradors, were Hindu; and most of the Company's Muslim subjects, who were poor farmers and artisans, were of no particular concern to the Company's officers. Indian Muslims, as I have already said, were and are as socially heterogeneous as Indian Hindus, and it is not at all surprising that the reactions to the Company *raj* should have varied from Muslim community to community.

The most hostile reactions came from lower, though not the lowest, rather than higher strata Muslim communities. And they came not long after the Company had established itself as the subcontinent's dominant power: almost four decades before the Mutiny. The best organized of these hostile reactions were the *fara'izis* of Bengal and an Islamic chiliastic movement centered in northern India, led and inspired by one Saiyid Ahmad Bareilly, and best-known (though imprecisely) in British India and Anglo-Indian literature as ''Wahhabi'' after its Arabian counterpart. Though they differed in their *modus operandi*, both *fara'izi* and ''Wahhabi'' movements in India were Islamic and Islamicizing. They imposed on British India the Islamic stigma of *dar al-harb*: literally, the ''abode of war,'' a polity unacceptable as second-best. In opposition to its rulers the faithful must either fight – as did the *mujahadin* of Saiyad Ahmad – or take flight or, at the very least, withhold their allegiance and services. Thousands and thousands of ordinary Muslims became *fara'izis* and ''Wahhabis.'' From their movements' *mullahs* (legists) and *sheikhs* (*sufi* leaders) they learned about the theocratic ideal of Islam, about the *shari'ah* and about how they would have to cut away the vestiges of their Hindu origins in order to be bona fide Muslims.

The highest strata Indian Muslim community, by and large, combining landed wealth and the claim, at least, to aristocratic lineage, the best of Muslim ''good families,'' the most illustrious and influential were the Urdu-speaking *ashraf* (literally, nobility) of the Gangetic Plain: the political center of the Mughal empire and its other Muslim predecessors, the heartland of high Muslim culture on the subcontinent, the United Provinces in British India, now Delhi and Uttar Pradesh. As *ashraf* they were, or were assumed to be, in the forms and substance of their faith, bona fide Muslims; as distinguished from their quasi Hindu, peasant and artisan, run-of-the-mill coreligionists. The origins of many *ashraf* family landholdings were in court services. They or their ancestors served Muslim courts in various military-cum-civil capacities and were remunerated for their services – as were their medieval European counterparts – with service tenements, land grants. In sum, among landholding *ashraf* families there was the tradition of court service and the cultivation of the appropriate values and skills of literacy and numeracy. New *ashraf* families who succeeded old *ashraf* families on the land and emulated them, emulated their traditions, values and skills. Muslim courts disappeared as the Company *raj* advanced. Few *ashraf* families fell so far into ruin as those who served Muslim courts in less exalted capacities – musicians, artisans, menials, ordinary soldiers – but the *ashraf* fell from greater heights. When the mighty are fallen, the poignancy, felt most keenly by themselves and their rhapsodists, lies in where they have fallen from rather than fallen to. Quite comfortable obscurity, oftentimes. To be sure, some *ashraf* families lost their holdings as a consequence of British land settlements: but not because they were Muslim, and probably in no greater proportion than Hindu landholders. The *ashrafs'* greatest loss was their "honor": their status, real and emulated, as families of the nobility, of the court servants of Muslim rulers. One of their poets grieved:

> The master is turned slave, such is the will of fate:
> The owner of the palace is now keeper of the gate.[21]

Unreconciled to the will of fate, saddened, some *ashraf* (and *ashrafizing*) families withdrew into landed obscurity rather than serve the palace's new owners. But many did not. Many were applicants for gatekeepers' positions. Like that Christian empress, Maria Theresa, they wept and took. In the United Provinces, they were the Company *raj*'s most conspicuous collaborators. They took the benefits of the Company's laws as landlords. In positive disproportion to their numbers, they took positions in the Company's subordinate bureaucracies and they schooled their sons to succeed them as servants at the Company's court. In Punjab, too, in which there was a larger though less distinguished Muslim population than in the United Provinces, Muslim "good families" were not, in Anglo-Indian parlance, "backward," i.e., conspicuously under-represented in the Company's subordinate services or in educational institutions that prepared their sons for such service.

   In these terms, Bengal was the only place in India in which there was a large concentration of Muslims – the largest on the subcontinent – whose "good families" were markedly "backward." But for a handful of Muslims, Bengalis in Company service and in educational institutions which prepared candidates for Company service were almost all Hindu. Although among the Company's Bengali subjects, about two-thirds were Muslim. Various explanations are offered for this anomaly. "Good families" of Bengali

Muslims had a particular preference for placing their sons in traditional Muslim educational institutions which neither prepared these boys for Company service nor inclined them to it. ''Good families'' were a tiny proportion of Bengali Muslim families which were overwhelmingly poor, illiterate and converts from the lowest strata of Hindu, Buddhist and tribal societies. ''Good families'' of Bengali Muslims could not compete successfully against the *bhadralok* for places in modern colleges and in Company service because these Bengali Hindus got there first and entrenched themselves. Whatever the validity of these and possibly other explanations, it is certainly true that within large Muslim populations, ethnically and linguistically defined, Bengali Muslims of ''good family'' were ''backward.'' But among such families, this was peculiar to them.

It was generalized into a myth of *Indian* Muslim ''backwardness'' by the British in the decades after the Mutiny: even after it was shown to be no more than a myth in 1882 by an education commission of the British Indian government. From their immediate indictment of Muslim ''fanaticism'' as the Mutiny's primary cause, the British in post-Mutiny India soon came to the judgment that Muslim ''separateness'' from Hindus offered the *Raj* a political opportunity. The opportunity to use religious divisions among Indians to rule them. The myth of *Indian* Muslim ''backwardness'' was perpetuated and patronized by the British government. In the myth's elaboration, the British enjoyed the collaboration of one of the extraordinary men of his age, the leading Muslim modernist reformer of the nineteenth century: Sir Saiyid Ahmad Khan. The British and Sir Saiyid had complementary interests in the perpetuation of the myth of Muslim ''backwardness.''

For the British, in broad general terms, the myth could be used to patronize the ''natural leaders'' of almost one-quarter of their Indian subjects. It could be used to tie together with the interests of Muslim landlords the interests of the English-educated Muslim middle classes and thus divide them from the empire's most potentially ''seditious'' subjects, the English-educated Hindu middle classes. For Sir Saiyid the myth could be used to gain imperial patronage for Muslims in the non-Muslim regime under which they were fated to live. It could be used to secure against the encroachments of Hindus the positions of power and trust occupied by Muslims in an empire whose operations depended and would depend increasingly on the collaboration of its subjects from ''good families.''

Sir Saiyid was born in 1817 into a very "good family": an *ashraf* family of Delhi with a Pathan pedigree, landholders and Mughal court servants. But as the Mughal empire declined, so did the family's fortunes. In 1839, Sir Saiyid entered the British government's subordinate service. Here he established a distinguished career as a judicial officer and a personal reputation through his written work and lectures as a leading advocate of the reconciliation of Indian Muslims to British imperialism. He was awarded a knighthood in 1869. He built his monuments to this reconciliation, however, only after his retirement in 1876. He established a few associations which did not endure to promote the interests of Muslim "good families" and publicize their loyalty to the Queen Empress. He founded an educational institution which did endure and prosper under imperial patronage: the Muhammadan Anglo-Oriental College which was to become in 1920 the Aligarh Muslim University.

Between his British patrons and Sir Saiyid, the agreed upon remedy for his coreligionists' "backwardness" was a special position for Muslims under the *Raj* whose markers were "reservations" and "weightage." In order for Muslims from "good families" to shed their "backwardness" – indeed, to keep them from falling further "backward" – it would be necessary to reserve for Muslim candidates a proportion of places in British imperial service and in educational institutions which trained such candidates. For Muslim politicians and Muslims enfranchised to vote by virtue of their wealth or educational status, it would also be necessary to reserve a proportion of separate constituencies in the municipal and provincial councils which the British began to establish in India after the Mutiny.

It would do justice for the number of these reserved places and constituencies to be in positive disproportion to the Muslim population, i.e., to be weighted to the advantage of Muslim "good families" against those of Hindus. Sir Saiyid argued the case ideologically, and in a way that was compatible with the ideology of empire. Again, India was not a nation, but a congeries of nations. Among these the largest and most inclusive groups, defined by what is most important about them and fundamentally different between them, were Hindus and Muslims. Muslims were not a minority of the Indian population. There was no Indian population, as such. The British empire in India had a population, but it was of two nations which inhabited the same Indian space. The Muslim nation was the smaller, but the importance of nations is generally and properly judged qualitatively: in terms of their history, culture, political and economic significance and so forth. Nations are not measured in the mere quantities of their populations. More, can one even say that the Hindu nation is the larger or even a nation when on the basic criterion of nationhood, religion, Hindus divide themselves into multitudes of sects and castes, about one-fifth of which, the scheduled castes, are placed by Hinduism beyond its pale?

Sir Saiyid certainly knew that the *ashraf* were *not* "backward" but rather advantaged in professional and administrative imperial employment in northern India. But that the *ashraf*, without the protection of "reservations," *might become* "backward" in the post-Mutiny empire, even if only to the point of losing or having to share their advantages: that seems to have been Sir Saiyid's apprehension. Queen Victoria's promise of 1858 that Indians would be "freely and impartially admitted to offices in our service" was not welcomed by Sir Saiyid. It implied in post-Mutiny India, the admission of Indian candidates to the empire's superior services, based upon their performances in competitive examinations in English and predicated on British or British-model university education. It implied to Sir Saiyid the domination of the superior services by Hindu Bengali "babus": the empire's "competition-wallahs" *par excellence*. In comparison to the sons of Hindu "good families," even the *ashraf* were underrepresented in university enrolments and comparatively disadvantaged in English-language education and education in English.

Sir Saiyid's language of employment had been Urdu. The language for employment in which his Muhammadan Anglo-Oriental College students were being trained was English; and although it contained some Islamic studies, the College's curricula were modelled on those of British institutions. The College was meant not only, nor even primarily, to provide modern, English-language education for more than a handful of Muslim boys, but rather to encourage them in substantial numbers to attain to such an education, wherever it was offered. To Sir Saiyid modern, English-language education was for Muslim "good families" the way out of their "backwardness." But the way would have to be lit by British favor: by reservations and weightage. Of what value, after all, would such an education be to Muslim families if even battalions of their sons were to be pitted against regiments of more experienced "babu" and *brahman* boys on British India's battlefields of competitive examinations for professional and bureaucratic employment. No. The interests of

Muslim "good families" would be served not by free and impartial competitive examinations, but by their sons' official nominations in weighted numbers to British service by officers of the *Raj*. On the battlefields of local politics, in the post-Mutiny empire's municipal and provincial councils, "babus," and *brahmans plus zamindars* (landholders) *and baniyas* (businessmen) would be joined in the Hindu regiments. They would outnumber and overwhelm Muslim forces. In general, Muslims were a minority of the population; and even where they were a numerical majority, as in Bengal, the enfranchised majority, by virtue of wealth and university education, would be of Hindus. Here, too the interests of Muslims would be protected if a special position were created for them: in every elected assembly, reservations of separate Muslim constituencies, their number weighted in positive disproportion to the Muslim population in that assembly's jurisdiction.

Although Sir Saiyid wanted the political advantages of reservations and weightage, he advised Muslims in general to eschew political activity as a way of getting them. Only the British could create a special position for Muslims in their empire, and they did not like political activity. The agglomeration of Sir Saiyid's coreligionists, their varied communities and quasi *jatis*, were probably incapable of organizing a political demand for reservations and weightage, and many would have little to gain by doing so. To the vast majority of Indian Muslim families, poor and illiterate, reservations and weightage were of no immediate concern.

A special position in their empire, could only be the self-interested gift of the *Raj*, and in the foreseeable future, Muslims of "good family" would enjoy it only so long as the *Raj* lasted. In return for British gifts, what Muslims of "good family" had most to offer was "loyalty"; their own and as the "natural leaders" of ordinary Muslims, theirs as well. Political inactivity was a demonstration of "loyalty." Sir Saiyid demonstrated his loyalty by advising Muslims not to join the Indian National Congress. It was a political organization. Behind its make-believe of Indian nationalism, it represented the interests of "babus" and *brahmans*. It was in their interests, and contrary to Muslims', that Congress supported an examination procedure in which Indians could really compete for positions in the Indian Civil Service. Congress was an organization of India's Hindu nation; or more accurately, of its twice-born middle classes.

Saiyid Ahmad's efforts to produce a modernist interpretation of

Islam, an Islam reconcilable to modernity, although intellectually impressive, had no great effect, even on Muslims of his "Aligarh school." Within his ideological framework, however, his specific arguments in favor of Muslim reconciliation to the realities of British imperialism and their solicitation of a special position in it enjoyed a warmer reception among Muslim "good families." The British *Raj* did not interfere with Islamic worship, Saiyid Ahmad argued, it was sufficiently respectful of Islamic institutions, it supported the *shari'ah*'s application to the regulation of Muslims' personal and family affairs, it was sensitive to the interests of its Muslim subjects, and last but not least, it protected Muslims from the crueler fate of a Hindu *raj*. Although its rulers were not Muslims, the British *Raj* was for Muslims an acceptable second-best, albeit not of the first division.

In 1906, some years after Sir Saiyid's death, in one of the most fateful of such meetings in modern Indian history, a delegation of Muslim dignitaries – mostly landlords – led by the Aga Khan presented the viceroy, Lord Minto with an "address."[22] In it, they expressed their appreciation of "the incalculable benefits conferred by British rule" on India, pledged the "unswerving loyalty [of Muslims] to the Throne," and asked, in effect, for reservations and weightage for Muslims in government service and on representative bodies from district boards to the viceroy's council.

The year before, Minto's predecessor, Curzon, doubtlessly aware of this Muslim mood of separatism and of the imperial opportunities it presented, partitioned Bengal with a provincial border that separated its Hindu-majority districts from its Muslim-majority districts. The Indian National Congress bitterly opposed the partition, as did the Hindu *bhadralok* who were the leading Congressmen and nationalists in Bengal. Not all Muslims of "good family" supported partition, but many did. And British officials, including Curzon, told them that they should. Liberated from the dominance of Calcutta's *vakils* (lawyers) and "babus," the Muslims of East Bengal were meant to enjoy unprecedented opportunities for English-language education and political representation. "Muslims in East Bengal," writes Peter Hardy, "were coming closer to Muslims in the upper provinces, in that they were slowly acquiring something to lose."[23] They lost it in six years.

Reservations and weightage endured, however. Minto and his Secretary of State for India, John Morley, were pleased to accede to the "prayer" of the Aga Khan's delegation of Muslim notables. For all of India, reservations and weightage first appeared in the Indian Councils Act of 1909. They reappeared in both subsequent omnibus India acts passed by the British parliament, in 1919 and 1935. Over almost four decades, until 1947, Muslims of "good family" had the opportunity to develop a vested interest in being Muslim.

What endured less well among them was "loyalty." There had, of course, always been Muslims who were *not* "loyal": Muslim Congressmen, for example, who opposed "loyalty" as politically shortsighted, and *'ulama* who opposed it as religiously errant. The reunification of Bengal in 1911 tested and dismayed the "loyal." Apart from frustrating the expectations of upper and middle class Bengali Muslims, the reunification gave all the appearances of a British retreat: a rout of the Muslim's mighty patron by the Hindu "babus" and *brahmans* of the Indian National Congress. On another front, the interface between ordinary Muslims and "loyal" Muslims of "good family," the credentials of the latter as "natural leaders" of the former were being opened by events to serious question.

In comparison to the Congress, certainly, Muslim "natural leaders" were laggard in leading: themselves, much less their ordinary coreligionists. Although founded in 1906, the Muslim League barely existed, even as an organization of Muslim elites until the 1920s. From then it existed largely in factions, and it became a disciplined organization with some command over constituencies of ordinary Muslims only after the late 1930s, under the leadership of Mohammad Ali Jinnah. Until then, the usual, functioning "natural leaders" of ordinary Muslims were the *'ulama*. It was mostly they who from the turn of the century organized the resistance and counterattacks to the revival of militant Hinduism – in northern India and Maharashtra, for example – and its calls for the prohibition of cow slaughter and the reconversion of Muslim quasi *jatis* to their original Hinduism.

While ordinary Muslim families of farmers and townspeople were little concerned with reservations and weightage they were apparently very concerned with a matter no closer than these to their immediate, material interests: the fate of the Ottoman *khalifah*, the Prophet's last successor. It was for him, and not for the British monarch, whom Muslims in mosques all over India, Friday after Friday, offered that particular prayer for their ruler (*khutba*). It was in defense of his empire, and not of Britain's, that ordinary Muslims rallied. And they rallied against Britain. They rallied against Britain's role in the parcelling out of bits of the Ottoman empire in the decades before the First World War. They rallied against Britain's role as the *khalifah*'s enemy in the war and as one of the disintegrators of his empire afterwards.

The Khilafat movement, the mobilization of Indian Muslims in defense of the Ottoman *khalifah*, from 1916 to 1924, was the first mass movement among ordinary Muslims – thousands upon thousands of them – in the twentieth century. The second would be the Pakistan movement. Like the *fara'izi* and "Wahhabi" movements, the Khilafat movement was Islamic and Islamizing in this sense: its rallying cry, the sentiment which called it into being, whatever its underlying causes, was drawn from the political ideals of Islam. Among its leaders, there were some Muslims from "good families" – but rarely from the "best." Even before the Khilafat movement, Muslims from particularly "good families," including the aged Sir Saiyid Ahmad Khan, who offered the British "loyalty" as the *quid pro quo* for reservations and weightage, suffered the affection of ordinary Muslims for the Ottoman *khalifah* as an embarrassment. It called into question not only their "loyalty" but the leadership of their "natural leaders."

For Mahatma Gandhi and the Congress, on the other hand, the Khilafat movement was an opportunity: to put together a mass movement of Hindus and Muslims in opposition to British imperialism. To the leaders of the Khilafat movement, for their alliance, Gandhi was willing to pay in the "Lucknow Pact" of 1916 the price of reservations and weightage. Particularly from the 1920s, however, the alliance foundered. It was a nationalist alliance, but only of complementary interests in opposition to British imperialism. Gandhi insisted on non-violent opposition, but *khilafatists* had no more interest in *ahimsa* than Congresmen had in the Ottoman *khalifah*. Muslims were fearful of the growing influence in Congress and on it of Hindu *qua* Hindu politicians, and of the Congress tail wagging the *khilafatist* dog. The mobilization of Hindus and Muslims for political action, in whatever cause, then as now, seems inevitably to result in their turning on one another. In the 1920s, there was a marked increase in the number of localized clashes between groups of Hindus and Muslims, even before the Congress–*khilafatist* alliance collapsed. It finally collapsed in 1924, when not the British but the Turkish republic abolished the *khalifah*.

The lasting effect of the Lucknow Pact was that it opened to negotiations *with the Congress* the questions of the special position enjoyed by Muslims of "good family" in British India. The British government, of course, continued to be a party to such negotiations, directly and indirectly; but increasingly, and decisively in the end, it was with the Congress that Muslim politicians had to settle.

In 1927, the British government sent a commission to India led by Sir John Simon to recommend constitutional reforms in furtherance of 1919's and further toward responsible government. To the Simon Commission, no Indian member was appointed. That blunder inspired hostile demonstrations all over India and a conference of almost all political parties in India to produce its own constitutional reforms for Indian self-government.

The Muslim League, or a faction thereof, was represented at this All-Parties Conference by Mohammad Ali Jinnah. His problem was to adjust the special position of the Muslim elite in British India to a political situation in which there was likely to be considerable devolution of power to Indian politicians. His proposed (and rejected) solution in 1928 was much the same as it would be during the *Raj*'s remaining two decades: reservations and weightage were, in part, negotiable in favor of the constitution of an Indian federation or confederation whose political power would be less at its center and more in its provinces.

Weak center/strong provinces in all its variations were formulae that were likely to maximize Muslim political power in a *raj* of responsible government and quasi democracy. In Bengal, Punjab and the lands to its north and southwest, Muslim majorities would presumably produce Muslim-majority provincial governments. If they had the constitutional power to do so, they could, *de jure* or *de facto*, by offers of cooperation or threats of secession or obstruction, exercise a veto on the central government of a Hindu majority.

The "Pakistan Resolution" passed in 1940 at the Lahore session of the League, then fairly firmly under Jinnah's control, was not only a response to the League's debacle in the 1937 elections but the explication of Jinnah's alternative to the 1935 act's division of power between Delhi and its provinces. The resolution nowhere calls for the establishment of "Pakistan." That name does not appear in the resolution, and it is written in language that seems calculated to obscure rather than make clear what it does call for. Thus, a "constitutional plan" for India would be acceptable to the Muslim League only if it were "designed on the following basic principles":

that geographically contiguous units are demarcated into regions which should be so constituted, with such territorial adjustments as may be necessary, that the areas in which the Muslims are numerically in a majority should be grouped to constitute "independent states" in which the constituent units should be autonomous and sovereign.[24]

The idea of a Muslim-majority state in northwest India separate from Hindustan, Hindu India, was certainly not new. The leading Indian Muslim poet Muhammad Iqbal revived it in 1930, and a few years later it was called "Pakistan" by a group of Indian Muslim students at Cambridge. But was the "Pakistan Resolution" really about "Pakistan"? In light of Jinnah's subsequent behavior, it seems more likely, in 1940 at least, to have been: on the one hand, an over-bid in his negotiations with the Congress and the British; and on the other, his attempt to concretize *dar al-Islam*, as the Ottoman *khalifah* had, in a bid to use Islam to mobilize ordinary Muslims in support of the League and a weak center/strong provinces constitutional settlement for the subcontinent.

In 1946, India held its last elections under British auspices. The Muslim League swept the field of Muslim constituencies. Jinnah established himself as the *quaid-i-azam* of Indian Muslims, their authoritative spokesman, an equal in negotiations with Congress and the British. In 1946, too, a Cabinet Mission from the British government recommended a constitutional settlement, like the Cripps Mission's of 1942, based on a variation of the weak center/strong provinces formula. Jinnah accepted it. Nehru finally rejected it for the Congress. Jinnah, his negotiating time at an end – the British were to leave in a year – declared August 15, 1946 to be "Direct Action Day" for Muslims. The horror began. The subcontinent was partitioned and Pakistan was born in a whirlwind of death and destruction.

Who was responsible for Partition and for what Jinnah himself called a "moth-eaten" Pakistan, to be bitten in half again in 1971 when its Bengalis seceded? There is enough responsibility to share. Politicians of Hindu parties and persuasions, from the 1928 All-Parties Conference to the present, have refused to recognize Muslim communalism as a reality of Indian political life, deniable only at its peril. In the name of secularism and at a particularly crucial time, after the 1937 elections, Nehru also denied the reality of Muslim communalism, as secularists now deny its legitimacy. Ayesha Jalal, in particular, has questioned the conventional opinion that Congress was the party of Indian unity and the Muslim League of Partition and Pakistan.[25] Rather, she argues, that given the choice between Jinnah's acceptance of a united subcontinent of autonomous provinces, on the one hand, and on the other, a partitioned subcontinent with a politically centered Indian Union, the Congress duumvirs, Jawaharlal Nehru and Vallabhbhai Patel, opted for the latter. Pakistan, they expected or hoped – again denying the reality of Muslim communalism – would be reabsorbed into India before long.

But Congress's complicity does not absolve Jinnah of his responsibility: of being too clever by half, at least, of assuming, apparently, that in his negotiations with viceroys and the Congress "high command," he could fight a barrister's war of words with "Pakistan," keep its meaning ambiguous and negotiable, while at the same time, with calls to throw off the Hindu yoke, he could rouse ordinary Muslims to whom, increasingly, the *quaid-i-azam*'s "Pakistan" meant only Pakistan.

British imperialism did not create Pakistan certainly, but it did help to develop the context in which it was created. Simply by ruling the subcontinent, the *Raj*, indissolubly foreign, neither of Hindus nor Muslims in a society organized by their communities, bred its own opposition from them and their differentiating impingement on one another: *fara'izis*, "Wahhabis," Arya Samajis, khilafatists, Hindu Mahasabites. Calculatedly, by acceding to the pleas of Muslim "good families" for a special position under the *Raj*, it vested them with political and economic interests in being Muslim, gave them something to lose in an India that was either "secular" or "Hindu." In the related context of bourgeois revolution, British imperialism facilitated the diversion of most of the subcontinent's Muslim "good families" from the Indian middle-class mainstream in which capitalism and parliamentary democracy had begun to develop together.

Political and economic development in the Indian Union and its international politics

In broad general terms, and with variable consistency and success, Indian governments have pursued two major policy goals: political and economic development. "Democracy," "secularism" and more qualifiedly, less certainly, and now all but discarded, "socialism" are at once officially designated means to these ends and their official designations. Democratic political development is meant to produce democracy, and so forth. In the first section of this chapter, I discuss democratic and secular political development and the development of secular, parliamentary democracy (see table 6). I discuss economic development in the second section, but with only an allusion to socialism. It has never been much more than a slogan in India; and even as that, it recedes. In reality, parliamentary democracy has developed together with capitalism, private and state: an officially sponsored, subcontinental variant of bourgeois revolution. It began and continues as a revolution from the top down. But increasingly as it proceeds, it becomes as well a revolution from the middle, at least, up. Appropriately, the middle classes are central to my discussion of the means and ends of Indian development in this chapter's first and second sections.

Finally, my third section deals with India's international politics. These are connected to bourgeois revolution in India: partially and as elsewhere, an external manifestation of things domestic. But to approach India's international politics by way of bourgeois revolution would probably strain the concept beyond its limits.

Political change: democracy, secularism and the cultivating middle classes

Again, for all but three of India's forty-two years of independence until 1989, the ruling party in New Delhi had been Congress and its continuation, Congress (I). In December 1989, the Indian Union

Table 6. *Major political events in the Indian Union's history, 1947–1992*

1947	India becomes an independent state, in effect governed by the Congress Party under the duumvirate of Jawaharlal Nehru and Sardar Vallabhbhai Patel.
	Managed by Patel, the integration of princely states into the Indian Union begins, to be completed by 1950.
	An independent Pakistan, of two wings on India's east and northwest, separated by ethnicity and 1,500 kilometers of hostile territory, emerges from the subcontinent's partition.
1948	India and Pakistan are at war in Kashmir.
	Mahatma Gandhi is assassinated by a Hindu militant.
1950	The secular, quasi federal constitution of the "sovereign, democratic republic" of India comes into effect.
	Death of Sardar Patel leaves Nehru as *the* leader of both the Government of India and Congress Party.
1952	First general elections for parliament and state legislative assemblies establish the pattern of Congress's one-party dominance.
	States begin to pass and enforce land reform legislation that will lead in a decade or so to the formation of cultivating middle classes.
1953	The formation of "linguistic states" begins with the creation of a Telegu-speaking Andhra Pradesh.
1955	The first of the major Hindu Code Bills becomes law, the marriage act.
1956	Nehru presents his Industrial Policy Resolution to parliament.
1957	Import-substitution industrialization begins in earnest under the second Five Year Plan.
	In the second general elections, Communist Party victory in Kerala is the first major challenge to Congress dominance.
1959	Center uses "president's rule" to dismiss Kerala's communist government.
	Panchayati raj systems make their first appearance, in Rajasthan.
1961	Indian forces "liberate" Goa from Portuguese rule.
1962	Third general elections are held.
	War with China. The US and the USSR come to the aid of non-aligned India.
1964	Jawaharlal Nehru dies, succeeded by Congress stalwart, Lal Bahadur Shastri.
1965	War with Pakistan. Truce mediated by the Soviet Union at Tashkent in 1966.
1966	Lal Bahadur Shastri dies. The Congress "syndicate" chooses Indira Gandhi to succeed him.

Table 6. *(cont.)*

Sikh-majority *Punjabi Suba* (Punjabi language state) is carved from
the northern half of pre-existing Punjab. The south becomes
Hindu-majority Haryana.

1967   Congress does its worst to date in fourth general elections:
reduced majority in parliament; and in the states, the beginning
of the end of one-party dominance.
"Green revolution" begins.
Short-lived "Naxalite" rural insurgencies led by revolutionary
communists begin in West Bengal and spread to Andhra Pradesh
and Kerala.

1969   Major commercial banks are nationalized.

1971   India wins Bangladesh War against Pakistan and facilitates the
secession of East Pakistan, which becomes Bangladesh.
Indira Gandhi routs the "syndicate" and wins decisive control
over the Congress Party by her resounding victory in the fifth
parliamentary elections.

1972   The first legislative assembly elections "delinked" from elections
for parliament. Congress polls well, but does not re-establish one-
party dominance.

1975   India annexes Sikkim and it becomes a state of the Union.
In response to a rapidly growing movement against her and her
party, particularly in Bihar and Gujarat, Indira Gandhi proclaims
an "emergency" which effectively suspends the operation of
democracy in India.

1977   In its sixth parliamentary elections, India elects its first non-
Congress – now, Congress (I) – central government: of the
patchwork Janata Party, under the prime ministership of Morarji
Desai, a former member of the Congress "syndicate."

1980   After the disintegration of the Janata Party and its government,
Indira Gandhi leads Congress (I) back to power in the seventh
parliamentary elections.

1981   Mandal Commission report encourages "other backward classes'"
movements.
Sanjay Gandhi is killed in an accident, and succeeded as his
mother's political heir by his older brother, Rajiv.
First stirrings of the Khalistan movement for a sovereign Sikh
state in a seceded Punjab.

1984   Indian troops storm the Golden Temple precincts, the holiest of
Sikh holy places, in response to its use as an armory and
sanctuary by Sikh gunmen. In revenge, Mrs. Gandhi is
assassinated by Sikh members of her bodyguard. A brief but
murderous anti-Sikh pogrom follows, mostly in Delhi. Rajiv

Table 6. *(cont.)*

Gandhi leads the Congress (I) to its greatest election victory in the eighth parliamentary elections.

1985 The Government of India's budget is the most comprehensive plan to date for liberalizing the "license-permit *raj.*"

1986 Beginning of the *Ramjanmabhumi Mandir–Babri Masjid* controversy and its use as a focus by the forces of *Hindutva.*

1987 The Bofors Scandal surfaces, with allegations of corruption and dissembling at the highest level of Indian government, over the purchasing of Swedish howitzers. The scandal brings to national prominence V.P. Singh, who resigns from Rajiv's cabinet and then from the Congress (I) to form an opposition party, the Janata Dal.

1989 A National Front of opposition parties wins the ninth parliamentary elections. V.P. Singh becomes prime minister, but his government survives for less than a year before the front disintegrates. The Bharatiya Janata Party (BJP), the party of *Hindutva* begins its climb to national prominence in these elections.

1990 National Front parties win in most major states in legislative assembly elections.
Armed secessionist movement in Assam begins.

1991 Rajiv Gandhi is assassinated during the campaign preceding the tenth parliamentary elections. Congress (I) forms a minority government under the prime ministership of P. V. Narasimha Rao, and begins, largely as a result of IMF pressure, to liberalize India's floundering and heavily indebted economy.

1992 The Union budget for 1992–93 manifests the new Congress (I) government's commitment *as a matter of policy* to the dismantling of Nehruvian "socialism" and the establishment of a free-market economy in India.

held its ninth parliamentary elections. Led in only twice-briefly-interrupted dynastic succession by Rajiv Gandhi, the son and grandson of his predecessors, in control of the Union's treasury, its military and paramilitary forces, its civil services, its broadcasting and telecommunications facilities and so forth, the Congress (I) government was defeated at the polls. And it resigned from power. It was returned in the parliamentary elections of 1991 as a minority government under the leadership of P. V. Narasimha Rao, a party stalwart. Because of the logistical problems in holding elections among so large and widely dispersed an electorate, parliamentary polls in India are held over a period of days. Rajiv Gandhi was assassinated in May, after the voting had begun but before it was half complete. The bomb blast that ended the Nehru–Gandhi dynasty delayed the completion of India's tenth parliamentary elections by only a fortnight.

Political development in India has been most notably of parliamentary democracy. In four decades, one of the world's few stable parliamentary democracies has been produced by a society that is more populous and diverse in every way than Europe's, scattered over more than half-a-million localities in a vast subcontinent, largely parochial and illiterate and fundamentally anti-democratic in its traditional institutions and cultural biases.

How can this remarkable development be explained: the adaptability of parliamentary democracy to the politics of Indian society? Really, we can only speculate. Of what relevance to this adaptability has been the Congress and Congress (I) parties' "one-party dominance"? What has this been and how has it worked? In this section, I address most of my discussion to these and related questions. In addition, I have expressed some thoughts on three other matters relevant to the development of parliamentary democracy in India: political corruption, secularism and communalism, and the growth of the cultivating middle classes.

In general, it seems possible for parliamentary democracy to enjoy reasonably wide acceptance not as an ideology nor even as a set of immutable "rules of the game" but only as a currently workable *modus operandi* for resolving conflicts over distributions of power and pelf. Democracy is likely to provide such a *modus operandi* under these circumstances: if it is acceptable to those social groups which enjoy and can aspire to power, wealth and status. If the imposition of an alternative system is clearly beyond the capacity of those groups which neither enjoy power, wealth and status nor can aspire to them. And if no one group or alliance of groups can reasonably aspire to a monopoly of political power, i.e., if political majorities are only transient coalitions of minorities. So it is in India.

Groups which have benefited less than the middle classes from parliamentary democracy have through its various means the chance, at least and however slim, of emulating the success of those who have benefited more. Thus, other backward classes have followed dominant *jatis* in their use of parliamentary means to expedite their embourgeoisement: to demand, for example, the legislated reservation of places for their children in universities and government employment. In their use of parliamentary means, the best chances of the nether quintiles probably lie: better and less slim certainly, than in various extra-parliamentary arenas where they confront the coercive power of their betters and the forces of law and order.

Common to those groups that are relatively powerful in India, in state parliamentary arenas and the center's, to those that aspire to power in these arenas and to those that are relatively powerless are such multiplicities of cross-cutting diversities – class across *jati, jati* across faction, faction across class – that no group nor even alliance of groups can reasonably aspire to gain or hold a monopoly of power. This may change, if as it now seems possible, Hindus *qua* Hindus can be organized into political majorities. But that hasn't happened yet and may not. Nowadays to get what they can get, all groups have got to negotiate: compromise, hold themselves together, ally with others. Negotiations in India's democracy do not preclude the use of violence. Indeed, violence is ordinary. But its use is less often meant to achieve directly some end than to achieve it indirectly by establishing the user's negotiating position. This democracy has become the *modus operandi* of group conflict in India. It has demonstrated its workability over the past four decades: the political lifetime of a generation.

So, in a society whose social ideologies are fundamentally anti-democratic the workability of parliamentary democracy may be explicable in part because its acceptance is not as an ideology but as a means sufficient to the day's political business. A paradox, it may owe something to the British *Raj*. Perhaps because so much of modernity in India was originally and is still exogenous, the consequences of imperialist and urban importations, Indians seem particularly adept at fitting rules to suit their contexts. So, it may be recalled, the rules of purity/pollution which villagers are expected to observe in their village contexts, they are expected *not* to observe on the train, in town, at the factory or university. In like manner, there are old rules which define access to village wells and other, new rules which define access to polling booths. That the new rules may eventually impinge on the old is a matter of concern, no doubt, to those who consider eventualities. Ordinary people don't seem to.

The paradox may owe something to parliamentary democracy's adaptability to non-democratic Indian society. For example, the myth that democracy's fundamental right, the franchise, is exercised individually, in substance as in form, is only more palpably a fiction in India than it is elsewhere. Everywhere, people exercise their franchise socially, as members of social groups. In India, this produces, as Ravinder Kumar suggests, a conservative irony:[1] many people exercise their democratic right to vote according to instructions they receive from traditional, non-democratic authorities. Patrons issue voting directions, for example, as do *gurus*, i.e., preceptors of one sort or another, communal or *jati* or tribal elders, lineage or family heads. Parliamentary democracy has certainly challenged some non-democratic relationships in India, as between *jatis*, for example. But it has also reaffirmed other non-democratic relationships, as within families, by providing new and important opportunities for the exercise of traditional hierarchical authority.

Parliamentary democracy has been adaptable both to traditional Indian beliefs in dynasticism, or more exactly, familialism, of which dynasticism is a manifestation, and to beliefs about the quality of breed or blood. One thinks immediately of the Nehru–Gandhi dynasty of prime ministers. Here parliamentary democracy adapted to virtually all the elements combined of traditional political authority. The founder of the line, Jawaharlal Nehru, established his right to rule through his charisma, the manifestation of his innate ruling capabilities. Not the first brahman to do this, certainly! There can be to *kshatriya*-hood an achievement criterion. Who rules successfully demonstrates that he or she was born to rule. To his daughter and grandson, Nehru passed on his rule because they were his heirs, albeit of lineal irregularity. His capabilities passed to them through his blood. Lions come from a lion's den. And there are many of them in India's parliamentary democracy.

Were we to name a founding father of parliamentary democracy in India and the one-party dominance of the Congress and Congress (I), it would be Jawaharlal Nehru. Nehru adopted the role of parliamentary democracy's preceptor to the Indian electorate. Preceptor is an ordinary politician's role in India, adopted by ordinary politicians, particularly in their discourses to "peasants." In Nehru's case, the role was credible. Although he was the towering figure of post-independence Indian politics, Nehru was a democratic ideologue: truer than most bourgeois politicians, certainly, to his ideology. He might have succumbed easily, as did many of his contemporaries in Asia and Africa, to the self-serving revelation that parliamentary democracy is for any number of reasons inappropriate to a "third world" country and declared himself chief guide in a "guided democracy," first person in a "people's democracy," president-for-life, great helmsman, whatever. But he did not. Instead he led his party in India's first three democratic elections and tutored its electorate in parliamentary democracy, tolerated dissent within Congress, suffered the rivalry of opposition parties – left and right, regional and national, secular and religious; and bore the restraints that democracy imposes on executive power: by cabinet and party colleagues, a lively parliament, an articulate opposition, a free press, an independent judiciary, and an unpoliticized civil service. He was a preceptor in practice.

Congress's one-party dominance was initially a legacy from the Congress movement for Indian independence. The Congress and Congress (I) parties have been post-independence manifestations of the Indian National Congress; and from this ancestor, both movement and party in British India, its successor parties have inherited the following characteristics, at least: they have been goal-oriented rather than ideologically committed and the goal has been winning; they have accommodated different ideological positions and social classes under their umbrellas, but like most umbrella organizations they have been most comfortable to those in the middle. In a proper parliamentary democracy, proper centrist parties! Their ideological explications notwithstanding, the underlying inclinations of the Congress and Congress (I) have been primarily to middle-class welfare, i.e., to the discouragement of class conflict, the maintenance of law and order, the protection of property, the encouragement of upward social mobility and the patronage of increasing agricultural and industrial production. In a word, the Indian National Congress was a bourgeois nationalist movement and its progenitors have been bourgeois nationalist parties. Their bases have been in the middle classes, not least because the Congress Party got to them first. In 1947, it partook of Mahatma Gandhi's charisma and it was the party of Jawaharlal Nehru. Britain's transfer of power had been to it. Congress was the best and most widely organized political party in India, a party of demonstrated "responsibility" in provincial government. The party most likely to win elections and deliver the goods.

Measured against what actually happens in most elections in most parliamentary democracies most of the time, elections in independent India have usually fallen within the range of "free and fair." One party has usually won them, however, albeit with decreasing frequency: the Congress and, from 1977, the Congress

(I). Through three general elections, from 1952, Congress governed in New Delhi and in virtually all of India's state capitals (except Kerala's, briefly), until 1967, when it lost several state elections. It governed the Union through five parliamentary elections, until 1977; through two more elections, as Congress (I), from 1980 to 1989; and from the 1991 parliamentary elections to now.

The more elections they won, the more the Congresses became parties of, by and for election winners: for those who wanted to exercise political power and those who wanted to profit from its exercise. The more the Congresses became parties of, by and for election winners, the less explicitly ideological they became; or more exactly, the less their concoctions of Gandhian and socialist rhetoric described their policies, and the more they came to be determined by the interests that they served: primarily, of the middle classes, rural and urban. One-party dominance has depended on them. But its success has compelled the support of others. It was William Faulkner, I think, who said that the world's wisdom is summarized in a dozen clichés: "nothing succeeds like success."

However much they opposed land reform and decried Nehru's "socialist pattern of society," landlords and great industrialists understood that in order to serve their interests they had no better alternative than to support, if only from their purses, Congresses and Congressmen. Officials were not slow to appreciate that, elections after elections, whoever their political masters were, of whatever family, *jati*, community and class backgrounds, they were almost certain to be Congressmen. Groups of the weak and despised, untouchables and Muslims, for example, sought the Congresses' protection by becoming their "vote banks." For although they gained little from their support of the ruling parties, they feared to gain even less by impeding their way to certain electoral victories.

On the Congresses's peripheries, in virtually ceaseless fission and fusion, have been parties of opposition. Some have been more or less ideological, like the communists and socialists on the left and the short-lived Swatantra Party on the right. The communists are now split into two competitive parliamentary parties and a number of revolutionary fragments. The socialists appeared as fragments, reappeared as reconstituted fragments, and finally disappeared in the 1970s. The Swatantra Party evaporated. Some opposition parties have been of a particular community or *jati*. The Akali Dal is a Punjabi party of Sikhs. The Kashmir National Conference of Kashmiri

Muslims. The Republican Party of Maharashtrian untouchables. The Bharatiya Janata Party (BJP), which used to be the Jana Sangh, is primarily a party of Hindi-speaking Hindus; although of late it has had considerable success in carrying its message of *Hindutva* (literally, Hinduness) to Gujarat, Maharashtra and elsewhere, and bodes well to become a national party.

Almost all parties that are particular to a community or a *jati* have also been particular to a region. Parties that are ostensibly of a region, are often dominated by a particular *jati* in that region. The Lok Dals of the Hindi region, for example were dominated by Jats; the Telegu Desam by Kammas, the Dravidian parties of Tamil Nadu by non-*brahmans*. In addition factionalism is rife and party loyalty weak in most opposition parties. They fissure between and within their constituent *jatis*, between their state units and within them, between and within the personal followings of their leaders and on the lines of individual opportunism and fearfulness. The general failure of opposition parties to oppose effectively, particularly at the Union's center, to offer alternatives to the Congresses, has been one of the primary causes of one-party dominance.

No less than most opposition parties, on the whole, have the Congresses been profuse in their factions and insecure in the loyalties of their members. But the results of this have been ambiguous: at once to facilitate one-party dominance and to undermine it. Parties of factions, unburdened by ideological commitment, inclined to promote middle-class welfare, purposeful primarily in winning elections and positioned to deliver the goods to its voters, the Congresses have patched together their pluralities and majorities from India's vast heterogeneity. Here from one village faction, there from another. Here from one *jati* or *jati* subgroup, there from their rivals. From a constituency alliance here that includes a particular community, from another there that excludes it. From a state coalition here that depends on the support of dominant and twice-born *jatis*, from another there dependent on the support of other backward classes. The myriad, separate cost-benefit calculations that have held the Congresses together in fragments and factions can, however, undo them in fragments and factions. Factions want to know what's in it for them. If Congress (I) is likely to lose this time, how can they avoid the loss or, better still, by a switch in time, gain from it?

The Congresses' dominance has always been tenuous. Where it has been most long-lived, at the center, Congress and Congress (I) have in no parliamentary elections ever won a majority of the popular vote. The Congresses' governments have commanded majorities of 70 to 80 percent of the seats in the lower house of parliament (Lok Sabha). But these have been the magnifications by a first-past-the-post electoral system of popular vote pluralities of 40 to 49 percent. When opposition parties have come together and the Congresses' patchworks have come unstitched, invariably related events of intersecting and complementary cost-benefit analyses, one-party dominance has been vulnerable. In the parliamentary elections of 1967, 1977, 1989 and 1991 Congress or Congress (I) faced more or less "united" fronts of opposition parties and dissident Congressmen. Opposition "unity" has been primarily electoral: an allocation by the Congresses' opponents of electoral constituencies amongst themselves in such ways as to confront the Congresses in "straight fights." The programmatic unity of anti-Congress and Congress (I) opposition fronts has been of their lowest common denominator or largely decorative: the purgation of Congress's sins and policies more favorable to the countryside.

In 1967, a 4 percent loss in Congress's popular vote cost the ruling party more than 15 percent of its seats in the Lok Sabha. In 1977 and 1989, Congress (I)'s popular vote dropped below 40 percent, and it lost its parliamentary majorities and its governments. Largely because of a decline in opposition "unity," Congress (I) gained more seats – enough to form a minority government – with a smaller percentage of popular votes in 1991's parliamentary elections than it had won in 1989's. In the Congresses' defeats, dissidence within them has been as crucial as opposition to them. Of India's four non-Congress prime ministers, all have been dissident Congressmen. Two, Morarji Desai (1977–79) and V.P. Singh (1989–90), had been Congress chief ministers and cabinet colleagues of Congress prime ministers.

Morarji Desai had also been a member of the Congress Party's "syndicate." It was one of Jawaharlal Nehru's instruments for establishing and maintaining a parliamentary democracy that was dominated by one party. The syndicate was the nickname given to the collectivity of Congress's senior state and regional bosses. Nehru acknowledged and accommodated their power. They, in turn, from their bases in local and state politics, produced the patchwork whose sum was Congress's dominance. Under Nehru's guidance, one-party dominance served as a system of tutelage in democratic conflict resolution for a society in which parliamentary democracy was culturally and experientially foreign and in which conflicts were many, inveterate and multiplex.

Peasants, i.e., subject cultivators, learned that through *jati* and factional alliances they could turn ballot papers into wealth, status and power. That they would not in the process turn Congress out of office was the syndicate's job to ensure: by its members' separate and collective knowledge of provincial politics, their positions as leading provincial politicians, their demonstrated political abilities and their common interests in keeping Congress in power. When popular agitation in the 1950s for "linguistic states" threatened Congress's dominance in various parts of India, for example, it was largely within the syndicate that the matter was negotiated and successfully resolved. One-party dominance was maintained. Congress's dominance allowed democratic competition but limited its consequences. My guess is that one-party dominance served to maintain parliamentary democracy by providing it with a cut-off mechanism that kept it from being worked beyond its capacity.

Too, we can only guess as to whether Nehru's faith in parliamentary democracy would have withstood creditable and widespread challenges to Congress's dominance. No less than his successors, India's first prime minister believed that the real alternative to Congress rule in India was chaos. We do know that under cover of the constitution, i.e., its provision for the imposition of "president's rule" from the center, Nehru sanctioned the removal from office in 1959 of the duly elected Communist Party government of Kerala. It may have been no more than a misjudgment, but it was a portentous one.

Among his confidants, none advised Nehru more strongly in favor of deposing the Kerala communists than his daughter. As prime minister, Indira Gandhi, established her personal dominance within Congress, from 1977, Congress (I), and used one-party dominance as her instrument for centralizing in herself political power in India. In this she was assisted by her son and heir-apparent Sanjay, who was killed in an airplane crash in 1981. Within the framework, more or less, of parliamentary democracy, mother and son worked to establish her political hegemony: to reduce to subservience to her, or beholdence, at least, institutions that generate political power and people who exercise it. The rewards of Mrs. Gandhi's regime went to those who professed loyalty to her and her sons, Rajiv succeeding Sanjay, however self-serving the profession or incompetent and dishonest the professor. "Indira is India," proclaimed one of her toadies, "and India is Indira."

She destroyed the syndicate, of course. She vitiated the offices of Pradesh (state) Congress Committee (I) chairman, state chief minister and governor. Henceforth the placemen of Mrs. Gandhi and, after her assassination in 1984, Rajiv, would serve as the leaders of state Congress (I) organizations and legislative assembly parties. The Gandhis appointed them, they hastened to Delhi to be instructed by the Gandhis, and served at their pleasure. Governors, particularly of states ruled by opposition parties, would become the Gandhis' men-on-the-spot: to intervene on their behalf in state Congress (I) politics, to encourage defections from the ranks of non-Congress (I) parties, to give the benefit of post-election doubts to state Congress (I) party claims to government, to find pretexts for recommending the dismissal of "unstable" non-Congress (I) state governments and the imposition of "president's rule" from the center. Gandhi apparatchiks, other than governors, regularly meddled in the factional disputes of opposition parties: fatefully for the prime minister in the Akali Dal's, but no less elsewhere. First, in the series of connected events that culminated in Mrs. Gandhi's assassination, were her efforts and those of her entourage to undermine the dominant position in their party of Akali Dal moderates. They patronized one Sant Jarnail Singh Bindranwale: a murderous Sikh zealot who turned on his Congress (I) patrons and died as commander of the Golden Temple in Amritsar when it was finally stormed by Indian troops in 1984.

The Gandhis' autocratic rule of Congress (I)'s state parties may well have increased, rather than reduced, factionalism and opportunism in them. I suggested earlier, in chapter 4, that for their efforts to rule India's states from Delhi the Gandhis may have decreased the capacities of state Congress (I) parties to reconcile within themselves their factional conflicts, and instead pushed these out into opposition, and provided opposition parties with a rallying cry: the *Dilli Durbar* versus the folk.

In any case, from Indira's first electoral victory in 1967 to Rajiv's defeat in 1989 and 1990, Congress (I)'s dominance all but disappeared from Indian state politics. During those years there were non-Congress (I) governments, however briefly, in all but a handful of states; and in some, Tamil Nadu and West Bengal, for example, non-Congress (I) governments have apparently become the rule. In virtually all states, non-Congress (I) governments have become a possibility, at least, even where there has never been one: in Maharashtra, for example. After the 1990 state legislative assembly elections, all but three of India's large states were ruled by non-Congress (I) governments. With the apparent demise of one-party dominance in state politics, however, the emergence of a conventional European-like system of multi-party competition seems less likely than some Indian variation: for example, competition that is apparently multi-party but whose parties are basically uncertain and shifting alliances of provincial factions.

At India's center, in its national parliamentary politics, a vestige, at least, of Congress (I)'s dominance persists. Though short of a majority, it was the largest single party elected in 1989 to the parliament that was dissolved in 1991 for lack of a viable non-Congress (I) government. After the 1991 elections, again parliament's largest single party, Congress (I) formed a minority government. In ten parliamentary elections, in forty-five years of parliamentary democracy, no viable alternative to the Congresses have emerged at India's center. The coalition front that "united" in 1977 to vindicate parliamentary democracy after two years of Mrs. Gandhi's "emergency" rule, beat her at the polls and formed India's first non-Congress central government. But it disintegrated into its factions after two years in office. Mrs. Gandhi returned to power with her largest parliamentary majority in 1980. The National Front of V. P. Singh that defeated Rajiv's Congress (I) in 1989 was apparently no wiser for its predecessor's experience and shorter lived: it disintegrated into its constituent parties and factions in less than a year. It was then succeeded by one of its factions. On the sufferance and apparently at the behest of Congress (I), the leader of that faction, Chandra Shekhar, served as prime minister for four months until he quit. His faction, turned party for the 1991 elections, virtually disappeared in them.

Factionalism pervades Indian politics. Of party discipline and loyalty, or expectations of them, there is not much. The defection from their parties of members of parliament and state legislative assemblies has become such an ordinary event, that a law was passed during Rajiv Gandhi's prime ministership that compelled individual defectors to recontest their seats. This has probably stemmed the tide of individual defectors. But it hasn't stopped factional politics. It didn't stop, for example, Rajiv Gandhi conniving to award the prime ministership in 1990 to Chandra Shekhar, whose faction numbered about sixty-odd defectors (in a Lok Sabha of 525 members) from the "united front" that defeated the Congress (I) in 1989.

For factionalism's pervasiveness and its corollary, the non-development of stable multi-party competition in India's politics, there are probably a combination of explanations. Politics in India incline towards localism. Parties tend to choose their candidates, particularly for state legislative assemblies, because they are local faction leaders or enjoy their support and/or because they "match" the particular *jati* and communal configuration on which the parties base their local support. Legislative assembly factions are midpoint, so to speak, in factional networks, factions of factions, that connect village *panchayats* to the Lok Sabha. Factions are networks of personal, *jati* and communal relationships between leaders and led, and they are often reinforced by familial dynastic ties. Factions, in general, rather than parties, particularly those which are neither communal nor communist, command their members' loyalties and represent their perceived interests. Parties are primarily the instruments which enable factions to aspire to political power, to attain it and its benefits. Other than in communist and communal parties, factions are non-ideological and function largely to arrange through the political system for the delivery of goods, material and non-material, power and status, electricity and esteem, to their members. If one party can't or won't deliver, then perhaps another can and will. In an economy of real and perceived scarcity, where government decides so much of who gets what, getting the goods and winning in politics are inextricably connected. So, the urgency to win draws factions to the party most likely to win, and if it wins and uses its access to public resources to deliver the goods to the factions that enabled it to win, it may well keep on winning. Here perhaps is the nexus between factionalism and dominance.

It may be that the faction rather than the party will continue to be the basic competitive unit in Indian politics, and that factional competition will incline these politics to the dominance of winning parties. One-party dominance has been an Indian variation on the parliamentary democratic theme, and multifaction competition may be as well. On the other hand, multi-party competition, closer to the European and North American models, may develop as Indian parties reach out for more diverse and mutually competitive groups, other backward classes versus dominant *jatis*, for example; or as these politics become more ideological: *Hindutva*, for example, as opposed to India's constitutional secularism.

Along with and certainly related to the failure of democracy in India to serve its nether quintiles so well as its upper one, the most noted disappointment of democratic political development in India has been the growth in parallel of political corruption and criminality. The "folklore of corruption," as Gunnar Myrdal calls it,[2] is pervasive in India. It is generally believed that political transactions are routinely tainted with corruption. The public servant acts according to how and by whom he is bribed or intimidated. The businessman uses "black money" to buy favors from politicians and bureaucrats. The politician sells his loyalty and pays for votes. And so forth. Any number of politicians have criminal connections and employ thugs to intimidate opponents and "capture" polling booths during elections. There are politicians who are themselves criminals.

A serious comparative study of political corruption and criminality, if such were even possible, might well reveal that these take some particular forms in India but are no more prevalent there and substantial in their economic and social costs than they are now or have been recently in other countries – democratic and non-democratic, bourgeois and Marxist-Leninist, Western and non-Western, "developed" and "developing." Such a study would probably observe that "corruption" is socially defined: what is corrupt in one society is not corrupt in others, ends that are served by corruption in one society are served by legitimate means in others. So, for reasons which are probably clear by now, Indian society is more tolerant of "nepotism" than are Western societies and more censorious of "greed." The tax evasion which is illegal in India and produces great hoards of "black money" is elsewhere managed by notable firms of chartered accountants and produces legitimate investments in foreign tax havens.

There are possible explanations, then, for corruption in India, those above and others. One-party dominance itself, perhaps: in self-evident fulfillment of yet another cliché: that "power tends to corrupt, and absolute power corrupts absolutely." The legal requirements, now disappearing, on businessmen to secure various licenses and permits from bureaucrats in order to carry on their business was a standing invitation to corruption. And even with the passing of this infamous and enterprise-destroying "license-permit *raj*," the carrying on of private business in India is still heavily dependent on government regulations and patronage, i.e., the regulations and patronage of politicians and bureaucrats. Increasing demands on middle-class salary earners, employed in the public sector – for children's school fees, holidays, consumer goods, keeping up with the Joneses of the private sector – explains some corruption. And doubtlessly there are other explanations as well. But comparisons with other places and explanations notwithstanding, corruption is widespread in Indian politics. Outright political criminality is only less so. The "folklore of corruption" probably reflects as much as it affects reality. The fuel of corruption in India is unreported income, i.e., "black money," and some estimates – guesstimates, really – have it as high as 50 percent of India's gross national product. It is common knowledge, for example, that black money pays for 40 to 60 percent of the price of urban real estate: including its most salubrious laundries, the peri-urban "farms" of the gentry. Black money is a major, perhaps *the* major, source of election campaign funding and was the treasure trove of one-party dominance. It is also inflationary, depletive of poverty and drought alleviation programs, conducive to the production of luxury goods and, increasingly, an exacerbation of India's burden of foreign debt. In general class terms, the effects of corruption are to slow economic trickle-down to the poor and to redistribute income within the middle classes. It is one of the darker sides of the development together in India of capitalism and parliamentary democracy.

Another, in some part, at least, is "communalism." In India's political lexicon, "communalism" is antithetical to "secularism." Forever reiterated by their successors, the goal of the founders of the Indian republic was to establish a state that was democratic *and* secular. India's constitutional commitment to secularism is much the same as the United States'. Everyone has the right, within justiciable reason, to profess and practice any religion or none; but there is no "established," i.e., state, religion; and the state is prohibited from favoring any religion or members of any religious community over others.

Secularism in India does not, however, bar legislation which interferes with the religious practices of any community. Again, the Indian constitution specifically outlaws the practice of untouchability, although it was (and still is) a religious practice of some Hindus, *pace* Mahatma Gandhi. The constitution has been interpreted to allow legislation, like the Hindu Code, which makes illegal certain socio-religious practices of Hindu families, e.g., barring daughters' inheritance from their families' landholdings, although these practices may enjoy the sanction of Hindu injunctive scripture.

As one of its "directive principles," article 44 of the Indian constitution commits the Union to the establishment of a "uniform civil code applicable to the entire country." Before the adoption of the constitution in 1950, judicially recognized civil codes of Indian families were not uniform; but derived largely from the separate religions of litigants, sanctioned by their separate injunctive scriptures and modified by their separate *jati* and quasi *jati* customs and usage. So, the promise of a uniform civil code was, by definition, the foreshadowing of legislation that would displace sacred rules from the regulation of Indian family life by rules that were secular – however respectful of religious sensibilities. After forty-two years, it is a promise that has yet to be kept. Most notably, the civil code for Indian Muslims is still derived from the *shar'iah*.

Why? Charitably: because allowing Muslims to regulate at least their family affairs in accordance with the *shari'ah* has been a pattern in politics which Muslims have accepted as second-best, in varying degrees of acceptability: from the Mughal empire to the British *Raj*. By following this pattern in the Indian Union, article 44 notwithstanding, Hindu leaders of the republic's overwhelming Hindu majority have: first, secured the allegiance of Muslims to the Indian Union by assuring them that they are honored citizens of an honored faith; and second, discredited the Muslim League's old bogey, adopted by the Pakistani government, that an Indian republic could only be a Hindu *raj* that discriminated against Muslims. Uncharitably: because Muslims have been Congress and Congress (I)'s vote banks: one-party dominance's pillars, which demonstrated their criticality particularly in 1977 and 1989 when their collapse helped to bring down the edifice.

Taken together, both explanations for the failure of the Union government to legislate a uniform civil code provide a summary, more or less, of why secularism has fared less well in India than has democracy. Obviously, it is, in part, because democracy has fared well. In a democracy, people vote to vindicate those things which they regard as important; politicians appeal for votes by promising to vindicate those things which their constituents regard as important. Most Indians regard their religions and their religious communities as very important: so important that I could not write my introduction to Indian society without extensive reference to these.

Over the twentieth century, Hindus and Muslims have been more and more separating their religions and religious communities one from the other, and the growth of communalism and communal violence has given the separation a fighting edge. So to the basic problem of asking people to adopt secular values when much of what they cherish is sacred and when they have the political power to refuse the request, has been added the exacerbation of conflict within the realm of the sacred. As I write, three of the most worrying issues in Indian politics are communal. The terrorism of Sikh desperadoes in Punjab and general disaffection within its Sikh majority. The terrorism of Muslim desperadoes in Kashmir, the general disaffection within its Muslim majority and Pakistan's involvement in the matter. And, finally, the ongoing escalating and spreading violence between Hindus and Muslims ostensibly over the future of a prayer house of mixed provenance in the Uttar Pradesh town of Ayodhya.

"Awakened" Hindus have argued for some time that the structure in question was originally *Ram Janmabhumi Mandir*: literally, the Lord Ram's birthplace temple. It was destroyed, they allege, by a Mughal emperor in the sixteenth century and Babur's mosque – *Babri Masjid* – built on its ruins. In subsequent centuries, the *mandir-masjid* witnessed the usual eclecticism and tolerance of ordinary Indian worshipers: it was used for prayer by both Hindus and Muslims of the locality. In the late 1940s, however, it was padlocked by a prudent Indian court which declined to decide whether it was *either* a temple *or* a mosque. In 1986, another court opened it to Hindu worshipers, on the plea of the Vishva Hindu Parishad and over the outraged objections of Muslim religious and communal organizations. Now, the Parishad wants to move or demolish the old *mandir-masjid* and build on its ruins a great, new temple to the Lord Ram. Ayodhya has become the focal point for political Hinduism: a place to which pilgrimages are organized, and saffron-robed pilgrims bring consecrated bricks. The furor over Ayodhya's *mandir-masjid* was the cause, in part, of the collapse of the National Front's government at the center in 1990, the most serious rash of communal tensions and violence in India since Partition and the election in 1991 in Uttar Pradesh of a state government ruled by the BJP. Again, it is the party of *Hindutva*; but not, at least among its hierarchs, of reckless, uncompromising *Hindutva*. The Muslim population of Uttar Pradesh is about 15 million.

Hindutva, Hindu nationalism, the belief that in some constitutional, legal, official way the Indian Union ought to be made over into a Hindu state, a state of India's overwhelming religious majority, a tree of its ancient roots, is the great challenge to Indian secularism.

A constitutional commitment to secularism, in India as in the United States, is most critical, I think, as a symbolic commitment by the majority to self-restraint. Except where a minority has secured a monopoly of coercive force, as in South Africa, ethnic, racial and religious minorities, under whatever constitution, live almost everywhere on the sufferance of the majority. Of this, minorities are constantly reminded, in the United States and India, for example, by the infiltration of Christian and Hindu ritual into public ceremonies and by some stark social and political realities. More critical to the maintenance of secularism in India than the constitution's commitment to a uniform civil code is the constitution's embodiment of the Hindu majority's commitment to self-restraint. Indeed, secularism might be better served in India if the Hindu political leaders of India's Hindu majority continue to act as if article 44 were not there. Although this now seems unlikely. Most Indian Muslims would certainly regard the legislation of a uniform civil code not as a vindication of constitutional secularism but a vindictive act of Hindu nationalism: another indication of the majority's decreasing commitment to self-restraint.

The indications are there and growing. In the increasingly, self-conscious Hinduization, ideologically as well as ritually, of ordinary Hindus and sometimes related to their embourgeoisement. As cause and effect of the turmoil and violence that has become ordinary, commonplace and increasingly murderous in inter-communal relations everywhere in northern India and spreading southward. In the solicitation of an inchoate "Hindu vote" by secular politicians; not least when their political fortunes were at risk by the daughter and grandson of Jawaharlal Nehru. In the manufacture of a formulated "Hindu vote" and its consolidation by parties, most notably the BJP, which question the validity of constitutional secularism and secular Indian nationalism.

From winning two Lok Sabha seats and less than 8 percent of the popular vote in the 1984 parliamentary elections, the BJP in the 1989 parliamentary elections leapt to win eighty-eight seats and 12 percent of the popular vote. In 1990, for the first time in the Indian Union's history, a party of Hindu *jagaram* (awakening) was elected to *gaddis* of Indian states: three, Hindi-speaking. In one other, a non-Congress (I) government was formed with BJP support. During the 1980s, the BJP had become increasingly militant and unequivocal in its demands for *Hindutva*, and its strength spread from its base in the Hindi-speaking states to Gujarat and Maharashtra. As a result of the 1990 elections, the BJP became an almost equal partner in Gujarat's governing coalition. In Maharashtra, the BJP in alliance with the Shiv Sena (Lord Shiva's army), a local party of even greater Hindu militance, became a creditable challenge to the Congress's hitherto unchallenged monopoly.

In the 1991 elections, the BJP did even better than it had two years earlier. It won 119 seats in the parliamentary elections and 20 percent of the popular vote. Thus, it became the second party in the Lok Sabha: the leading party of the opposition. Although it lost votes and seats in parliamentary elections in some Hindi-speaking states in 1991, in Uttar Pradesh, the largest of them, and the largest state in India, the home state of the Nehru–Gandhi dynasty, the BJP was voted into government. It lost some ground in Maharashtra, but gained some in Gujarat. In the states of Karnataka and Andhra Pradesh in the south and West Bengal in the east, the BJP established electoral toeholds at least. The BJP's successes in 1991 are all the more impressive because: first, the party fought these elections entirely on its own (except in Maharashtra) and *not* as in 1989 and 1990 after having negotiated seat distribution "unity" with other non-Congress (I) parties; and second, but for the sympathy votes garnered by the Congress (I) after Rajiv Gandhi's murder, the BJP probably would have done even better in 1991 than it did.

Hindutva's fortunes are likely to ebb and flow, from elections to elections. But that it is an idea or more, perhaps a massive urge whose time has come, I have no doubt. So, however destructive *Hindutva* may appear to ideologues of Indian secularism, they can neither ignore it nor argue it away. Neither, of course, will be done by politicians who want to win, whose guiding "ism" is opportunism.

India's constitutional secularism is analogous to its constitutional quasi federalism in this regard: they are both being reconciled with the realities of Indian politics. The reconciliation is largely inexplicit, incremental, ambiguous and the product of time. Not unlike, since the 1960s, the reconciliation of the constitutional provisions for Hindi as the Union's "official language" with the multilingual composition of the Union and the persistence of English as the national elite language. Here are three constitutional provisions: all derived from the conceptions of English-educated elites, all predicated on models of Western parliamentary democracy. All were the determinate gifts of bourgeois revolution from above, all have been made increasingly ambiguous by four decades of parliamentary democracy from below. The Indian tolerance for ambiguity, which I have already noted, is a mechanism for survival in a world which defies rational ordering, but in which there are rational though indeterminate solutions to particular problems.

My guess is that constitutional secularism, in content if not in form, will continue to be reconciled with the political reality that India is a Hindu nation, but nonetheless multi-religious and religiously tolerant. I do not regard as entirely propagandistic the assertion of the BJP supremo that "the Hindu belief is essentially secular,"[3] not second-handedly from the West, but of itself. Historically, constitutional secularism is a restraint on the Abrahamic religions' proclivities to ideological intolerance. It was adopted from this tradition by the English-educated framers of the constitution. But it may be inapposite to Hinduism. Even now, Hinduism does not demand the exclusive adherence of its worshipers to a creed as do the Abrahamic religions; neither does it impose any ideological test on them; nor, as a general rule, does it discriminate against non-Hindus on *ideological* grounds. It was not a usual function of Hindu princes to enforce orthodoxy, discourage heterodoxy and punish heresy. Indeed, these words have virtually no meaning in the lexicon of Hinduism. There is no prescribed path to a God immanent in his universe. The *dharma* is a code of conduct and not a creed. Exceptions of this century notwithstanding, a brief time in the subcontinent's history, a time of European imperialism, of the imperialism of a *raj* whose religious notions were derived from Abrahamic tradition and of the aftermath of that imperial experience, religious tolerance has been ordinary to Hinduism.

If not Hindu tolerance, however, than the prudence of Hindu politicians would seem to compel the conciliation of India's Muslim minority. A uniform civil code or any other legislation that impinges on Muslim concerns will almost certainly be the product not of Hindu diktat but of negotiations between Hindus and Muslims. Muslims know that they negotiate from a position of weakness: a minority, mostly of poor and uneducated people. But not entirely. They are a very large minority, too large and sufficiently well-organized to be trifled with. And their representation in the middle classes, though disproportionately small, is large enough to matter. For more than a millennium, as we noted earlier, Indian Muslims have been inextricably tied – by language, other ethnic traits, and even religious observances – into village and larger Hindu societies in which religious toleration has been the norm, and is so even in these troubled times. On their side, Hindu negotiators represent an ancient religion and a modern India: the one unrivalled among the world's great faiths in its history of religious toleration, the other driven largely by Hindu middle classes which have no interest in avenging the past at the cost of destabilizing the present and endangering the future.

Of India's middle classes, those that earn their incomes from cultivation are most notably the products of the post-independence development of parliamentary democracy in India. I want, here and in one place, to collect and recapitulate some of my scattered observations about the cultivating middle classes and in doing so to supplement and develop these observations. I have demarcated the cultivating classes at *more or less* the upper quintile of landholding farm families. Note the emphasis! What these families have in common is that they are *not* primarily subsistence cultivators. They sell most or much of some of what they produce. In this sense, they are capitalist or at least quasi or protocapitalist producers. Again, that over 80 percent of the wheat grown in India and over 60 percent of the rice is the produce of modern high-yielding varieties, green revolution technology, is some measure of the considerable development of commercial agriculture in India over the past four decades. Moreover, the commercialization of Indian agriculture has taken place through the processes of parliamentary democracy. In this, upper peasantries, at least, and, increasingly, those of the middle, have participated and become through their participation cultivating middle classes. Capitalist agriculture and parliamentary democracy have developed together in the post-independence Indian countryside.

There are regional variations. A family with fewer acres in Punjab, where there is a well-developed infrastructure for capitalist agriculture, may be more paradigmatically capitalist, as well as doing better, than a family with larger holdings in Bihar. While commercial agriculture has not spread at the same rate across India, it has spread steadily and inexorably. Yesterday's line demarcated the cultivating middle classes at half the upper 20 percent of farm families, tomorrow's line may demarcate them at twice these upper 20 percent. The green revolution's spatial and social spread, the momentum of backward classes' and farmers' movements, now having transcended their state arenas to become forces in national politics, propelled by provincial assertiveness and Hindu *jagaram*, are pushing the demarcation line steadily downward. Now, its only foreseeable floor is between the approximately 55 percent of farm families which are effectively landed, i.e., their holdings are more than "marginal" by today's nonuniform and changing standards of marginality, and the 45 percent of farm families which are effectively and absolutely landless: the poor by any standard.

The cultivating middle classes have appropriated for their own benefits the rural reform legislation which was meant by urban reformers to benefit rural society, in general, and particularly the poor: community development, land reform, *panchayati raj*. The green revolution was a rural reform given knowingly to the cultivating middle classes by a Union government which had hitherto failed to foster India's self-sufficiency in food grains, and by its failure had become particularly vulnerable to pressure from Washington. Its success in increasing India's food production and serving the interests of the cultivating middle classes virtually insures the continuation of the green revolution as India's *strategy* for agricultural development, for the development of commercial agriculture.

The cultivating middle classes have been able to make the most of Congress's rural reforms because they were given the political power to do so. It too was the gift of urban reformers: the Indian constitution, a union of quasi federal states, universal adult suffrage and parliamentary democracies at both levels, the Congress system. The cultivating middle classes took the power, and have used it consistently and with notable success to serve their own interests. They threatened Congress's hegemony in the 1950s and 1960s in order to turn the states of the Union into ethnic homelands in which their dominant *jatis* would be concentrated and thereby dominant in their state legislative assemblies. They established state and cooperative financial institutions which meet their demands for credit and for forbearance in the collection of their debts. The levying by any state of a tax on agricultural income they have made politically unthinkable. In bids to pay for and buy the votes of cultivating middle-class families, particularly of backward-classes' *jatis*, the Union and state governments and their parties have vied to forgive the repayment of agricultural loans up to about Rs. 10,000. About half of these have already been "forgiven" *de facto*, i.e., forgotten. Legislative assemblies dominated by cultivating middle classes have established universities in which their sons could find places and bureaucracies and public sector corporations in which they could gain employment. State police organizations have generally shared the cultivating middle classes' dislike of "communists," other "outside agitators" and malcontents among the local hoi polloi who threaten "law and order" in the countryside.

Although divided by *jati* and religious community, the cultivating middle classes have been able to aggregate their interests in order to serve them. They are aggregated, automatically, as it were, in the calculations of politicians who *know*, for example, that upper village households of whatever *jati* will respond in the same punitive way to any government that enhances their irrigation charges. They are aggregated in ministries and the councils of governing parties by representatives of different *jatis* who share the same middle-class interests. They are aggregated in *panchayat samitis* by patrons of different *jatis* who share the same middle-class interests.

Nowadays cultivating middle classes are made up of families from dominant *jatis* and families of, usually, other touchable Hindu *jatis* which form backward classes. In the political scramble to appropriate state resources, particularly since the 1970s, dominant *jatis* whose political center is in upper village households have been joined by backward classes whose political center is in middle village households. Their joinings have been both contentious and collaborative. It would be a pointless exercise, I think, to argue that the lines of contention are *basically* those of *jati or* those of class. They are basically those of *jati and* class, as I suggested in chapter 3.

Contention between dominant *jatis* and backward classes takes place in all the usual politicians' arenas, within and across party lines. The backward classes have at their particular service a constitutional provision which allows Indian governments to discriminate in their favor; by reserving places for students from backward-class *jatis* in medical and engineering colleges, for example, or in government employment. At the service, too, of backward classes is the conclusion (based on evidence that is, at best, seriously flawed) of the relevant official body, the Mandal Commission of 1980, that the appropriate constituent units of "backward" classes are "backward" *jatis*. Thus served, backward classes have been motivated to political action and backward *jatis* to form classes in which their interests can be aggregated and their efforts joined. Doubtlessly, they have also been motivated to aspire by the example of dominant *jatis* which have aspired and succeeded. As economic development proceeds, the apparent opportunities for backward *jati* families to succeed increase, as commercial farmers, for example, or as the families of university educated and professionally employed sons.

In the Indian countryside, as in Western cities, arrivistes must fight their battles with those who have arrived. From time to time, in Gujarat, for example, and in Bihar, regularly, contention between dominant *jatis* and *jatis* of backward classes has exploded into violence. The battle was joined at the center after the 1989 and 1990 elections. The leading party in the short-lived National Front government, the Janata Dal of prime minister V.P. Singh, had done well in the Hindi-speaking north among voters of other backward classes. Singh's post-election promise to establish discrimination in their favor for central government jobs, sparked incidents of violence, including a number of adolescent suicides, throughout India, and contributed to the dissolution of his government. The issue, for the first time one of national politics, has survived him; or more accurately, it has been virtually mooted, to the Janata Dal's disadvantage, by the Congress (I)'s growing interest in the backward classes and their votes. The backward classes are increasingly well-organized, and their *jatis'* members account for perhaps half the Indian electorate. From within the backward classes, the second wave of *embourgeoisées*, who promise to be more numerous than the first, are coming.

Collaboratively, in the guises of farmers' movements, the faces of upper village households of dominant *jatis* and middle village households of backward classes turn angrily together toward the city. From it they demand for all landed farmers "remunerative farm prices" and protest against their "negative terms of trade" for the manufactures of urban India. Their protest is buoyed with folkishness. India does not live in New Delhi's palaces, built on the toil of farmers, its office blocks and guarded bungalows and five-star hotels, but in its villages. Never Indira, but they, the sons of its soil, are India.

In October 1988, for the second time in a decade, thousands of farmers from the Hindi-speaking region converged on New Delhi to hold an extended protest rally against the Union government's alleged discrimination in favor of urban interests. It was an extraordinary event. For weeks the farmers occupied one of the capital's spacious lawns, a lawn laid by the British to imperial proportions, and turned it into their camping grounds. Here they cooked their food on *chulhas* (clay hearths); bathed from plastic buckets, washed their clothing, slept on bales of hay, chatted, played cards, read under the shade of tarpaulins stretched from their tractors, and listened to amplified harangues from their leaders and sympathetic politicians. Wandering into the scene from one of New Delhi's broad avenues the visitor entered what was apparently the enclave of another country. So little did its inhabitants resemble those of their temporary surrounds.

The scene seemed to illustrate the "*Bharat* versus India" juxtaposition that became in vogue among intellectuals a decade or so ago. *Bharat* is the Indian name for India as Deutschland is the German name for Germany, and may be equally evocative of folkishness. *Bharat* is Indian India, the real India, the countryside! "India" is the city: the home of the modern educated and business middle classes.

But appearances and epigrams may deceive. The rural middle classes become increasingly parts of wider middle classes. They are certainly connected to the urban middle classes of the provincial city. It is the cultivating middle classes and not their urban counterparts which are the dominant blocs in the politics that radiate from state capitals. Led by upper village households, the cultivating middle classes become increasingly attached to the provincial city through their investments and participation in local small businesses and through the occupations of their sons. The horizons of the cultivating middle classes tend to be provincial. They are, after all, classes of village-based small holders. Usually circumscribed by state borders, their *jatis* and quasi *jatis* are their primary organizations and their interests are aggregated in state legislative assemblies and *panchayati raj* institutions. In the Indian constitution's division of powers, most of what closely and immediately concerns the cultivating middle classes is allocated to the states: agriculture, land tenure, irrigation, education, local government, administration of justice and police.

But, the farmers rallying in New Delhi in 1988 did not address their demands to their governments in the states. The demands were of the Union government: the government that in various ways determines "remunerative" farm prices and sets the "terms of trade" between agricultural and manufactured goods in an increasingly national market. Of course, the farmers made their demands in the name of the eternal countryside. Like that of any sophisticated interest group, their rhetoric elevates their cause above mere self-interest. But their demands tell their own story. They are the demands of the cultivating middle classes. The sectorial conflict is not between *Bharat* and "India." Quite the contrary, it is within

India. It is an indication, as were the elections held since 1989 and their aftermaths, of the nationalizing of the cultivating middle classes' interests and of the arenas in which they must contest to vindicate them. The sectorial conflict, in other words, is of bourgeois revolution, within the dominant Indian middle classes. On the one side, there are the cultivating middle classes which are politically dominant in the states, but must have power at the center to maintain their dominance as Indian capitalism matures. The educated and business middle classes which have been dominant at India's center are on the other side, and on the defensive.

Industrial development and the educated and modern business middle classes

I do not suggest that independent India's policy for industrial development was consciously formulated to perpetuate the pre-independence alliance of English-educated and modern business middle classes. But this has certainly been one of its major social accomplishments. And it, in turn, has had its economic consequences. How was the alliance perpetuated, by whom, where is it now and with what success has it effected industrialization?

The alliance was perpetuated, built into the very cornerstones of India's policy of industrial development: planning; import-substitution; the occupation by the "public sector," i.e., government-owned and operated companies, of the Indian industrial economy's "commanding heights"; and below these, the stimulation of a "mixed economy" of public and private sector enterprises.

The industrialization that began under the British *Raj* has been continued within the framework of comprehensive, officially planned economic development. Since 1951–52, the basic planning documents have been occasionally interrupted sequential five-year plans issued by the Indian government's Planning Commission. Driven by Nehru, planned industrialization was begun in earnest in the second plan, from 1956–57 to 1960–61. For their periods of operation, the plans establish objectives and priorities of national economic development, specify targets within these in terms of particular goals and/or physical achievements, and recommend requisite public expenditure, private investment and fiscal and regulatory controls to achieve these targets. Under Nehru's chairmanship, the Planning Commission was probably the most powerful decision-making body in India.

But gradually, planning has lost its centrality to Indian economic development. Much of Nehru's enthusiasm for planning died with him, as did much of the relatively unpoliticized planning that he superintended. In general, the second and subsequent plans failed to meet their major objectives, at least until the sixth plan of 1980–81 to 1985–86. Since then, and even before, Indira and Rajiv Gandhi's half measures to liberalize the Indian economy, their partial disempowerment of "license-permit *raj*," has made planning decreasingly relevant to an increasingly buoyant private sector. Coupled with India's experiences, the collapse of eastern Europe's economies from 1989 is unlikely to enhance the enthusiasm of India's middle classes for a planned economy. Still, there is in India a huge public sector of government-owned and operated enterprises, which accounts for about two-thirds of the fixed capital in India's factories and about one-third of the value of their manufactures. Plans are, more or less, the blueprints for its development. The eighth plan began in 1990–91.

Import-substitution has been India's basic strategy for industrialization. Its goals were to make India industrially self-reliant and, ultimately, a major industrial power: to realize its industrial potential and the political ambitions of its rulers. In general, and applicable to heavy basic no less than light consumer industries, India's policy has been to import only those manufactured goods that enhance India's capacity itself to manufacture them. Behind this comprehensive barrier to imports, with little regard to social and economic costs and "comparative advantage," and in spite of a relatively low rate of industrial growth at least until recently, India has become one of the world's twenty major industrial economies. It manufactures virtually everything that is manufactured anywhere: from tinned fruit to nuclear energy. Since the 1970s, the government has encouraged Indian industrialists to export; and although India is still a minor exporting country, the value of its exports has increased, albeit from a very low base, about twenty-fold over the past two decades and about 60 percent of it is in manufactured goods.

In accordance with the landmark Industrial Policy Resolution, which Nehru presented to parliament in 1956, in anticipation of the second plan, the commanding heights of the Indian economy are in the public sector. The government has become the dominant or monopolistic producer and/or supplier of military ordnance, basic iron and steel, ships, heavy engineering and foundry goods, energy from all sources, telecommunications and broadcasting, rail and air transport. India's major financial institutions are also commanded by the government. The life insurance business was nationalized in 1956, as was India's largest bank, the State Bank of India. In 1969 and 1980, Mrs. Gandhi's government nationalized twenty of India's largest commercial banks.

Below these heights, there is a mixed economy in which private industry is encouraged, subject to the government's fiscal and regulatory controls. And subject to competition from public-sector corporations, which have among their activities the manufacturing of automobiles, cement, electronic goods; the operations of hotel chains, warehousing, wholesaling and even retailing facilities.

The architects of this comprehensive policy for industrialization, before and after independence, were an elite of the English-educated middle classes: the premier Indian middle classes of the British *Raj*, of the opposition to it and of the Congress *raj* that succeeded it. They were the same elite it should be recalled, which decided that India should be a secular state and that the family rules of its religious majority should be reformed by a Hindu Code. When Nehru read his Industrial Policy Resolution, they were, in profile: few in number and largely self-perpetuating, urban and high *jati*, educated in English and trained in the law, employed in the bureaucracy or the professions or politics. They were, in a word, a predemocratic, non-business elite: "guardians" as Philip Mason, following Plato, called their British predecessors.[4] They were inclined to the view that educated men know what is best for their society, by the example of the British *imperium* of bureaucrats and from the inspiration of their own *brahman*-hood or equivalents thereof. In establishing a policy for industrializing India, they were not ostensibly concerned to articulate and accommodate the interests of industrial groups which would be affected by such a policy. Rather they were themselves deciding what was best for India.

India's industrial revolution was to be engineered from the top. But definitely *not* from the business top, not by the families of "merchant princes"-cum-industrial magnates of British India. For the educated elite, industrialization was simply too important a matter to be entrusted to Indian industrialists. First, they lacked the resources necessary to initiate an industrial revolution. Second, they lacked the proper motivation. Not the good of society but profit would be their spur. Finally and *sotto voce*, Indian industrialists were at heart still *baniyas*, traders who buy cheap and sell dear. Only the state, i.e., the preserve of the educated middle classes, could industrialize India: by accumulating the necessary resources and allocating them productively and in the interests of society. Those interests, according to the Industrial Policy Resolution, would be best served in a "socialist pattern of society." A society whose government, in accordance with the preamble and directive principles of India's constitution, is committed to providing all its citizens with social, economic and political justice; reducing disparities among them in income and wealth; and preventing the "concentration of wealth and means of production to the common detriment."

So the alliance of urban middle classes, with reference to which I began this discussion, was certainly not a conspiracy, but rather the emergent of circumstances, an entente in consequence of complementarities of real interests rather than compatible ideological positions. The real interests of the educated middle classes were never served in a "socialist pattern of society." It was a pattern that existed only on paper. The real interests of the English-educated middle classes were served in a pattern of industrialization that established them as its directors. By making themselves the premier middle classes of an industrializing India – as its planners, regulators and adjudicators, technical experts and managers – English-educated professionals retained the primacy that they had enjoyed under the bureaucratic *Raj*. India's four largest corporations, for example, are in the public sector and run by bureaucrats.

Indian industry's private sector, the realm of its business middle classes, was ruled in 1956 by the great industrial houses – conglomerates, in modern terms – of a handful of business families: Tatas, Birlas, Dalmias, Singhanias, Goenkas, Thapars and so forth. They were mostly Marwaris from Rajasthan and Gujarati-speaking Hindus, Jains and Parsis. Their operations were concentrated in Bombay and Calcutta. Disparaged in the ideology which underlay the "socialist pattern of society" and relegated by it to second place in India's industrial future, the heads of these great business families were by no means opposed to the general substance of Nehru's Industrial Policy Resolution. Indeed, in their Bombay Plan of 1944, they suggested active roles for the government of independent India in planning, financing and managing industrial development. They understood that in an India that was overwhelmingly rural, agricultural and poor, only government could husband and economically allocate the resources necessary to the development of an industrial infrastructure. It was certainly beyond the capacities of private business, and it was clearly unprofitable.

An import-substitution strategy of industrial development suited the great business houses. The British *Raj* had protected British interests primarily and not theirs. They wanted an Indian government to protect them. However tardily, they had voted with their purses for the protective shield of a Congress *raj, not* for its prod to use their "comparative advantages" in competition with the Japanese on world markets. They had already gone to the British *Raj* to shield them from the Japanese! No, they wanted the vast Indian market for themselves and for whatever they manufactured and without competition from abroad.

They would have preferred fewer government regulations on their activities and less government operation and control of industrial enterprises. In the 1960s, a few industrialists even funded and flirted with a short-lived "free enterprise" party, the Swatantra (freedom). As it turned out, however, it was they who profited most from the "license-permit *raj*" that they berated. In spite of government policies to favor small business in the manufacture of certain items, e.g., leather goods, and to prevent the monopolizing of manufacturing by established big-business houses, they were advantaged *vis-à-vis* smaller and newer businesses in competing for permits to expand their operations and licenses to import. Big business was advantaged not only by their superior resources as such, but by the privileged access these provided to decision-making bureaucrats and politicians. By the mid-1970s, economic power and wealth in the private sector of Indian industry was probably no less concentrated in its twenty largest business houses than it had been two decades earlier.

Over the decades, and particularly from the mid-1970s, this mutually beneficial industrializing entente between elites of the English-educated and modern business middle classes has become *embourgeoisée* into an industrializing scheme of things among the Indian middle classes. As they have grown, so to the pattern of their growth has industrialization, and more recently, the services sector of the Indian economy.

It has grown in size. It is some indication of this, for example, that the number of public-sector companies has trebled from about 6000 in 1961, and that their paid-up capital has grown from about Rs. 10 million to about Rs. 150 million. In the private sector, mostly large and medium size limited, i.e., incorporated, firms have grown in number from about 20,000 to more than 120,000, and their paid-up capital has increased from less than Rs. 10 million to almost Rs. 300 million. The most spectacular industrial growth since the mid-1970s has been in small-scale modern industries. Beginning with the production of simple consumer goods, small industries have now come to hold an important, if not dominating position, in the manufacture of sophisticated electronic goods and precision equipment. In the decade and a half or so since the mid-1970s, the number of small industrial firms has quadrupled to almost 200,000, the value of their manufactures has increased seven-fold to about Rs. 800 million. Small industry employs about 80 percent of India's factory workers, accounts for more than 50 percent of the value added in India's manufacturing industries and about one-third of its exports. Garments and jewelry, India's two major exports, are manufactured almost entirely by small businesses.

Indian industry has grown in its diversities. When Nehru's government announced its Industrial Policy Resolution, about 70 percent of India's manufacturing was in food and textile industries. Now these produce only about one-third of India's manufacturing output which, as I have said before, includes a complete range of capital, intermediate and consumer goods. The growth in size and manufacturing diversity of Indian industry, in both public and private sectors, has been paralleled by a growth in size and diversity of its entrepreneurial and salaried workforce. India's services sector is largely of, by and for its middle classes; and that sector has grown since the 1970s to become larger than either the manufacturing or agricultural sectors of the Indian economy.

I don't know to what extent, but there has certainly been a diversification in the social backgrounds of successful entrepreneurs as a consequence of small business's exponential growth in manufacturing and the provision of services. Self-made and university trained people of other than traditional business *jatis* and families have become small businessmen, and some of them have been notably and exemplarily successful. The great business houses, even their newest and most spectacular rags-to-riches member, the Ambanis, are still largely from traditional business communities, and employ their sons and nephews – and occasionally daughters and nieces – in top management positions. However, as Indian industry moves further from the insularity of import-substitution and more into the mainstream of international commerce its demands for MBAs and the like increase. They, like the technologically and scientifically trained personnel who have made the diversification of Indian industry both possible and Indian, are from an increasingly wide variety of social backgrounds: including, particularly in the public sector, employees from scheduled castes and tribes and backward classes. Indian industry has become increasingly diversified in its sources of capital and technology. Indian share markets have boomed over the past decade or so. The number of stock exchanges has doubled to fifteen. From fewer than 2 million investors in 1980, there are now more than 10 million, and the value of all shares in the market increased from about Rs. 65 million in 1980 to about Rs. 600 million in 1990. In recent years, both through investments and arrangements for technological collaboration, foreign firms have increased their stake, notably in India's industrialization. Through various collaborative arrangements between Indian and foreign firms, foreign investment in India has grown from about Rs. 32 million in 1973 to more than Rs. 1 billion in 1990. Ubiquitous reminders of what until recently was the closed Indian industrial economy are the hyphenated trade names in Indian advertising: Tata-Burroughs in computers, Hero-Honda in motorcycles, DCM-Toyota in light commercial vehicles, BPL-Sanyo in sound systems are just a few of many. In response to India's fiscal crisis of 1990 and as part of the radical liberalization of the Indian economy begun by the Congress (I) government of P.V. Narasimha Rao (about which, more below), a policy of actively encouraging foreign investment in India's industrialization has been adopted in Delhi.

To date Indian governments have been particularly successful in tapping the resources of non-resident Indians (NRIs) for investment in India. Deposits in India under schemes for non-resident Indians, in both rupee and foreign currency accounts, have increased from a value of about Rs. 13 billion in 1981 to about Rs. 110 billion today. Companies owned by non-resident Indians have become major collaborators with Indian firms. Non-resident Indians who have returned to India have brought with them technological skills and consumer goods expectations that they have learned abroad.

Finally, at all levels, the participation of bureaucrats and politicians in Indian industrialization has increased, as has the influence of the cultivating middle classes.

Although the Indian industrial economy has become increasingly liberalized, from the mid-1970s, nevertheless the public sector has grown: from employing about 66 percent of the workforce outside of agriculture and household industries to now employing over 70 percent of that workforce. An area of substantial growth in the public sector has been in administration. "License-permit *raj*" has been partially disempowered, but there are still giant public-sector corporations to run, "sick" industrial units to nurse, export incentive schemes to superintend, and central and state laws, rules and regulations pertaining to industry and almost beyond number to be enforced and not enforced. In India, for every industrial issue, problem, and change of direction, there has been an appropriate bureaucratic response. This, of course, is not surprising when we remember that the public sector is the bastion of the educated middle classes, that they are leading partners in the Indian industrializing entente and that their interests in industrialization are great: as income earners, consumers and Indians.

Though by no means exclusively, Indian politicians are the brokers *par excellence* of India's industrialized economy. The sum of their brokerage fees is doubtlessly staggering, even allowing for fantasy in the Indian "folklore of corruption." Typically politicians collect their "rents" by intervening on behalf of their families or others' into either the bureaucratic or corporate parts of the public sector. Needless to say, they have a great interest in that sector and in its intrusiveness into the private sector. They are the middle classes' middle men.

The Indian states have become major industrializers, in both the public and private sectors. Most of India's public sector belongs to the states. The total value added in factories owned by state corporations is about twice that of factories owned by the center, and more than half of the factory workers in the public sector are employed by the states. State governments – not least and antedating *perestroika*, the communist government of West Bengal – have bid to attract private industries of all sizes by offering land, water and power at concessional rates, promising disciplined or docile labor forces and so forth. By constructing industrial estates and through such institutions as their financial corporations, state governments, and of course, their bureaucrats and politicians, have become major patrons of small-scale private-sector manufacturing.

Government programs to disperse and encourage the dispersal of manufacturing to non-industrialized, "backward" areas and away from overcrowded cities have not been notably successful. Still, in contrast to the all but complete concentration in 1947 of manufacturing in the "presidency" towns of British India, i.e., Calcutta, Bombay and Madras, the geographical spread of Indian industry today is almost as remarkable as its growth in size and diversity. About 15 percent of India's national product is produced by manufacturing. Seven states and territories do better than this, and in only seven small states and territories does manufacturing contribute less than 10 percent to their domestic products. The Indian industrial landscape of today is dotted with large provincial cities: Bangalore in Karnataka, Ludhiana in Punjab, Saharanpur in Uttar Pradesh, Bhilwara and Kotah in Rajasthan, Vadodara (Baroda) and Bhavnagar in Gujarat, and so forth. India's town and city dwellers who were about 17 percent of its population at the time of independence are now about 25 percent. The major growth has been in large and medium size cities, and it has been driven largely by industrial development. An urban population has emerged in independent India which reproduces itself, rather than depending on rural immigration for its reproduction.

From their state bases, the cultivating middle classes have long been the industrializing entente's sleeping partner in this sense: they have imposed their constraints on industrialization. Of these, obvious examples are the uses of their considerable political power to prohibit governments from taxing their incomes or denying them a generous procurement price at which the government guarantees to buy their produce. Of late, the cultivating middle classes seem to be taking a more active role in industrialization, in ways that I have already suggested: in the arenas whose politics they dominate, the states; through investments and participation in small businesses, and by exploiting the employment opportunities now available to their sons in their state's public and private sectors. Their increasing presence in national politics may have some effects on government decisions about the pace and emphases of industrialization.

With what success have the Indian middle classes effected the industrialization of their country? Indian industrialization has been least successful in realizing the social goals of the Industrial Policy Resolution. It has had mixed success in itself. It has been most successful in serving the interests of the middle classes.

That "objective of social and economic policy," including industrialization, accepted by the Indian parliament in 1954, the establishment of a "socialist pattern of society," has never been reached. Indeed, it has never been seriously approached: unless government-orchestrated capitalism is taken to mean "socialism." Although it

Table 7. India in Asia, 1990–91: social and economic indicators (figures below should be regarded as indicative)

	Pop. (m)	Pop. growth rate (%)	Infant mortality (per 1000)	Literacy (%)	People per doctor	GNP per cap. ($US)	GDP growth (%)	Exports 12 mos. ($US)	Sur./def. cur. a/c ($US)	Foreign debt ($US)	Inflation CPI (%)
Bangladesh	116	2.7	108	33	6,219	179	6.2	1.5b	−800m	10.8b	9.3
Burma (Myanmar)	43	2.1	59	79	3,797	278	4.5	0.7b	−400m	4.5b	35.0
Cambodia	8	2.2	116	48	36,000	110	0.0	0.04b	NA	0.6b	10.0
China	1,150	1.4	27	73	724	325	5.0	62.1b	6,270m	45.4b	2.1
Hong Kong	6	0.9	6	88	1,024	12,069	2.4	82.0b	4,820m	0.0	11.9
INDIA	843	2.1	88	41	2,522	350	4.5	19.3b	−8,900m	69.8b	10.0
Indonesia	183	1.8	65	74	8,010	555	7.0	26.8b	−2,400m	65.7b	9.1
Japan	124	0.4	5	100	635	23,570	4.9	290.0b	33,820m	0.0	3.3
Laos	4	2.9	97	84	6,495	180	9.1	0.6b	−94m	0.6b	18.6
Malaysia	18	2.3	14	73	2,656	2,305	10.0	29.1b	−1,740m	15.5b	3.1
Nepal	20	2.3	118	21	20,356	170	2.0	0.2b	−300m	1.5b	11.5
Pakistan	115	2.9	98	26	2,086	365	5.6	6.0b	−1,700m	19.5b	6.0
Philippines	63	2.3	40	89	1,090	727	3.0	8.2b	−2,983m	29.4b	14.9
Singapore	3	1.1	7	90	753	11,575	8.3	52.2b	1,898m	0.0	3.4
South Korea	43	0.9	21	93	1,216	5,569	8.6	65.0b	−2,050m	30.4b	12.0
Sri Lanka	17	1.3	24	86	7,253	430	5.1	1.8b	−300m	5.3b	21.3
Taiwan	21	1.2	5	91	1,010	7,990	5.2	66.8b	10,870m	0.0	4.1
Thailand	55	1.4	24	89	5,564	1,418	10.0	20.3b	−3,236m	27.3b	6.0
Vietnam	68	2.2	54	94	3,140	200	2.4	2.1b	−500m	14.6b	90.0

Source: Asiaweek, August 9, 1991, pp. 6–7.

survives in the visions of ideologues and the verbiage of politicians, a "socialist pattern of society" has not survived four decades of Indian industrialization as its real or realizable objective. Still to be laid by Indian industry are "the economic foundations for increasing opportunities for gainful employment and improving living standards and working conditions for the mass of the people." Nowadays, fewer than one-fifth of Indian workers are employed in industry. Ironically, the limited opportunities for industrial employment in India are the consequence of the strategy of industrialization endorsed by the Industrial Policy Resolution: to develop behind the protective wall of import-substitution basic and intermediate goods industries which are inherently capital rather than labor intensive. Small businesses were meant to be *the* mass employers, but they have not employed masses large enough to ameliorate India's chronic unemployment and underemployment. Over the past decade and a half there has *not* been an increase in employment by small businesses commensurate with their boom in productivity.

At various points earlier in this work, I indicated and appreciated the achievements of Indian industrialization *qua* industrialization: and once again, these have been considerable. But less considerable than they might have been. Starting from a very low base, India's annual growth rate of GDP from manufacturing was about 7 percent until the drought years of the mid-1960s. But then for various reasons of supply and demand, over which economists contend, industrial growth declined to about 4.5 percent annually – a very low rate of industrialization – for almost two decades until the mid-1980s. From then, briefly, industrial production grew at an Indian record rate of about 8 percent annually until it was slowed by drought in 1986–87 and finally brought to decline, however temporarily, in 1991 by fiscal crisis and the new Indian government's efforts to meet it and in the process to restructure radically the Indian economy. In any event, save Bangladesh, Sri Lanka, Myanmar (Burma) and the war-torn and strife-ridden countries of Southeast Asia, India has over the decades since 1960 the slowest industrial growth rate in Asia (see table 7 for other comparisons).

In general, industries in the public sector have been disappointing and expensive industrializers. Indian public-sector firms have used more capital to produce a smaller output than comparable firms in the Indian private sector. Indian private-sector firms, sheltered by import-substitution, are less efficient producers than many comparable firms abroad. To reduce these inefficiencies was one of the goals of the liberalization of the Indian economy that began in the mid-1970s, and accelerated, for a while, particularly after the budget brought down by the Rajiv Gandhi government in 1985. But while these liberalizing reforms reduced some of the worst excesses of "license-permit *raj*", e.g., confiscatory tax rates which invited evasion and labyrinthine licensing procedures which reduced efficient manufacture, they left its bureaucratic structure largely intact, and the structure – buttressed by its political allies – soon overwhelmed the reforms.

Another goal of the Gandhis' reforms was to encourage exports and export-led industrialization. As I have noted, exports increased during the 1980s. But imports increased more rapidly and substantially. India's balance of payments deficit trebled over the decade as did its external debt. It became one of the "third world's" major international debtors; and by the end of 1990, it was desperately short of hard currency reserves to pay its debts and buy its necessary imports, e.g., petroleum. Over the 1980s, India's internal debt, too, grew exponentially: largely as a result of excessive government borrowings to prop up an economy that was closed, inefficient, regulated and subsidized. Relatedly, and exacerbated by the "oil shock" of the Gulf War, inflation climbed to 12 percent, in a country where half the population lives in relative to dire poverty; and prominent among those items whose prices rose most dramatically were "wage goods": items of ordinary consumption, mostly food-stuffs, the consumables of the poor. In January 1991, hat in hand, the government in Delhi asked the International Monetary Fund (IMF) for an emergency loan to rescue the Indian economy.

Yet again: though *generally* insufficient, the benefits of India's economic growth over the past forty years have accrued *particularly* – though not entirely – and with relative sufficiency to the middle classes. Reasonably, this should elicit neither surprise nor concern, given that economic growth in India has been an integral part of the more comprehensive growth of capitalism and parliamentary democracy in more or less tandem. The cause for concern is this: that the middle classes over these decades have developed vested interests in patterns of economic growth that now constrain the liberalization of the Indian economy, that now constrain further growth. In this sense, the constraints on economic growth in India are political. To illustrate this, a brief recapitulation.

A planned and regulated economy with a vast public sector where import-substitution has been the basic policy for industrial growth, however inadequate that growth, has nonetheless vested the educated middle classes, including politicians, with positions as patrons, promoters, regulators, directors and managers of industry, technicians and other privileged members of the industrial salariat. It has made available to them "rents" whose total is incalculable. From the British *Raj* to the "license-permit *raj*," they have remained India's premier middle classes.

Indian manufacturers, large and small, have vested interests in protecting from the competition of foreign imports or the intrusion of foreign firms the vast domestic markets for Indian-made goods that are more than sometimes overpriced and shoddy. "Black money" buys Indian industrialists, among other things, grease for the bureaucratic and political wheels within wheels on whose turnings the fortunes of almost every Indian enterprise depends.

The cultivating middle classes exchange their votes and local influence for politicians' assurances that farmers' incomes will not be taxed, that fertilizer and other inputs which they must buy will be subsidized by the government; that the government will maintain remunerative floor prices for their products, supply them with virtually free electricity and irrigation waters, and forgive their debts.

These patterns may now be changing. The shock of India's fiscal crisis, its depth and the fear of its adverse consequences for further economic growth and bourgeois well-being; the IMF's stringent loan conditions – "deflate, devalue, denationalize and deregulate"[5] and the growing realization among Indian businessmen and bureaucrats that liberalization of its economy is Hobson's Choice for India – all this made certain that the issue of economic liberalization would be seriously addressed by P.V. Narasimha Rao's Congress (I) government rather than being fiddled with or finessed. Indeed, one of this government's first acts was to devalue the rupee by about 20 percent. Led in its drive to economic liberalization by a competent and determined finance minister, Manmohan Singh, the government has apparently begun on an irreversible course toward meeting squarely the IMF's other "de-" conditions:[6] a radical departure for India from its economic path of four decades, an abandonment of the Nehruvian legacy – at once embraced and scorned – of "license-permit *raj*" in favor of a comprehensive and alternative economic policy.

"India is an economic miracle waiting to happen."[7] Perhaps! We know that the wherewithal is there. But it seems unlikely that the economically miraculous will happen directly or quickly. And it may not happen at all. For example, with no proportionate increase in agricultural production, government subsidization of fertilizer, which is of disproportionate benefit to upper village households, increased ten-fold in the decade to 1991 – twice the rate at which total government expenditure increased. Had the Delhi government not capitulated to farmers' protests in 1991 against Manmohan Singh's plan to cut fertilizer subsidies by 40 percent, it is likely that Congress (I)'s factions would have torn the party apart, the opposition parties which support the Narasimha Rao minority government would have abandoned it, and the government would have fallen.

Vested interests in India are interdependent. Fertilizer subsidies compensate farmers for the relatively high price of manufactured goods. Government subsidies to manufacturers, e.g., tariffs, which are the world's highest, contribute to the high price of manufactured goods. But they are also a major source of government revenue. If tariffs are reduced, from whose pockets will the revenue come? Devaluation will increase inflation, and more rather than less may have to be spent on food subsidies for the poor – now about half the cost to the government of fertilizer subsidies. The argument that savings can be effected through more efficient administration collides with the reality of educated middle classes' interests in inefficient administration. Their interests also collide, of course, with denationalization and deregulation. And so forth.

Liberalization is more likely to resemble, at best, the surgeon's scalpel or, at worst, his triage than the magician's wand and before there are any economic miracles, things are likely to get worse before they get better, for some people at least. Which people? Whose vote banks? With one-party dominance either dead or dying or in suspended animation, liberalization of the Indian economy is unlikely to succeed unless it is supported by a wide consensus among politicians across factional and party lines. Or in other words, a necessary, though in itself insufficient prerequisite for any economic miracle in India is a general acknowledgement among Indian politicians of the Indian economy as a subject for policy-making, primarily, rather than as a great milch cow to nurture their separate vote banks. This is the political miracle waiting to happen.

And it just might. The Union Budget for 1992–93, presented by Manmohan Singh and passed by parliament may become a landmark in modern Indian history. It portends the death-knell, finally, for "license-permit *raj*," Nehruvian "socialism" and signals the gradual establishment of a market economy that, rather than "free," is likely to be much freer than it has been. More, the budget holds open to the Congress (I), at least, and its fellow-travellers the possibility of their commitment to a *program* of economic reform: long-term, comprehensive, internally consistent and politically calculated – but without the vote-catching gimmickry that has in recent years been paraded as policy. In 1992, no parliamentary government in New Delhi would or could alter the dominant pattern of change in India from bourgeois revolution. The new Indian economy envisaged by Manmohan Singh will promote bourgeois revolution, certainly, but only by breaking the nexus between it and economic inefficiency and unproductiveness.

International politics

There is a persistence in India's international politics. Pakistan has always been their concern: primarily, most of the time, and at other times collaterally. The issue of Kashmir has almost always been at the center of this concern, or close to it. In their political relations, there is an underlying contentiousness between India and Pakistan which from time to time has burst into violent conflict. They have fought three wars: in 1948, 1965 and 1971. During the last war India facilitated the secession from Pakistan of more than half its population, of East Pakistan, now Bangladesh. Between wars, across the guarded, mountainous borders that separate these unfriendly neighbors, there have been recurring exchanges of artillery fire and other military incidents. India has at times denied its airspace to Pakistan, and Pakistan has appointed itself the champion of Indian Muslims against Hindu "oppression."

The ongoing quarrel between India and Pakistan conflated with the Cold War, Sino-Soviet and Sino-Indian hostilities, was exacerbated by them, and has survived their apparent amelioration. These conflations gave immediate and circumstantial meaning to India's stated foreign policy, longstanding and well known, of "nonalignment." But nonalignment's underlying meaning with regard to South Asia, i.e., India's abiding claim to regional predominance, continues to be thwarted by Pakistan, in spite of New Delhi's increasing assertiveness. So India's relations with Pakistan are as contentious as ever and as centered in Kashmir. An armed secessionist movement of Muslims, abetted, at least, by Pakistan, now operates in the Indian state of Jammu and Kashmir. Increasingly,

India's domestic politics have become communal and militantly Hindu. Pakistan's domestic politics have become increasingly "Islamic," and that has probably aggravated its "inability to solve its problem of national identity except in anti-Indian [and/or anti-Hindu] terms."[8]

For India, the issue of Kashmir is not open to negotiations with Pakistan. It is a domestic matter. A former princely state, Jammu and Kashmir, of which the latter is all but a southwestern corner, has been part of the Indian Union since its inception: from the time of the subcontinent's partition and legally, under terms established by the departing British government. By vote of its constituent assembly, Jammu and Kashmir became an Indian state in 1957, and its statehood has been popularly affirmed in the regular exercise by Kashmiris of the same democratic rights enjoyed by all Indians. At least in theory. Given the chance, the party that most Kashmiri Muslims would have voted for, the Plebiscite Front, was illegal until 1975.

The right to secede is not a democratic right in India. The Indian government represses secessionism wherever it occurs, including Kashmir. But really, secessionism in Kashmir is different. A secessionist movement of Indian Muslims – and Kashmiri Muslims are Indian nationals no less than their coreligionists in Kerala – which enjoys the moral, material and diplomatic support of Pakistan, strikes at the rawest edges of India's domestic politics: between defenders of secularism and champions of *Hindutva*, between guardians of the *shar'iah* and advocates of a uniform civil code, between Hindus and Muslims.

By no means was Kashmir the only unfinished business of Partition. India and Pakistan squabbled for years over the division of government assets, refugee property, irrigation waters. But while all of these conflicts have been resolved, the issue of Kashmir has not. Its history is briefly this. Jammu and Kashmir was ruled by a Hindu dynasty, but most of its subjects, concentrated in Kashmir, were Muslims. The principality bordered on India to the south and Pakistan to the west. Its maharaja might have acceded to either. But he hesitated. He was in a difficult position, to say the least; and, in desperation, perhaps, or folly, toyed with the idea of independence.[9] Pakistan tried to force the issue by joining the efforts of armed Muslim tribesmen to depose the maharaja. Frightened, he acceded to India. Indian soldiers were airlifted to Kashmir where they fought a year's war with Pakistani soldiers, only yesterday members of the same army. The fighting ended with a cease-fire agreement signed in January 1949 and negotiated through the United Nations.

The agreement left both sides in temporary control of those portions of Jammu and Kashmir that were occupied by their troops. About two-thirds of the area was held by India, including its core, the Vale of Kashmir. The Pakistanis held a corner in the northwest. Both parties agreed that the issue would be permanently resolved and the future of Jammu and Kashmir decided by a plebiscite of its people. But subsequently, time and again, and always to Pakistan's infuriation, India found grounds to renege on its agreement. A plebiscite has never been held in Jammu and Kashmir.

Had it been, it is most unlikely that Jammu and Kashmir would now be a state in the Indian Union. Whenever taken, the votes of its Muslim majority would almost certainly have been either to join their coreligionists in Pakistan or, if given the option, to become an independent country. Either way, in New Delhi's estimation, the consequences would probably have been disastrous for India. A hostile government in Pakistan's Islamabad or Jammu and Kashmir's Srinagar would hold hostage the Himalayan headwaters of the Indus River's tributaries which irrigate Punjab's agriculture. The southern borders of a hostile Jammu and Kashmir, well below the Himalaya's sheltering peaks, would be dangerously close to the Gangetic Plain, northern India's heartland.

But the direst consequences of a Muslim electorate voting to separate itself from India would certainly be in its shock to communal relations between Hindus and Muslims in India, and, relatedly, to the secular legitimacy of the Indian Union. Would such a vote not seem to confirm Pakistan's contention, inherited from the Muslim League of British India and broadcast throughout the subcontinent and to the world that: if ordinary Muslims were given the choice they would live in a Muslim country and not in some "secular" Indian *raj* that was really a Hindu sham. They would affirm by plebiscite the argument of Muslim middle-class nationalists from Sir Saiyid Ahmad Khan to Mohammad Ali Jinnah to Islamabad's current rulers that the subcontinent was the home of "two nations."

And what would have been the likely consequences in India of this affirmation? The fear, not unfounded, has been of spontaneous and instigated anti-Muslim pogroms in spates across northern Indian, in particular. For years after Partition, its wounds festered. North-Indian towns, particularly Delhi, accumulated large populations of refugee families and their remnants of Sikhs and Hindus who had experienced the horror and escaped from it with no kindly feelings toward Muslims. Communal relations in many north-Indian towns have not been easy, in some cases since the 1920s; and in the past two decades, the recorded number of violent communal incidents here and elsewhere has been steadily increasing. Today, communal relations are at their worst since Partition.

Would a Kashmiri Muslim vote in favor of seceding from the Union not have given credence to the reiterated accusations of Hindu militants that India's Muslims are, in effect, Pakistan's "fifth column": not merely a religious minority but a subversive presence. And if such an accusation were widely accepted by Hindus, and they denied the reality of equal citizenship to their Muslim neighbors, what would have been the nation-building consequences for India? And what then of India's constitutional commitment to secularism? What then of the validity of its founders' rejection of the Muslim League's contention that India had two nations and Congress's claim to have established a secular state on the subcontinent: one nation of religiously diverse Indians?

Nowadays, of course, there are many Indians who argue that such a claim should never have been made. So, these days, the proponents of a plebiscite in Kashmir, the "liberation front" and its friends in Pakistan, confront not only an unmovably defensive secularism, but a militantly aggressive Hinduism. It, certainly, will never surrender to Muslim votes the Himalayan abode of the Lord Siva, and the sacred sites and pilgrimage places associated with Him in Kashmir.

Finally, would secessionism in Kashmir not have encouraged it elsewhere: among Sikhs and tribes of the northeast, for example, in Assam and Tamil Nadu? And if the army, already overused to quell domestic disturbances, were to become the force that held the Union together, what would be the consequences for it, for Indian democracy, for the integrity of the Indian Union. No, a handful of Kashmiri Muslims – about 5 million, now – will not be permitted to determine the Indian Union's fate. There has not been and there will be no plebiscite in Kashmir.

There will probably be no war, either. To keep Kashmir, India need not fight one. And Pakistan cannot win one to capture it. It can only use the Kashmiri issue as grist in its domestic politics and to embarrass India internationally, and particularly in Muslim countries. The "liberation front" is not fighting Indian troops to make Jammu and Kashmir a Pakistani province. It wants an independent state, which would include, of course, Azad (free)

Kashmir – Pakistan's portion. In its efforts to (re)"internationalize" the Kashmir issue, Islamabad enjoys virtually no support from either of its great friends in Washington and Beijing or in the post-Cold War United Nations, among whose sovereign states secessionism has never been a popular cause.

The conflations of Indo-Pakistani contentiousness with the international politics of the United States, the Soviet Union and China have largely determined the course of India's nonalignment. Nonalignment may be understood as a moral and rational position for third parties in a cold war among nuclear armed superpowers. Or it might be understood in the spirit of George Washington's farewell address as a general prescription for serving one's own interests by remaining aloof from the quarrels of others and profiting from their distress. And, of course, it may be understood as both. They are not mutually exclusive. India has understood them as both. In any case, Pakistan responded predictably to India's nonalignment by becoming the United States' SEATO and CENTO ally. Smaller and weaker than India, of less Cold War significance, Pakistan nonaligned was less well-positioned than India nonaligned to profit from the quarrels of the superpowers. Pakistan was more likely to profit, *to strengthen itself vis-à-vis India*, by joining its quarrel with India to the global strategy of the United States. In the 1950s, Washington offered its diplomatic and military assistance to allies on the periphery of the great, mythic Sino-Soviet land mass.

There was in Pakistan, a persistent belief that the Indian government had accepted the subcontinent's division in 1947 not as a final settlement but only to get rid of the British. Finally, the Congress *raj* would try to undo Partition and reabsorb Pakistan into Hindustan. In a sense, Pakistan's insistence on a plebiscite in Kashmir, its claim to a Muslim irredenta in the Himalayas, was the offensive thrust of a defensive strategy. It was to support this thrust, India feared, that Pakistan had become an American ally, for whatever ostensible Cold War reasons the alliance had been offered. In international politics, certainly, an enemy's enemy is a friend.

From the alliance between Pakistan and the United States, a growing entente between nonaligned India and the Soviet Union was the consequence. Only with eastern Europe did India consistently maintain a balance of trade surplus. The Soviet Union became India's major supplier of arms and its champion in the United Nations and elsewhere on the issue of Kashmir. India was most reluctant, to say the least, to censure Soviet military ventures: from its suppression of the Hungarian revolution in 1956 to its invasion of Afghanistan in 1979. Thus was the issue of Kashmir incorporated into the Cold War and the Cold War incorporated into the issue of Kashmir.

In 1962, Cold War lines blurred momentarily on the subcontinent and nonalignment was momentarily vindicated. Having separately and in spite of their mutual hostility identified China as their Asian enemy, the United States and the Soviet Union provided India with diplomatic and military support during and after its lost border war with China. But the moment passed. Pakistan, perturbed by American military aid to India, for the same reason that SEATO and CENTO aid to Pakistan perturbed India, moved toward an anti-Indian rapprochement with China.

In spite of its membership in the United States' Cold War alliance system, Pakistan's relations with China had been generally amicable. Presumably, China shared India's understanding of Pakistan's primary motivation for becoming an American ally. After 1962, India's two most threatening foreign policy concerns seemed to merge into one: a Sino-Pakistani axis on the subcontinent. It troubled India's defeated and demoralized army with the terrible apprehension of concerted attacks across the borders of West Pakistan and China into Rajasthan, Punjab and Kashmir and across the borders of East Pakistan and China into the short and narrow corridors that connect India's northeastern wing (of Assam and the tribal states) with the rest of the Union.

When in 1965, war finally came, however, it was a much less dramatic, more modest affair: a limited conflict between India's and Pakistan's armies that began in the Rann of Kachchh and ended, predictably, in Kashmir. China supported Pakistan with arms and anti-Indian invective, but did not join the battle directly. A truce between the belligerents, which more or less restored the *status quo ante* was mediated by the Soviet Union at Tashkent in 1966. Afterwards, Islamabad resumed its ties to the United States which had been more or less neutral in favor of Pakistan during its second war with India and regarded Pakistan still as useful in the Cold War. At the same time, Washington, by some heavy handed use of its intelligence agencies and the levers of its aid programs to intrude into India's domestic affairs and influence its foreign policy, raised the specter of ''neocolonialism'' in New Delhi. The complementarity of Soviet and Indian interests *vis-à-vis* the Sino-Pakistani entente was undisturbed by the 1965 war, and New Delhi renewed its special relationship with its most steadfast and unobtrusive supporter.

Moscow had long accepted and encouraged India's claim to being the predominant power in South Asia: again, the regional corollary of its nonalignment policy. As a consequence of the Bangladesh War in 1971, India seemed to have achieved its predominance. For two and a half decades the West Pakistani ruling elite of their country had exploited, repressed and disparaged the Bengalis of East Pakistan. In response, their demands for provincial autonomy had become increasingly strident, and in the elections of 1970 they had voted overwhelmingly for the party of East Pakistani autonomy, the Awami League. The Pakistani government nullified the elections and sent its army to occupy East Pakistan and suppress its autonomy movement. The suppression was done with great brutality. Millions and millions of refugees fled into India, many if not most of them Bengali Hindus. They brought to their refuge the unhealable wounds and the nightmare stories of a holocaust, and the great economic and political burdens of their maintenance. The Indian army mobilized and trained a *mukti bahini*, an irregular "liberation army," of former East Pakistani soldiers, and finally led them in a successful, lightning war of secession. Under India's aegis, East Pakistan became the independent republic of Bangladesh in 1971.

While these events unfolded, President Nixon and his Secretary of State, Kissinger, were busily engaged in arranging the United States' rapprochement with China. Pakistan's military government was their intermediary. American foreign policy "tilted" toward the support of Pakistan; and presumably to make this clear to Indira Gandhi, a United States naval task-force was dispatched to the Bay of Bengal. "Madam" was unintimidated. While in two weeks the Indian Army defeated the Pakistanis and the Indian navy destroyed the port from which they might have been evacuated, the *U.S.S. Enterprise* and its sister ships stood at anchor off Chittagong. Then they sailed away.

Presumably, Mrs. Gandhi's courage was fortified, in part, by the Indo-Soviet treaty of friendship and cooperation, signed in 1971 before India invaded East Pakistan. It was not quite a mutual security pact, but close enough. It is an irony of India's nonalignment that it should have produced for it one of the most durable and unwavering alignments in post-World War II's international politics. The *Enterprise*'s departure signalled a lesser fidelity: that America's interests in South Asia and Pakistan's territorial integrity were worth bluffing but not fighting for. In any case, General Yahya Khan had maneuvred Pakistan and its army into a political and military cul-de-sac in the east from which only the most committed or reckless ally might have tried to save them. The United States was neither. Nor was China. It made the appropriate gestures in support of Pakistan, but Beijing did not intervene directly.

Post-war, the political configuration of the subcontinent seemed to change dramatically in India's favor. At a stroke, a hostile Pakistan had disappeared from India's eastern flank to be replaced by a poor, war-ravished neighbor which owed its independence to New Delhi. Of Pakistan, only its former western province remained: its population, about one-tenth of India's, smaller than its Muslim minority. Its army defeated, its allies having failed it, its domestic politics in turmoil, its economy weakened, Pakistan turned for assistance and acceptance to the Muslim west, to the Shah of Iran and friendly Arab countries. It seemed to turn away from India and the futility of trying to redeem Kashmir from it. Indeed, Kashmir seemed irredeemably India's. In 1975, Mrs. Gandhi offered the chief ministership of the Indian state of Jammu and Kashmir to India's long-serving and most famous political prisoner, head of the proscribed Kashmiri Plebiscite Front, champion of self-determination for his people, the Lion of Kashmir, Sheikh Mohammad Abdullah. He accepted the offer. He accepted that there would be no plebiscite. The issue of Kashmir seemed closed.

After its easy defeat by China in 1962, India made costly and strenuous efforts to improve its army. Its offensives in Kashmir in 1965 and in East Pakistan in 1971, were notable and the reinforcement of its defenses on China's borders was formidable. In its next war with the Chinese, the Indian Army was likely to be a well-matched opponent. To strengthen its defenses, India annexed its Himalayan protectorate, Sikkim, in 1975. The year before, as a message to China, particularly, India exploded a nuclear "device" in the Rajasthan desert.

Although the contested borders over which India and China fought in 1962 have never been settled *de jure* by negotiations and treaty they seem to have been settled *de facto* by inaction, time, an exchange of prime ministerial visits and a return to diplomatic business as usual. There is still the occasional exchange of angry words, but neither side is willing to fight for territory that it doesn't have, and both sides have under their control the territory that they most want. The Indians have the area south of the Tibetan–Chinese border in Arunachal Pradesh, formerly the North East Frontier Agency. That territory, like Sikkim, is incorporated in India's defenses of its militarily vulnerable northeastern wing. The Chinese have the Aksai Chin plateau in northern Kashmir, more than 30,000 square kilometers of barren waste, through which they have a strategic road connecting Xinjiang and Tibet. The plateau is of no particular interest to India, except that it is in Kashmir. For that reason, primarily, India will not negotiate a border settlement based on lines of control, in spite of China's willingness to do so. To every government of the Indian Union, in principle, if not in fact, the territorial integrity of the state of Jammu and Kashmir is non-negotiable. And not, of course, because China holds some of Kashmir, but because Pakistan does, too, and all of it is Pakistan's irredenta.

Although the future is no more certain in South Asia than it is anywhere, than it was in the Persian Gulf in mid-1990, nowadays at least, China is less a source of worry to India than the yardstick against which New Delhi measures its international stature. To be a great power of the second division, a predominant regional power, India must measure up to China, particularly in its military capabilities. The standard of measurement is costly and unimaginative, to be sure, when Japan is a great power of the first division, for example, but it is still in use, and not only in South Asia. So, most of the competition between India and China these days is not so much with one another but against a common standard. With the apparent end of the Cold War and the return to amicability of Sino-Soviet relations, China's interests in South Asia have become minimal. It is not China that thwarts India's ambition to be the predominant regional power, but Pakistan.

With 10 percent of India's population and a much smaller industrial base, Pakistan has been able to retain a rough military parity with its great neighbor to the southwest. It has managed this by keeping a large and competent military establishment and availing it, as I have already suggested, with the military resources or resources for military use of countries outside the region, but with some interests in it that can be served by Pakistan. Of these the United States and China have been the most prominent. Arab wealth has funded the ''Islamic [nuclear] Bomb'' that Pakistani technologists have been working to develop for years, and may well have developed. Israel is perhaps the model of a small country which can do better than hold its own against hostile and more populous neighbors by combining a good military force, access to the military resources and diplomatic support of a great friend and, more problematically, a nuclear deterrent.

For its services as Washington's front-line state in its proxy war with the Soviet Union in Afghanistan, Pakistan was rewarded with an arsenal of some of the best American military hardware. Indeed, to India's great displeasure, American military largess to Pakistan since 1979 has probably readjusted, though not redressed, the South Asian balance of power that tipped so decidedly to India's advantage after the Bangladesh War. Today, Pakistan would probably be able to keep up with and perhaps better India in their usual short–sharp war. But on the issue over which it would be fought, Kashmir, India would not accept a short–sharp rebuff. It might even welcome the opportunity to substantiate its claim to regional predominance by beating Pakistan soundly, once and for all, and, if need be, in a war of military attrition.

In lieu of this, and in spite of Pakistan's unwillingness to acknowledge it, India's predominance in South Asia is being more and more aggressively displayed in New Delhi's demonstrations of military and political force. India's rapidly and expensively developing blue-water navy has virtually no defensive function except to vindicate India's claim to regional predominance. New Delhi anticipates no war at sea. Apart from the acknowledged nuclear powers, including China, and Israel, only India has developed an intermediate-range ballistic missile capability. The Indian army's "peace keeping" enterprise in Sri Lanka from 1987 to 1989, may have produced a debacle but it delivered New Delhi's message. If there is to be foreign intervention into the domestic affairs of South Asian countries, other than Pakistan, it will not be by Pakistan or its friends, but by India. India intervened to frustrate a *coup d'état* in the small Indian Ocean state of Maldives in 1988. In 1989, it imposed a partial economic boycott on Nepal, in part to punish it for looking to buy arms from China.

Pakistan had troops in the Gulf War. If it is able to attach itself to Washington's efforts to establish its post-Cold War global predominance or, more modestly, to Riyadh's purse strings, Pakistan may continue for a while to frustrate India's ambitions for regional predominance. But only for a while. The Indian Ocean's predominant power, the United States, seems to be coming more and more to a recognition of India's "managerial role"[10] in South Asia, and tacitly acknowledged it in the Maldives affair. The withdrawal of Soviet troops and American arms from the war in Afghanistan, in particular, and the apparent end of the Cold War, in general, is likely to have more dire implications for Pakistan's position on the subcontinent than for India's. Simply, Pakistan is more in need of American aid to frustrate India's claim to regional predominance than India will miss Soviet aid to assert it. In addition, without the Cold War's rationale, there is little point in the United States continuing to favor a secondary power in South Asia in preference to the predominant one. In all the ingredients of quality and quantity that make a great power, the disparity between India's and Pakistan's are too substantial, and India is too determined to be South Asia's predominant power.

Postscript. What is the connection between India's aspirations to regional predominance and bourgeois revolution? Or to put the same question differently: why is India spending vast sums of money to develop its military establishment when about half of its people live in poverty? Certainly, India's defense concerns are not illusory. It has fought three wars with Pakistan. On its Kashmiri salient Pakistan poses an indirect long-term threat to India's territorial integrity and domestic order. India was humiliated in a war with China. And while hostilities are unlikely to resume *today*, there is unfinished business between India and China, a politically unstable border of about 2,000 kilometers, and the unfixed ambitions of expanding great powers of the second division. But India has armed not simply for self-defense. Witness its naval expansion! It is armed and interventionist to fulfill its self-appointed managerial role in South Asia.

There are any number of reasons for India to aspire to regional predominance. The most obvious is that countries which can aspire to great-power status usually do. It becomes a goal in itself. India's interests in the Indian Ocean's mineral resources are another reason. And yet another reason, which I cannot prove although I am certain of it, is that India's domestically predominant middle classes aspire to be the citizens of a great power, secular or Hindu, and to travel on a great power's passport. Our hypothetical Indian doctors from part I are likely to find that the "third-world" status of the country in which they were born and trained is an impediment to their practices in Sydney and southern California.

Notes

Introduction

1 Barrington Moore, *Social Origins of Dictatorship and Democracy* (Boston: Beacon Press, 1966), p. 427.
2 Ibid.
3 Ibid., p. 439.
4 D. P. Chaudhri, "Recent Trends in the Indian Economy," working paper no. 88/2, Canberra: National Centre for Development Studies, the Australian National University, 1988.
5 Alexis de Tocqueville, *Democracy in America*, vol. I, translated by Henry Reeves, revised by Francis Bowen and further edited by Phillip Bradley (New York: Vintage Books, 1956), p. 452.
6 From Rabindranath Tagore's *Songs of Kabir*, quoted in *Sources of Indian Tradition*, compiled by Wm. Theodore de Bary *et al.* (New York: Columbia University Press, 1958), pp. 360–61.

1 Families and villages

1 It was about one-fifth in 1965, according to a survey of forty-five medical colleges reported in Jagdish N. Bhagwati, "Education, Class Structure and Income Equality," *Wealth and Power: Essays in Development Economics*, vol. I, a collection of the author's essays (Oxford: Basil Blackwell, 1985), p. 191. Doubtlessly, the percentage is now greater than one-fifth.
2 The concerns expressed below and some of their supporting data are taken from the landmark study, *Status of Women in India: A Synopsis of the Report on the Status of Women* (Delhi: Indian Council of Social Science Research, 1973).

2 Caste: *varna* and *jati*, Muslim quasi *jatis* and untouchability

1 Quoted in de Bary, *Sources of Indian Tradition*, pp. 16–17.
2 Louis Dumont, *Homo Hierarchicus: The Caste System and its Implications*, translated by Mark Sainsbury (Chicago: University of Chicago Press, 1970).

3 Mahatma Gandhi, *An Autobiography* (Ahmedabad: Navajivan Publishing House, 1966), p. 183.

4 *The Bhagavad Gita*, translated from the Sanskrit by Swami Nikhilananda (New York: Ramakrishna-Vivekananda Center, 1952), p. 202.

5 Premchand, *Godan or The Gift of a Cow*, translated by Jai Ratan and P. Lal (Bombay: Jaico Publishing House, 1979), p. 203.

6 Thanks to Don Ferrell and Jayanti Banerjee.

7 For a good exposition of his theories of "sanskritization" and "westernization" see, M. N. Srinivas, *Social Change in Modern India* (Berkeley: University of California Press, 1966).

8 M. Mujeeb, *Indian Muslims*, 1st Indian edition (Delhi: Munshiram Manoharlal, 1985), p. 13.

9 Imtiaz Ali, "Endogamy and Status Mobility among the Siddiqui Sheikhs of Allahabad," *Caste and Social Stratification Among Muslims in India*, edited by Imtiaz Ahmad (Delhi: Manohar, 1978), p. 190.

10 A comprehensive discussion and collection of data relevant to the current status of untouchables appears in, Ministry of Home Affairs, Government of India, High Power Panel on Minorities, Scheduled Castes, Scheduled Tribes and Other Weaker Sections, *Report on Scheduled Castes*, December 1983.

11 Gilbert Etienne, *India's Changing Rural Scene 1963–1979* (Delhi: Oxford University Press, 1982), p. 130.

3 Class: primordial group representation, stimuli-response and patron–client relationships

1 "Class, Status, Party," *From Max Weber, Essays in Sociology*, translated, edited and with an introduction by H. H. Gerth and C. Wright Mills (New York: Oxford University Press, 1946).

2 Pranab Bardhan, *The Political Economy of Development in India*. (London: Basil Blackwell, 1984), p. 107.

3 *Sydney Morning Herald, Good Weekend*, October 10, 1987, p. 42.

4 Weber, "Class, Status, Party."

5 *India Today*, November 30, 1987, p. 50.

6 Planning Commission, Government of India, *The Report of the Balwant Rai Mehta Committee on Community Development and National Extension Services*.

7 Rambir Singh, "Haryana," *Patterns of Panchayati Raj in India*, edited by G. Ram Reddy (Delhi: Macmillan Company of India, 1977), p. 115.

4 Homelands, "linguistic" and tribal states: nation provinces and bourgeois revolution

1 Robert W. Stern, *The Process of Opposition in India: Two Case Studies of How Policy Shapes Politics* (Chicago: The University of Chicago Press, 1970), ch. 2.

2 *India Today*, October 15, 1981, p. 89.
3 Paul R. Brass, "The Punjab Crisis and the Unity of India," *India's Democracy: An Analysis of Changing State–Society Relations*, edited by Atul Kohli (Princeton: Princeton University Press, 1988), p. 212.

5 British imperialism, Indian nationalism and Muslim separatism

1 B. R. Tomlinson, *The Political Economy of the Raj: 1914–1947* (London: The Macmillan Press Ltd., 1979), p. 157.
2 Ibid., p. 6.
3 Morris D. Morris, "The Growth of Large-Scale Industry to 1947," *The Cambridge Economic History of India*, vol. II (Cambridge: Cambridge University Press, 1983), pp. 668–76.
4 Ibid, pp. 588–92.
5 Neil Charlesworth, *British Rule and the Indian Economy: 1880–1914* (London: The Macmillan Press Ltd., 1982), pp. 51–55.
6 Ibid.
7 Quoted in P. E. Roberts, *History of British India Under the Company and the Crown*, 3rd edition, completed by T. G. P. Spear (Oxford: Oxford University Press, 1958), pp. 383–84.
8 "The Rajput States of India," *Asiatic Studies: Religious and Social*, a collection of essays by Alfred C. Lyall (London: John Murray, 1982).
9 M. V. Pylee, *Constitutional Government in India* (London: Asia Publishing House, 1960), p. 114.
10 Judith M. Brown, *Modern India: The Origin of an Asian Democracy* (Delhi: Oxford University Press, 1985), p. 297.
11 Quoted in Damodar P. Singal, *Pakistan* (Englewood Cliffs, New Jersey: Prentice-Hall, Inc., 1972), pp. 58–59.
12 Claude Markovits, *Indian Business and National Politics, 1931–1939* (Cambridge: Cambridge University Press, 1985), pp. 165 and 3.
13 Robert W. Stern, *The Cat and the Lion: Jaipur State in the British Raj* (Leiden: E. J. Brill, 1988), chs. 6 and 7.
14 Markovits, *Indian Business*.
15 Ibid., p. 30.
16 *Subaltern Studies: Writings on South Asia*, vols. I–VI, edited by Ranajit Guha (Delhi: Oxford University Press 1982–).
17 Eric Wolf, *Peasant Wars of the Twentieth Century* (New York: Harper and Row, 1969).
18 Quoted in K. M. Prasad, *Sarvodaya of Gandhi*, edited by Ramjee Singh (New Delhi: Raj Hans Publications, 1984), p. 90.
19 A. R. Desai, *Social Background of Indian Nationalism*, 4th edition (Bombay: Popular Prakashan, 1966), p. 371.

20 Ishtiaq Husain Qureshi, *The Muslim Community of the Indo-Pakistan Subcontinent, 610–1947* ('S-Gravenhage: Mouton and Co., 1962), pp. 84 and 270.

21 Quoted in Mujeeb, *Indian Muslims*, p. 477.

22 Quoted in Ram Gopal, *Indian Muslims: A Political History, 1858–1947* (London: Asia Publishing House, 1959), pp. 329–35.

23 Peter Hardy, *The Muslims of British India* (Cambridge: Cambridge University Press, 1972), p. 151.

24 Quoted in ibid., p. 231.

25 Ayesha Jalal, *The Sole Spokesman: Jinnah, The Muslim League and the Demand for Pakistan* (Cambridge: Cambridge University Press, 1985) and Asim Roy, "The High Politics of India's Partition: The Revisionist Perspective," *Modern Asian Studies*, vol. 24, no. 2, 1990.

6 Political and economic development in the Indian Union and its international politics

1 Ravinder Kumar, "The Past and Present: An Indian Dialogue," *Daedalus*, 118:4, Fall 1989, pp. 27–49.

2 Gunnar Myrdal, *Asian Drama: An Inquiry into the Poverty of Nations*, abridged by Seth S. King (New York: Vintage Books, 1972), pp. 202–10.

3 *India Today*, March 31, 1990, pp. 22–28.

4 Philip Mason, *The Men Who Ruled India*, 2 vols. (London: Jonathan Cape, 1953–54).

5 *India Today*, July 15, 1991, p. 36.

6 *Far Eastern Economic Review*, October 31, 1991, pp. 61–62.

7 Clive Crook, "India," *The Economist*, May 5, 1991, survey pp. 3–18.

8 Mohammad Ayoob, "India in South Asia: The Quest for Regional Predominance," *World Policy Journal*, Winter 1989–90, vol. 7, no. 1.

9 V. P. Menon, *The Story of the Integration of the Indian States* (Bombay: Orient Longmans, 1969), p. 377.

10 Ayoob, "India in South Asia."

Guide to further reading

There is a rough parallel between *Changing India*'s chapters or their parts and the categories in this section. In these there is, inevitably, a measure of arbitrariness, as there is in my placement of works in particular categories. For example: "Family, *jati* and villages" tend to be written about together, but not always; and works so categorized my differ only from those listed under "Class" more or less according to their emphasis or the ideological persuasions of their authors. I have listed Bardhan, *The Political Economy* under "Class" because that is the most interesting aspect of the book to me, but it might more appropriately be put under Economic Development. And so forth. Readers in search of anything in particular will have to fossick; here, in the bibliographies of the works cited, and – I suggest – in the comprehensive *Bibliography of Asian Studies*, published as a delayed annual by the Asian Studies Association, Ann Arbor, Michigan.

In the works cited here, I have, in general, preferred more or less recent publications, books to journal articles (useful periodicals are cited in the next section), edited collections to their separate pieces, more to less comprehensive studies, variety to consistency in theoretical underpinning and methodology. Only if they suit these preferences are footnote citations repeated below.

Works of general reference and relevance

The Cambridge Economic History of India. 2 vols. vol. I, *c.* 1200–1750 AD, edited by Tapan Raychaudhuri and Irfan Habib; vol. II, *c.* 1757–1970, edited by Dharma Kumar with Megnad Desai. Cambridge: Cambridge University Press, 1981–82.

Cohn, Bernard S. *India: The Social Anthropology of a Civilization*. Englewood Cliffs, New Jersey: Prentice-Hall, 1971.

de Bary, Wm. Theodore; Stephan N.; Weiler, Royal and Yarrow, Andrew, comp. *Sources of Indian Tradition*. New York: Columbia University Press, 1958.

Dobb, Maurice. *Studies in the Development of Capitalism*. Revised ed. New York: International Publishers, 1963.

Heesterman, J.C. *The Inner Conflict of Tradition: Essays in Indian Ritual, Kingship and Society.* Chicago: University of Chicago Press, 1985.

Inden, Ronald. *Imagining India.* Oxford: Basil Blackwell, 1990.

Lannoy, Richard. *The Speaking Tree: A Study of Indian Culture and Society.* Oxford: Oxford University Press, 1971.

Moore, Barrington, Jr. *Social Origins of Dictatorship and Democracy.* Boston: Beacon Press, 1966.

Muthiah, S., ed. *A Social and Economic Atlas of India.* Delhi: Oxford University Press, 1987.

Naipaul, V.S. *India: A Wounded Civilization.* New York: Knopf, 1977.

India: A Million Mutinies Now. London: Heinemann, 1990.

Robinson, Francis, ed. *The Cambridge Encyclopedia of India, Pakistan, Bangladesh, Sri Lanka, Nepal, Bhutan and the Maldives.* Cambridge: Cambridge University Press, 1989.

Schwartzberg, Joseph E. *A Historical Atlas of South Asia.* Chicago: University of Chicago Press, 1978.

Sen, S. P., ed. *Dictionary of National Biography.* 4 vols. Calcutta: Institute of Historical Studies, 1972–74.

Major religions and religious communities

Ahmad, Aziz. *Islamic Modernism in India and Pakistan, 1957–1964.* Oxford: Oxford University Press, 1967.

Ahmad, Imtiaz, ed. *Modernization and Social Change among Muslims in India.* Delhi: Manohar, 1983.

Andersen, Walter K. and Damle, Shridhar D. *The Brotherhood in Saffron: The Rashtriya Swayamsevak Sangh and Hindu Revivalism.* New Delhi: Sage Publications, 1987.

Appadurai, Arjun. *Worship and Conflict Under Colonial Rule.* New York: Cambridge University Press, 1981.

Basham, A. L. *The Wonder that was India.* New York: Grove Press, 1954.

Bhagavad Gita. Translated by Swami Nikhilananda. New York: Ramakrishna-Vivekananda Center, 1952.

Bowes, Pratima, *The Hindu Religious Tradition: A Philosophical Approach.* London: Routledge and Kegan Paul, 1978.

Derrett, J. D. M. *Religion, Law and State in India.* London: Faber and Faber, 1968.

Dumont, Louis. *Homo Hierarchicus.* Translated by Mark Sainsbury. Chicago: University of Chicago Press, 1970.

Eaton, Richard Maxwell. *Sufis of Bijapur, 1300–1700.* Princeton: Princeton University Press, 1978.

Farquhar, John Nicol. *Modern Religious Movements in India.* New York: Garland, 1980.

Forrester, Duncan B. *Caste and Christianity: Attitudes and Policies on Caste of Anglo-Saxon Protestant Missions in India.* London: Curzon Press, 1980.

Gilmartin, David. *Empire and Islam, Punjab and the Making of Pakistan.* Berkeley: University of California Press, 1988.

Gopal, Ram. *Indian Muslims: A Political History, 1858–1947.* London: Asia Publishing House, 1959.

Hardy, Peter. *The Muslims of British India.* Cambridge: Cambridge University Press, 1972.

Jones, Kenneth W. *The New Cambridge History of India: Socio-Religious Reform Movements in British India.* Cambridge: Cambridge University Press, 1990.

Jordens, S. T. F. *Dayananad Sarasvati: His Life and Ideas.* New York: Oxford University Press, 1979.

Kapur, Rajiv A. *Sikh Separatism: The Politics of Faith.* London: Allen and Unwin, 1968.

Keyes, Charles F. and Daniel, E. Valentine. *Karma: An Anthropological Inquiry.* Berkeley: University of California Press, 1983.

Lele, Jayant, ed. *Tradition and Modernity in Bhakti Movements.* Leiden: E. J. Brill, 1981.

McLeod, W. H. *Who is a Sikh? The Problem of Sikh Identity.* Oxford: Oxford University Press, 1989.

Mujeeb, Mohammad. *Indian Muslims.* 1st Indian ed. Delhi: Munshiram Manoharlal, 1985.

Mushir-Ul-Haq. *Islam in Secular India.* Simla: Indian Institute of Advanced Study, 1972.

Neill, Stephen. *A History of Christianity in India.* 2 vols. Cambridge: Cambridge University Press, 1984–85.

Oddie, G. A. *Social Protest in India: Protestant Missionaries and Social Reforms, 1850–1900.* Columbia, Missouri: South Asia Books, 1978.

Qureshi, Ishtiaq Husain. *The Muslim Community of the Indo-Pakistan Subcontinent: 610–1947.* 'S-Gravenhage: Mouton and Co., 1962.

Radhakrishnan, Sarvepalli and Moore, Charles A. *A Sourcebook in Indian Philosophy.* Princeton: Princeton University Press, 1957.

Singh, Khushwant. *A History of the Sikhs.* 2nd edn, 2 vols. Delhi: Oxford University Press, 1977.

Stutley, Margaret and James. *A Dictionary of Hinduism, its Mythology, Folklore and Development, 1500BC–AD1500.* Bombay: Allied Publishers, 1977.

Smith, W. C. *Modern Islam in India.* New York: Russell and Russell, 1946.

Zimmer, Heinrich. *Philosophies of India.* Edited by Joseph Campbell. New York: Meridian Books, 1959.

Family, *jati* and villages

Ahmad, Imtiaz, ed. *Family, Kinship and Marriage among Muslims in India.* Delhi: Manohar, 1976.

   Caste and Social Stratification among Muslims in India. Delhi: Manohar, 1978.

Berreman, Gerald D. *Caste and Other Inequities: Essays on Inequality*. Meerut: Folklore Institute, 1979.

Béteille, André. *Caste, Class and Power: Changing Patterns of Stratification in a Tanjore Village*. Berkeley: University of California Press, 1963.

Gould, Harold A. *The Hindu Caste System: The Sacralization of a Social Order*. New Delhi: Chanakya Publications, 1987.

Gray, John N. and Mearns, David J., ed. *Society from the Inside Out: Anthropological Perspectives on the South Asian Household*. New Delhi: Sage Publications, 1989.

Hardiman, David. *Peasant Nationalists of Gujarat: Kheda District, 1917–1934*. New Delhi: Oxford University Press, 1981.

Ishwaran, K. *A Populistic Community and Modernization in India*. Monographs and Theoretical Studies in Sociology and Anthropology in Honour of Nels Anderson, 13. Leiden: E. J. Brill, 1977.

Joshi, Barbara R. *Untouchable! Voices of the Dalit Liberation Movement*. London: Zed Books, 1986.

Klass, Morton. *Caste: The Emergence of the South Asian Social System*. Philadelphia: Institute for the Study of Human Issues, 1980.

Kolenda, Pauline. *Caste, Cult and Hierarchy: Essays on the Culture of India*. Meerut: Folklore Institute, 1981.

Ludden, David. *Peasant History in South India*. Princeton: Princeton University Press, 1985.

Mandlebaum, David G. *Society in India*. 2 vols. Berkeley: University of California Press, 1970 and 1972.

Moffatt, Michael. *An Untouchable Community in South India: Structure and Consensus*. Princeton: Princeton University Press, 1979.

Östör, Ákos; Fruzzetti, Lina and Barnett, Steve, ed. *Concepts of Person: Kinship, Caste and Marriage in India*. Cambridge: Harvard University Press, 1982.

Parry, Johnathan P. *Caste and Kinship in Kangra*. London: Routledge and Kegan Paul, 1979.

Premchand. *Godan*. Translated by Jai Ratan and P. Lal. Bombay: Jaico Publishing House, 1979.

Raheja, Gloria Goodwin. *The Poison in the Gift: Ritual Prestation and the Dominant Caste in a North Indian Village*. Chicago: University of Chicago Press, 1988.

Sharma, Miriam. *The Politics of Inequality: Competition and Control in an Indian Village*. Honolulu: The University Press of Hawaii, 1978.

Srinivas, M. N. *Caste in Modern India and Other Essays*. Bombay: Asia Publishing House, 1962.

Social Change in Modern India. Berkeley: University of California Press, 1966.

Srinivas, M. N.; Seshaiah, S. and Parthasarathy, V. S. *Dimensions of Social Change in India*. New Delhi: South Asian Publishers, 1978.

Class

Ahmad, Saghir. *Class and Power in a Punjabi Village*. Introduction by Kathleen Gough. New York: Monthly Review Press, 1977.

Alavi, Hamza and Harriss, John. *Sociology of "Developing Societies": South Asia*. London: Macmillan Education, 1989.

Bardhan, Pranab. *The Political Economy of Development in India*. London: Basil Blackwell, 1984.

Breman, Jan. *Of Peasants, Migrants and Paupers: Rural Labour Circulation and Capitalist Production in West India*. Delhi: Oxford University Press, 1985.

Gough, Kathleen and Sharma, Hari P., ed. *Imperialism and Revolution in South Asia*. New York: Monthly Review Press, 1973.

Hasan, Zoya. *Dominance and Mobilization: Rural Politics in Western Uttar Pradesh*. New Delhi: Sage Publications, 1989.

India. Ministry of Home Affairs. High Power Panel on Minorities, Scheduled Castes, Scheduled Tribes and Other Weaker Sections. *Report on Scheduled Castes*. 1983.

Misra, B. B. *The Indian Middle Classes: Their Growth in Modern Times*. Delhi: Oxford University Press, 1961.

Sachchidananda. *The Harijan Elite*. Faridabad: Thomson Press, 1977.

Weber, Max. "Class, Status, Party." From *Max Weber, Essays in Sociology*. Translated, edited and with an introduction by H. H. Gerth and C. Wright Mills. New York: Oxford University Press, 1946.

Wolfe, Eric. *Peasant Wars of the Twentieth Century*. New York: Harper and Row, 1969.

Women

Chatterji, Shoma A. *The Indian Women's Search for an Identity*. New Delhi: Vikas, 1988.

Desai, Neera and Krishnaraj, Maithreyi. *Women and Society in India*. Delhi: Ajanta Publications, 1987.

Ghadially, Rehana. *Women in Indian Society, A Reader*. New Delhi: Sage Publications, 1988.

Jain, Devaki. *Women's Quest for Power: Five Indian Case Studies*. Assisted by Nalini Singh and Malini Chand. Delhi: Vikas, 1980.

Jeffrey, Patricia. *Frogs in a Well: Indian Women in Purdah*. London: Zed Books, 1979.

Karlekar, Malavika. *Poverty and Women's Work: A Study of Sweeper Women in Delhi*. Delhi: Vikas, 1982.

Khanna, Girija and Varghese, Mariamma A. *Indian Women Today*. New Delhi: Vikas, 1978.

Kishwar, Madhu and Vanita, Ruth, ed. *In Search of Answers: Indian Women's Voices from Manushi*. London: Zed Books, 1984.

Liddle, Joanna and Joshi, Rama. *Daughters of Independence: Gender, Caste and Class in India.* New Brunswick, New Jersey: Rutgers University Press, 1989.

Mandelbaum, David G. *Women's Seclusion and Men's Honor: Sex Roles in North India, Bangladesh and Pakistan.* Tucson: University of Arizona Press, 1988.

Mies, Maria, ed. *Indian Women and Patriarchy: Conflicts and Dilemmas of Students and Working Women.* New Delhi: Concept, 1980.

Minault, Gail, ed. *The Extended Family: Women and Political Participation in India and Pakistan.* Delhi: Chanakya Publications, 1981.

Papanek, Hanna and Minault, Gail. *Separate Worlds: Studies of Purdah in South Asia.* Columbia, Missouri: South Asia Books, 1982.

Ram, Kalpana. *Mukkuvar Women: Sexual Contradictions in a Southeast Indian Fishing Community.* Sydney: Allen and Unwin, 1991.

Status of Women in India: A Synopsis of the Report on the Status of Women. Delhi: Indian Council of Social Science Research, 1973.

Wignaraja, Poona. *Women, Poverty and Resources.* New Delhi: Sage Publications, 1990.

Ethnicity and ethnic movements

Brass, Paul R. *Ethnic Groups and the State.* London: Croom Helm, 1985.

 Language, Religion and Politics in North India. Cambridge: Cambridge University Press, 1974.

Das Gupta, Jyotirindra. *Language, Conflict and National Development: Group Politics and National Language Policy in India.* Bombay: Oxford University Press, 1970.

Duyker, Edward. *Tribal Guerrillas: The Santals of West Bengal and the Naxalite Movement.* Delhi: Oxford University Press, 1987.

Furer-Haimendorf, C. von. *Tribal Populations and Cultures of the Indian Subcontinent.* Leiden: E. J. Brill, 1985.

Gupta, S. K. *The Scheduled Castes in Modern Indian Politics: Their Emergence as a Political Power.* New Delhi: Munshiram Manoharlal, 1985.

Hardiman, David. *The Coming of the Devi: Adivasi Assertion in Western India.* Delhi: Oxford University Press, 1987.

Irschick, Eugene F. *Politics and Social Conflict in South India: The Non-Brahman Movement and Tamil Separatism, 1916–1939.* Berkeley: University of California Press, 1969.

Katzenstein, Mary Fainsod. *Ethnicity and Equality: The Shiv Sena Party and Preferential Politics in Bombay.* Ithaca: Cornell University Press, 1979.

O'Hanlon, Rosalind. *Caste, Conflict and Ideology: Mahatma Jotirao Phule and Low-Caste Protest in Nineteenth Century Western India.* Cambridge: Cambridge University Press, 1985.

Phadnis, Urmilla. *Ethnicity and Nation-building in South Asia.* New Delhi: Sage Publications, 1989.

Stern, Robert W. *The Process of Opposition in India: Two Case Studies of How Policy Shapes Politics.* Chicago: University of Chicago Press, 1970.

Weiner, Myron. *Sons of the Soil: Migration and Ethnic Conflict in India.* Princeton: Princeton University Press, 1978.

British imperialism and Indian nationalism

Ballhatchet, Kenneth. *Race, Sex and Class Under the Raj: Imperial Attitudes and Policies and Their Critics, 1793–1905.* London: Weidenfeld and Nicolson, 1980.

Bayly, C. A. *Rulers, Townsmen and Bazaars: North Indian Society in the Age of British Expansion.* Cambridge: Cambridge University Press, 1983.

Borman, William. *Gandhi and Non-Violence.* Albany: State University of New York Press, 1986.

Bridge, Carl. *Holding India to the Empire: The British Conservative Party and the 1935 Constitution.* Asian Studies Association of Australia, South Asian Publications series 1. New York: Envoy Press, 1986.

Brown, Judith M. *Modern India: The Origins of an Asian Democracy.* Delhi: Oxford University Press, 1985.

Chakrabarty, Dipesh. *Rethinking Working Class History: Bengal 1890–1940.* Princeton: Princeton University Press, 1989.

Charlesworth, Neil. *British Rule and the Indian Economy: 1880–1914.* London: Macmillan, 1982.

Chaudhuri, K. N. and Dewey, Clive J. *Economy and Society: Essays in Indian Economic and Social History.* New York: Oxford University Press, 1979.

Desai, A. R. *Social Background of Indian Nationalism.* 4th ed. Bombay: Popular Prakashan, 1966.

Dewey, Clive J. *Arrested Development in India: The Historical Dimension.* Riverdale: The Riverdale Co., 1988.

Fox, Richard G. *Gandhian Utopia: Experiments with Culture.* Boston: Beacon Press, 1989.

Gallagher, John; Johnson, Gordon and Seal, Anil, ed. *Locality, Province and Nation: Essays on Indian Politics, 1870 to 1940.* Cambridge: Cambridge University Press, 1973.

Gandhi, Mohandas Karamchand. *An Autobiography.* Ahmedabad: Navajivan Publishing House, 1966.

Guha, Ranajit. *Elementary Aspects of Peasant Insurgency in Colonial India.* Delhi: Oxford University Press, 1983.

Guha, Ranajit, ed. *Subaltern Studies: Writings on South Asian History and Society.* 6 vols. 1982–.

Hirschmann, Edwin. *"White Mutiny": The Ilbert Bill Crisis in India and the Genesis of the Indian National Congress.* Columbia, Missouri: South Asia Books, 1980.

Hutchens, Francis G. *The Illusion of Permanence: British Imperialism in India*. Princeton: Princeton University Press, 1967.

Jalal, Ayesha. *The Sole Spokesman: Jinnah, the Muslim League and the Demand for Pakistan*. Cambridge: Cambridge University Press, 1985.

Jeffrey, Robin, ed. *People, Princes and Paramount Power: Society and Politics in the Indian Princely States*. Delhi: Oxford University Press, 1978.

Kumar, Ravinder, ed. *Essays on Gandhian Politics: The Rowlatt Satyagraha of 1919*. Oxford: Clarendon Press, 1971.

Low, D. A. ed. *Congress and the Raj: Facets of the Indian Struggle, 1917–1949*. London: Heinemann, 1977.

Markovits, Claude. *Indian Business and National Politics, 1931–1939*. Cambridge: Cambridge University Press, 1985.

McGuire, John. *The Making of a Colonial Mind: A Quantitative Study of the Bhadralok in Calcutta, 1857–1885*. Canberra: Australian National University Press, 1983.

Menon, V. P. *The Story of the Integration of the Indian States*. Bombay: Orient Longmans, 1969.

Minault, Gail. *The Khilafat Movement: Religious Symbolism and Political Mobilization in India*. New York: Columbia University Press, 1982.

Moon, Penderel. *The British Conquest and Dominion of India*. London: Duckworth, 1989.

Nehru, Jawaharlal. *The Discovery of India*. London: Meridian, 1947.

Parekh, Bhiku. *Colonialism, Tradition and Reform: An Analysis of Gandhi's Political Discourse*. New Delhi: Sage Publications, 1989.

Prasad, K. M. *Sarvodaya of Gandhi*. Edited by Ramjee Singh. New Delhi: Raj Hans Publications, 1984.

Raj, Rajat K. *Industrialization in India: Growth and Conflict in the Private Corporate Sector, 1914–1947*. New York: Oxford University Press, 1979.

Rothermund, Dietmar. *Government, Landlord and Peasant in India: Agrarian Relations under British Rule, 1865–1935*. Wiesbaden: Franz Steiner Verlag GmbH, 1978.

Sarkar, Sumit. *Modern India, 1885–1947*. Madras: Macmillan India, 1983.

Seal, Anil. *The Emergence of Indian Nationalism: Competition and Collaboration in the Late Nineteenth Century*. Cambridge: Cambridge University Press, 1971.

Sisson, Richard and Wolpert, Stanley, ed. *Congress and Indian Nationalism: The Pre-Independence Phase*. Berkeley: University of California Press, 1988.

Stern, Robert W. *The Cat and the Lion: Jaipur State in the British Raj*. Monographs and Theoretical Studies in Sociology and Anthropology in Honour of Nels Anderson, 21. Leiden: E. J. Brill, 1988.

Stokes, Eric. *The Peasant and the Raj*. Cambridge: Cambridge University Press, 1978.

Tomlinson, B. R. *The Political Economy of the Raj: 1914–1947*. London: Macmillan, 1979.

Wurgaft, Lewis D. *The Imperial Imagination: Magic and Myth in Kipling's India.* Middletown, Connecticut: Wesleyan University Press, 1983.
Yang, Anand A. *The Limited Raj: Agrarian Relations in Colonial India, Saran District, 1793–1920.* Berkeley: University of California Press, 1990.

Economic development

Ahluwalia, I. J. *Industrial Growth in India: Stagnation since the Mid-Sixties.* Delhi: Oxford University Press, 1985.
Bala, Raj. *Trends in Urbanization in India.* Jaipur: Rawat Publications, 1986.
Balasubramanyam, V. *The Indian Economy.* London: Weidenfeld and Nicolson, 1984.
Bhagwati, Jagdish N. *Wealth and Poverty: Essays in Development Economics.* Vol. I. Oxford: Basil Blackwell, 1985.
Cassen, R. H. *India: Population, Economy and Society.* New York: Holmes and Meier, 1978.
Chaudhri, D. P. and Das Gupta, Ajit K. *Agriculture and the Development Process: A Study of Punjab.* London: Croom Helm, 1985.
Chaudhry, Mahinder D., ed. *Contributions to Asian Studies 13, Rural Development*, Leiden: E. J. Brill, 1979.
Chugh, Ram L. and Uppal, J. S. *Black Economy in India.* New Delhi: Tata McGraw Hill, 1986.
Crook, Clive. "India." *Economist*, May 5, 1991, survey pp. 3–18.
Etienne, Gilbert. *India's Changing Rural Scene, 1963–1979.* Delhi: Oxford University Press, 1982.
Food and Poverty: India's Half Won Battle. New Delhi: Sage Publications, 1988.
Frankel, Francine R. *India's Political Economy, 1947–1977.* Princeton: Princeton University Press, 1978.
Myrdal, Gunnar. *Asian Drama: An Inquiry into the Poverty of Nations.* Abridged by Seth S. King. New York: Vintage Books, 1972.
Rao, C. H. Hanumantha and Joshi, P. C. *Reflections on Economic Development and Social Change: Essays in Honour of V. K. R. V. Rao.* Bombay: Allied Publishers, 1979.
Rodgers, Gerry. *Population Growth and Poverty in Rural South Asia.* New Delhi: Sage Publications, 1989.
Sims, Holly. *Political Regimes, Public Policy and Economic Development: Agricultural Performance and Rural Change in the Two Punjabs.* New Delhi: Sage Publications, 1988.
Sundrum, R. M. *Growth and Income Distribution in India: Policy and Performance since Independence.* New Delhi: Sage Publications, 1987.
Suri, K. B., ed. *Small Scale Enterprises in Industrial Development: The Indian Experience.* New Delhi: Sage Publications, 1988.

Toye, John. *Public Expenditure and Indian Development Policy: 1960–1970.* Cambridge: Cambridge University Press, 1981.

Uppal, J. S., ed. *India's Economic Problems: An Analytical Approach.* New York: St. Martin's Press, 1979.

Politics

Brass, Paul R. *The New Cambridge History of India: The Politics of India since Independence.* New York: Cambridge University Press, 1990.

Calman, Leslie J. *Protest in Democratic India: Authority's Response to Challenge.* Boulder, Colorado: Westview Press, 1985.

Desai, I. P. *et al. Caste, Caste Conflict and Reservations.* Centre for Social Studies, Surat. Delhi: Ajanta Publications, 1985.

Galanter, Marc. *Competing Equalities: Law and the Backward Classes in India.* Berkeley: University of California Press, 1984.

Hart, Henry C., ed. *Indira Gandhi's India: A Political System Reappraised.* Boulder, Colorado: Westview Press, 1976.

India. Planning Commission. Committee on Plan Projects. *Report of the Team for the Study of Community Projects and National Extension Service,* 1958. [Balvantray Mehta Study Team Report.]

Jeffrey, Robin. *What's Happening in India? Punjab, Ethnic Conflict, Mrs. Gandhi's Death and the Test for Federalism.* Basingstoke, Hampshire: Macmillan, 1986.

Kohli, Atul, ed. *India's Democracy: An Analysis of Changing State–Society Relations.* Princeton: Princeton University Press, 1988.

Lele, Jayant. *Elite Pluralism and Class Rule: Political Development in Maharashtra.* Bombay: Popular Prakashan, 1982.

Masselos, Jim, ed. *India: Creating a Modern Nation.* Delhi: Sterling Publishers, 1990.

Nandi, Ashis. *At the Edge of Psychology: Essays in Politics and Culture.* Delhi: Oxford University Press, 1980.

Phadnis, Urmila; Muni, S. D. and Bahadur, Kalim, ed. *Domestic Conflicts in South Asia.* 2 vols. New Delhi: South Asian Publishers.

Prasad, V. Sivalinga. *Panchayats and Development.* New Delhi: Light and Life Publishers, 1981.

Radhakrishnan, P. *Peasant Struggles, Land Reforms and Social Change: Malabar, 1836–1982.* New Delhi: Sage Publications, 1989.

Reddy, G. Ram, ed. *Patterns of Panchayati Raj in India.* Delhi: Macmillan India, 1977.

Rudolph, Susanne H. and Lloyd, I. *In Pursuit of Lakshmi: The Political Economy of the Indian State.* Chicago: University of Chicago Press, 1987.

Singh, V. B. and Bose, Shanker. *Elections in India: Data Handbook on Lok Sabha Elections, 1952–1985.* 2nd ed. New Delhi: Sage Publications, 1986.

State Elections in India: Data Handbook on Vidhan Sabha Elections, 1952–1985. 5 vols. New Delhi: Sage Publications, 1988.

Vanaik, Achin. *The Painful Transition: Bourgeois Democracy in India*. London: Verso, 1990.

Weiner, Myron and Katzenstein, Mary Fainsod. *India's Preferential Politics: Migrants, the Middle Classes and Ethnic Equality*. Chicago: University of Chicago Press, 1982.

Wood, John R., ed. *State Politics in Contemporary India: Crisis or Continuity*. Boulder, Colorado: Westview Press, 1984.

Foreign relations

Ayoob, Mohammad. "Dateline India: The Deepening Crisis." *Foreign Policy*, Winter 1991–92, no. 85.

"India in South Asia: The Quest for Regional Predominance." *World Policy Journal*, Winter 1989–90, vol. 12, no. 1.

Barnds, William J. *India, Pakistan and the Great Powers*. The Council on Foreign Relations. New York: Praeger, 1972.

Cohen, Stephen P., ed. *The Security of South Asia: American and Asian Perspectives*. Urbana: University of Illinois Press, 1987.

Engineer, Asghar Ali. *Secular Crown on Fire: The Kashmir Problem*, Delhi, Ajanta Press, 1991.

Horn, Robert C. *Soviet–Indian Relations: Issues and Influence*. New York: Praeger, 1982.

Mansingh, Surjit. *India's Search for Power: Indira Gandhi's Foreign Policy, 1966–1982*. New Delhi: Sage Publications, 1984.

Rudolph, Susanne H. and Lloyd, I. *et al. The Regional Imperative: United States Foreign Policy towards South Asian States*. Atlantic Highlands, NJ: Humanities Press, 1981.

Strategic and Defence Studies Centre, Research School of Pacific Affairs, Australian National University, "India's Strategic Future." Conference papers. Canberra, 1990.

"Texts of Secret Documents on Top Level U.S. Discussions of Indian Pakistan War." *New York Times*, January 6, 1972.

Thomas, Raju G. C. *Indian Security Policy*. Princeton: Princeton University Press, 1986.

Periodicals

In different ways, these have been particularly useful: *Asian Survey* (Berkeley, California), *Asiaweek* (Hongkong), *Contributions to Indian Sociology* (Delhi), *Economic and Political Weekly* (Bombay), *The Economist* (London), *Far Eastern Economic Review* (Hongkong), *India Today* (Delhi), *Journal of Asian Studies* (Ann Arbor, Michigan), *Journal of Commonwealth and Comparative Politics* (London), *Keesings Contemporary Archives* (London), *Modern Asian Studies* (Cambridge), *Pacific Affairs* (Vancouver, British Columbia), *South Asia* (Armidale, New South Wales), *Seminar* (Delhi).

Statistical data

Unless otherwise noted, statistics relating to one thing or another that pepper *Changing India* have been collected as follows: either from such primary official Indian sources as the various rounds of the National Sample Survey or decennial Censuses of India, most recently of 1991, or from the following annual statistical compilations: Agrawal, A. N. *et al. India: Economic Information Yearbook.* New Delhi: National Publishing House; *India: A Statistical Outline.* New Delhi: Oxford and IBH Publishing Co.; India. Ministry of Information and Broadcasting, Research and Reference Division. *India: A Reference Annual*; Sachdeva, S. K. ed. *India Annual Review.* New Delhi: Competition Review; *Statistical Outline of India.* Bombay: Tata Services Ltd., Department of Economics and Statistics.

Index